HIGH PRAISE FOR

BAD

THE AUTOBIOGRAPHY

"For those interested in prison reform, Ja[...] is a must read. His life is a testimony to t[...] [...] changes in our system of prisons. We all will benefit if changes are made that stress education, rehabilitation, and employment opportunities instead of just incarceration. Reading Carr's autobiography forces us to think about just that."

— *Jim Beall, California State Senator*

"These are the stories I grew up with, the epic mythologies that sustained me during my long years of exile—gladiator tales of a legendary, furious hero who flew so very close to the sun, burning hot, reckless, ruthless. These are the great and terrible exploits of my godfather, the Black Spartacus who goes harder than all the rest and makes no apologies—vivid, visceral, vital, shining with charisma. His undying bond of comradeship with Uncle George [Jackson, *Soledad Brother*] serves as a crucial example for everyone in the struggle."

—*Jonathan Peter Jackson, artist; godson of James Carr*

"James Carr's autobiography escapes many traps that befall stories of incarceration and radicalization, confronting the reader with brutal honesty rather than framing the subject as a passive victim or martyr in order to further a political agenda or provide a moralistic argument. . . . Avoiding the sensational and the romanticized, he embraces the full complexity of his life and forces the reader to do the same. Carr demonstrates deep insight and sensitivity in his condemnation of the prison system, leaving us with lessons which resonate clearly with today's urgent mass incarceration crisis."

—*Alejandro Van Zandt-Escobar, Regional Field Manager,*
The Petey Greene Program

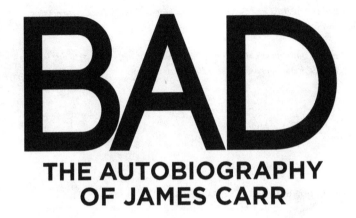

BAD

THE AUTOBIOGRAPHY OF JAMES CARR

JAMES CARR

THREE ROOMS PRESS

NEW YORK CITY

Special thanks to Dan Hammer and Isaac Cronin for working with James Carr to create the original edition of BAD: The Autobiography of James Carr.

Also, thanks to Isaac Cronin for introducing Three Rooms Press to the Carr family and helping to arrange for the publication of this edition.

And many thanks to the Betsy and Gea Carr for their kindness and dedication to making this edition a reality.

To read the original introduction to BAD *written by Dan Hammer, please go to this link on our website: http://threeroomspress.com/2016/04/original-intro-by-dan-hammer/*

COVER AND BOOK DESIGN:
KG Design International
www.katgeorges.com

INTRODUCTION AND AFTERWORD PHOTOS:
© Thomas P.E. Rothchild

COVER PHOTO AND PHOTO ON PAGE ix:
Courtesy © Betsy Carr

PUBLISHED BY:
Three Rooms Press, New York, NY
www.threeroomspress.com

DISTRIBUTED BY:
PGW/Perseus
www.pgw.com

CONTENTS

James Carr, with daughter Gea

INTRODUCTION

BY GEA CARR

On October 28, 2015 I woke up feeling incredibly ill. I think it was my mind's way of telling my body to stay in bed. The power of the mind is great, yet the power of Egyptian cotton can be even greater. If I rose from my sheets, the elusive San Quentin gates would open for me. For the first time I would visit the place where my father spent a great deal of his life and where his close friend, my uncle George Jackson (*Soledad Brother*), was murdered. My fear on this day was palpable; I had been waiting for it for forty-four years. Yet now, I didn't want to go. I was paralyzed by dread.

The prime piece of California real estate known San Quentin is one-hundred sixty-four years old. It houses California's only Death Row facility—the largest in the United States. San Quentin, or Q as my dad referred to it, is designed to hold 3,082 inmates but is currently home to 4,223 incarcerated souls. As a child I referred to it as my dad's house.

As one crosses the Richmond Bridge on the way to wine tastings in Napa or a mud bath in Calistoga, it's easy to regard San Quentin with admiration. It is a beachfront property perched on the San Francisco Bay worth hundreds of millions of dollars. It is situated just minutes from some of the most expensive homes and communities in the world. Looking out at the vista while standing under the gun tower that looms above the parking lot, you can almost picture Steve Perry singing *"When the lights go down in the city . . ."* or Otis sitting on the dock of the bay—until you turn around and remember where you are.

ONE COULD IMAGINE THAT Q IS filled only with the worst, most vile humans, humans that need to be removed from society. One could imagine that tax dollars are well spent funding its $210 million annual budget. That a society by the people, of the people, and for the people requires that these walls help to protect it.

Yet every time I have passed this building, I have felt the weight and horror of what really happens within those walls . . . what happened to my father there . . . what he had to do to survive in Q . . . what is currently happening to countless other children's fathers within those prison walls. I always find myself resenting Q for keeping my father from me during the beginning of my life. And I'm struck with a certain melancholy knowing that so little has changed. One in fourteen American children has a parent in prison: herein lies one of the deepest issues facing the future of our country.

I STARTED MY FIRST VISIT TO San Quentin in the warden's office, accompanied by my friend, a state senator in charge of designating and distributing funding for state prisons. Not surprisingly, the warden was lovely to us. I looked around his office and couldn't help but think, *man, if my dad could see me now.* It was surreal. After chewing the fat with the warden (we actually talked about the silk socks his wife had given him), we started our prison tour.

We passed through several identification checks, gates, and metal detectors, then stepped into the sunny yard. I was fighting back tears and had a lump in my throat. I couldn't swallow. Here I was, looking at the same granite blocks my father used to look at, walking on the same pavement he had once tread on. Little had changed at San Quentin since his time there. All the buildings he and George Jackson wrote about were still standing. My father's and George's words were jumping off the pages of their letters into reality. *So that's the gym where my dad pretended he was gonna let an old guy suck his dick and stabbed him instead for his Q initiation.* I peered into his very cell block. *So this is where he mixed moonshine in the toilet, sniffed glue and somehow amidst it all started planning a revolution.*

OUT IN THE YARD, INMATES EXERCISED freely. These men knew that America now had a black president. They were snacking, reading, and working out. I even saw one inmate feeding some seagulls part of his lunch. *This is the yard, those are the gun towers,* I thought, looking up. Men with rifles were up there. I scoured the ground, trying to imagine the very spot where my uncle George would have fallen, knowing that this was where he was murdered. No headstones here. Just blood, somewhere beneath the surface.

There is a new flock of men at Q now. They are new revolutionaries and old revolutionaries. Some of them are high. Some are sober. Some are conscious. And some don't give a fuck. Just like on the outside.

We visited the computer lab where inmates who had been confined less than an hour from Silicon Valley's booming technology are learning two kinds of computer coding. There I met a handsome man from San Jose who was the same age as me, but had been incarcerated for much of the technological revolution. Still, he was excited to tell me that Mark Zuckerberg had visited the week before. "When do you get out?" I asked him. "Seventeen years . . . " he said. I couldn't help but think that the coding he was learning would be obsolete by the time he hit the streets.

We visited the home of the *San Quentin News,* a newspaper where convicts write, design, and print the paper. Inmates were eager to share copies of their latest edition, which detailed stories about the Zuckerberg visit, the Prison University Project Graduation, and the recent visit and game between the Golden State Warriors and their very own San Quentin Warriors. I met an inmate who had been in for twenty-two years. He was excited to show me his "e-reader." He was overwhelmed by its touch screen and that fact that he could access several books on it. It was a slow tablet in a clear case like all prison electronics (they do that so you can't hide contraband in them). He used it to help earn college credits. "You have to remember I've been in here twenty-two years. I've never even had a cell phone," he told me.

SAN QUENTIN'S DEATH ROW HOUSES MORE than seven hundred inmates. The senator and I walked through the condemned yard and viewed the men in cages. They were showering, shitting on toilets, playing basketball and games in the sunlight.

We spoke to several of the inmates and asked them their opinion of the death penalty. Surprisingly, many of the men said they supported it. Condemned men had their own cells and were each assigned legal counsel. Serving time on Death Row was actually somewhat more palatable than serving time with the general population, according to some men.

California hasn't executed anyone since 2006. But in terms of prison reform, we have such a long way to go.

MY FATHER'S BEST FRIEND, GEORGE JACKSON, called himself Geo. He arranged for my mom and dad to be introduced, and, when my mother became pregnant, my dad assumed he would have a son and name him after George. This was the plan, but George was murdered in Q two weeks before I was born. My dad changed. He had lost his best friend, mentor and confidant and he knew *he* had to step up and try to fill George's enormous shoes.

I think my father wanted me to be a boy because he thought I could more easily fend for myself. But if you ask the parents of Trayvon Martin, Oscar Grant, or Michael Brown, they would hardly agree. And, certainly, being an African-American boy did not make my father's life easier. He burned his school down when he was nine years old. He didn't do it because he was a bad child. He did it because he was angry, because he was human, it was a reaction to the inhumane racism that he was subjected to by his so-called teachers because of his black skin. When my father was nine he faced his first incarceration at the Alexander Boys Home. By the time he was fifteen, he was locked up in a federal prison, charged as an adult.

BLACK MEN IN THIS COUNTRY HAVE the inalienable right to be angry. How can they not be? The system is stacked up against them from the moment they're born. In the forty-four years since my father was murdered, the United States would appear to have made some progress in the area of racial equality. But in that same period, the prison population has quintupled. According to the NAACP, African Americans are now incarcerated at nearly six times the rate of Caucasians. Statistically one in three black men can expect to go to jail in their lifetime. One in thirteen black adults can't vote because of their criminal records. In her stunning book, *The New Jim Crow*, Michelle Alexander argues that Jim Crow and slavery were caste systems, and that our current system of mass incarceration is also a caste system. The chain remains and the shoes are left to fill.

MY DAD WANTED ME TO BE a boy. When I was born, my dad was in County for a parole violation and was unable to be at the hospital. The nurse handed me to my mom and she took one look at me and named me George. The nurse told her I was far too pretty of a little girl to be named George so she came up with Gea. My middle name is Attica Jackson. I was born on the day of the prison riots in Attica where one thousand inmates took control of the prison in New York. My name carries as much weight as the blood that runs in my veins and the ghosts that haunt me.

I'm not sure what to do with all of this weight and this lump in my throat that just won't go down.

ON THE DAY I WAS BORN, my father wrote a letter to my mother.

> *As I think of the child, I can't help but think of Geo and the life we as brothers used to dream of, and said we would have. We decided long ago to negate our individuality, for only thus is it possible to serve those whom you claim to represent. A movement must never center around one or a group of people, for if it does, at that point it marks itself for its very doom . . .*

It's to this pledge that we dedicated ourselves back in 1960, and it has been eleven years now; looking back over my shoulder, I can see some good that has been done, but when I look to the forefront of the struggle, I see a sinister monster, that is capitalism. I see dollar-hands exchanging, heads rolling, and dust flying, which only indicates to me that there is a terrible lot to strive for, and therefore it shall be to the future that my eyes shall be cast—but with an occasional look over the shoulder, to witness the destruction of the people's enemies and the erection of the new.

I love you and baby Gea Jackson Carr. Power, love, caresses, and a thousand kisses,

Jimmy
Ghost of Geo

Tell the people thanks.

BAD

THE AUTOBIOGRAPHY
OF JAMES CARR

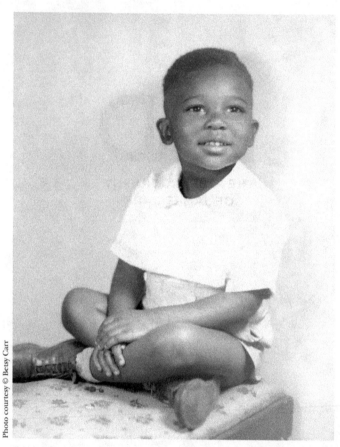

James Carr, age two

ONE

Slam! The heavy metal doors crash closed. It is so black. I can't see my arms. All I can hear is my own breath and the sound of the doors ringing around in my head. The cons call this place the "Black Hole," the hole within the Hole. No light. No air. The cell is fixed up with a set of double doors, the inner one padded with a lining of hard rubber that nothing gets through. It's the last stop in Tracy, a prison the authorities call Deuel Vocational Institution. I feel around for a bed of some sort, but there isn't any, only rough concrete painted black with a hole in the middle of the floor to shit in. It's a six-by-six dungeon designed to make me into a vegetable.

Instead of taking the long fall into limbo, I've learned a new trick for survival by reliving the past and slipping off into the future. I'm learning how to get out of the pen without leaving.

When I was nine years old I burned down my school. I didn't know the whole school would burn, I only wanted to get even with the playground coach, a big crewcut Mormon whose favorite game was to goad the nigger kids into beating the shit out of each other.

The playground was right down the hill from my house, at the Mellowbar Elementary School in East L.A. They had a ring set up down there, and this clean-living coach was the boxing instructor. The first day I went down and got in the ring with the gloves on, he got my cousin, who was older and more experienced, to beat me up. "Left! Jab! Now punch!" He kept yelling instructions at Larry until I'd been knocked down and had two puffed eyes and a bloody nose. Then he made me jump rope for an hour. I hated the guy, but I really wanted to learn how to box.

When he finally told me I could stop skippin' rope I said, "Fuck yes," and he heard me. He came over, got his hands on me and in his best flattop tones said, "We can't have that bad-mouthing around the ring. Get out of here. You're off the playground for a week!"

Larry was laughing his head off and I was mad as a mother-fucker. He didn't like the Mormon either, but he liked to see my ass whipped. That night when the playground closed down he came up to my house and we schemed awhile on how to get the coach.

Next day he took me down to show me where the coach had his office in the school. By standing on a step he made with his hands, I could look in. There were pennants, medallions, a trophy, and hanging on the door was a nice black leather jacket. My plan was to come back on Saturday, break in, and steal the dude's jacket.

Saturday morning I went down to the playground fence to wait for Larry. I stood there for two hours, but the fool never showed up. I went home, stole a pack of my father's Luckies, lit one up and looked down at that school. I couldn't possibly climb through the window and steal the jacket on my own, but I could burn it. I knew what gasoline could do from working in my uncle's junkyard: all I needed was fifteen cents' worth of gas and some cotton balls. I took some money from my little white piggy bank, got some cotton from the bathroom, and bought the gas.

The can was really heavy. By the time I got down to the fence, my hands were rubbed sore. I pulled the gate wide enough to slide the can in then slipped through myself. They had a chain on it, but if you pulled on it there was—enough slack for a skinny little kid like me to get through easy. There wasn't a soul around and the whole place was quiet and spooky. All the buildings were old, wooden things with chipped-up plaster and rotting timbers. I broke the windows out of the coach's office, soaked the cotton balls, stood on the gas can, and threw the balls onto the shelves, the desk, and all over the floor. Then I tossed a match in there.

I split up the hill. When I turned around, the whole school was going up, black smoke pouring out of the windows, flames and sparks filling the sky. I could hear the sirens. Cops, firemen, and a big crowd of people were watching the thing go down. I sat up on my hill and watched the mother burn, smokin' Lucky Strikes, trippin' hard on what I had done—and grinning.

RIGHT FROM THE START I GUESS I was a bad motherfucker. Watching that fuckin' school go down was the first time I realized how much hate I had in me, and how good it felt to let it out. When the cops finally tricked me into admitting it, catching me in a thousand lies, my father beat me in the bathtub with braided ironing cords for weeks. I had to sleep nights in the garage with the garbage and the rats. He wouldn't even put his car in it, the place was so bad.

Right after I burned down the school, my parents got a divorce. I went with my mother to live in Aliso Village, a square mile of crumbling concrete boxes which everyone called "Flats." The City of L.A.'s final solution: low-cost housing complete with dirt roads, Cadillac cockroaches, and thousands of welfare mamas.

The place was two-thirds Mexican and one-third black, and all the teenage dudes were in gangs. It was an unwritten law that any black kid caught outside at night was open game for the Mexican gangs. The cops sat back and laughed. You couldn't get a cop to come down to Flats. Gangs fighting like dogs and cats, fools killing each other . . . but the cops weren't interested because the only property around was the corner liquor store and all that concrete. Whenever my mother sent me to the store I ran like hell and stayed close to the buildings for fear I'd never make it back.

"You gotta be tough to stay alive," my uncle Joe told me when he got back from Korea. "You ain't got no choice, kid. You either learn t'fight now or get walked on all y'life." Then he proceeded to teach me GI fighting tricks, like the strangle hold and the schoolboy hold for gouging out eyes. Joe boxed with me every night till I was ready to take on the neighborhood. I had just meant to defend myself, but I soon found out that the only way to do that was to attack first. With Joe's tricks, and with the brass knuckles I stole from his drawer, I quickly developed a dangerous reputation, even though I was only ten. And the more I fought, the more I liked it.

Easter Sunday, 1953, 1 went over to Hollenbeck Park with a freshly stolen hunting knife in my coat pocket and nothing particular on my mind. Church had just let out, and all the folks were strutting around in their finest store-bought clothes. Down at the lake I saw a kid fishing with a beautiful new rod and reel. I stood watching him cast for a few minutes, fascinated with his rig till I just had to try it out. I walked over and asked him if I could; he said no without even looking back at me. Something inside me snapped. (I still don't know exactly what it was, though I know it wasn't really temper: at the time I wasn't very angry at the kid personally, and forgot all about his fishing pole.) I pulled the hunting knife out of my coat, stabbed the kid in the guts as hard as I could and said, "That's what you get, punk."

I turned and walked back up the hill. Hundreds of people were watching me, but no one tried to stop me. By the time I reached the street one of the Easter strollers must have gotten it together enough to tell a cop, because two of them grabbed me from behind just outside the park gate and hustled me into a squad car.

THE COUNSELORS AT JUVENILE HALL HAD a hell of a time interrogating me. They kept trying to discover some type of motive. Hell, I didn't know why I did it except that I had a knife and I was supposed to be tough, so I used it. I kept saying, "I don't know," while they kept thinking up possible reasons. It seemed like they were more nervous than I was, thinking up new lines of questions. Eventually they gave up, booked me, and took me around the corner for a physical.

When I walked into the room, this guy in a white uniform and thick round glasses greets me like a long-lost son. He had a voice like Oliver Hardy, a fleshy, pock-marked face with a brush moustache, and he managed to pack two hundred pounds into his five-foot-tall body. He made me take a shower, took my medical history, and checked my pulse.

"Sit down over here," he said, pointing to a metal stool right next to his desk. I was naked and that stool was cold. The next thing I see is his hand coming around the desk grabbing at my nuts.

"Cough!" he ordered.

I cough.

"No-no-no! Again!"

I cough again, louder.

"You're not doing it *right*," he says as he kneels down and grabs on to my penis. "Okay, try it now. I must make certain you don't have a hernia."

It took a long, long time to check me out. He was really getting into it when one of the counselors walked in. "You finished, Doc? I'm sposta put'm away."

After I put my clothes on, the counselor walked me down to Receiving, asked me a bunch of personal questions, then put me in the day room where boys of all ages were hanging around watching television. It was big and crowded, maybe four hundred guys in there. Mattresses were strewn all over the place but even so it was so packed that the younger kids were forced to sleep on the bare tile floor.

After three days of watching TV in the day room I was assigned to a company—a group of boys all the same age, patterned on an army platoon—and sent to the company room, which was nothing but a smaller version of the big day room.

By the time I got to the company I knew the ropes of Juvenile Hall enough to realize I'd have to fight or get chewed to bits. As soon as I walked into the room, this guy, a little bigger and a little older, came up to me. I figured this was it.

"Whass y' name, boy?"

"Carr. Whass yours?"

"Whatchya in for, Carr?"

"I stabbed a kid over in Hollenbeck Park."

"Think you're tough enough to fight, Carr?"

"I'll fight any—"

With that he smashed me in the mouth. I saw it coming and tried to duck, but I was too slow. My tongue was cut, and I was bleeding pretty bad. I kicked him hard in the shin and got in a punch, but he was too big for me. He hit me in the gut, spun me around, and pushed me into the wall. When I tried to get up, he kicked me down again. I was beat.

After he was sure all the other kids had seen me down for good, the kingpin walked over and stuck out his hand. "Y'did all right, Carr. My name's Clam." He pulled me up and shook my hand, then introduced me to the rest of the dudes. Clam was still the king, but everybody in the company knew I wasn't afraid to fight.

TWO WEEKS LATER I HAD TO appear in Judge Reed's court. Clam and some of the others who'd been in juvey before told me all about him. They called him "Max" because all he ever gave were maximum sentences. He never let anyone go home. "Go to Max's court man, an' it's off to camp, or to a foster home, or to fuckin' prison. There's jus' no way home."

I'd never been in a courtroom before. It scared me at first. My mother was sitting there crying her head off. When the clerk called my name, he called hers too. Judge Reed stuck his head out like a turtle, looked down at both of us, and started telling my mother what a bad boy I was. He had my whole history in front of him, from the fire on down to what he called my "brutal and callous disregard for others."

When he finished bad-mouthing me, he started in on her. "Some people are capable of raising children. Others are not. You certainly are not." It was like he was making a speech to the whole world. At the end of every line he'd look down hard at us, then back to all the other people in the courtroom as if we were both so bad everyone should take special note.

"In cases such as this where the parents are unfit and have repeatedly demonstrated their incompetence, the county must intervene for the good of the child as well as the good of the public. For this reason it is my responsibility to have James placed in a foster home for a period of two years."

When my mother started crying, Reed gave her a hard look and said, "Your own loose living and lack of moral instruction are in large part responsible for this boy's crimes." By this time even I thought she was fucked up—though I knew she hadn't had any idea about the things I'd done. In fact, she really didn't even know who I was.

THERE IS NOTHING PLEASANT ABOUT SITTING in your own shit in the dark for days on end, but it'd be almost tolerable if it weren't for the legendary Isolation Diet. In the entire California penal system there's no better food than on the Tracy mainline, and none worse than in Tracy's Hole. They make a loaf of squashed beans, squashed carrots, and squashed squash, all mixed together and baked. Twice a day I get an ice-cold slice of this between two slices of white bread, plus all the water I can drink. That's it. Drink plenty of water and walk real slow.

Sometimes all I can think about is food. I go on incredible food trips for what seems like days. Of course I don't know how long it really is: I've lost all sense of time. It speeds up and slows down to tremendous extremes, and I take off flying or walking under water. The only clock I have is the twice daily arrival of the isolation loaf, but the guards vary the meal hours, so even that doesn't mean a thing. You forget you've eaten shortly after they've left, and get delirious or go tripping again.

I keep telling myself stories in order to control the delirium. Putting the past in order saves me from the complete disorder of the present.

The first "prison" I was ever sent to was called Alexander's Boys' Home. I was eleven years old. I remember it was a real big, nice two-story white house right in the middle of the East L.A. ghetto.

Alexander himself was a big fat man with tiny shoulders— he looked just like a pear. Seemed like his gut started at his neck. His belt was hidden from sight up underneath there, and he wore pants with big old cuffs that were about four feet too long and hung all over his rundown shoes. And he had nerve enough to wear a tie. He looked like the top fool in the world, but when he first picked me up at juvenile Hall, he acted like the nicest guy you ever want to meet. It was just like Dracula picking you up in the woods. "How you doin' son? I come to get you outta this bad place!"

We get outside and he puts me in his station wagon. "Well, ya hungry? Let's you and me stop for a little bite to eat." He took me to a drive-in and got me a hot dog, then we drove out to his house.

Alexander was getting ghetto rich off the place. He had twenty-four kids at eighty dollars per month each, plus a salary for both him and his wife. They had it worked out so they fed us practically nothing: a peanut-butter sandwich with a glass of powdered milk in the morning, soup for lunch, and the famous Mama Alexander breadcrumb meatloaf for dinner.

Alexander got his pay from the county in return for rehabilitating his "children," but he sure didn't have to do much. He'd send us to public school all day, put us to work painting and pulling weeds all afternoon, then send us up to bed at seven. On weekends it was even neater: He'd just send us home so he wouldn't have to feed us.

When I first arrived there all the kids crowded around to tell me about how vicious Alexander was, how he beat them and pushed them around. But I was always devilish—I was going to have my fun no matter what.

"BUCKLEY!" I WHISPERED LOUDLY.

"Quiet, Carr! We don't want no one else wakin' up."

I hit my head on the window frame on the way out and couldn't see much except a dark shape as Buckley raced down the fire escape. By the time I got down both Campbell and Buckley had disappeared. I didn't even care if I found them; it was a good feeling just to be out of that house and on my own.

"Hey, Carr! Over here!" I saw Buckley and Campbell in the bushes across the street. Campbell passed me a cigarette as I snuck in beside them. We squatted there, smoking and talking in whispers, planning what to do next. As we sat and listened to the quiet night, we heard some pigeons cooing in back of the house next door. We looked at each other and grinned.

A couple of weeks later there was an article in the local paper about pigeon thieves in the neighborhood. We'd gotten together over three hundred birds in Alexander's backyard. Man, we had pigeons for *days*! It was all we could do to build cages fast enough to keep 'em all in.

One night we stole a whole coop from a doctor who saw and followed us back to Alexander's. When the police arrived we were in the backyard with a whole neighborhood full of pigeons. They had Alexander out there in his nightshirt asking him where he had got all the pigeons. The doctor was yelling at him on the other side, and the good Alexander was going out of his mind. The cops told him he had to return the pigeons and discipline us, and then left.

Alexander called us up to his office one by one—first Campbell, since he was the littlest.

"Where'd those pigeons come from?" we could hear him yelling through the door. "You'd better tell the truth, boy!"

"I don't know anything about it," said Campbell.

Alexander started screaming, "Bullshit, bullshit, *bullshit!*" and beating Campbell with a razor strop.

He didn't even bother to *ask* Buckley, because when Buckley went in he told Alexander he was a "fat-assed fool." After that all I could hear was the strop workin'.

Next it was my turn.

"Carr, I'm gettin' rid of you! I'm sendin' you back to Juvenile Hall unless you come clean an' tell me who those pigeons belong to, an' right now!"

I was ready to break out laughing. There was this slobbering crook sweating away in his ridiculous nightshirt with a razor strop in his hand threatening to send me *away*.

"I don't know nothin' about 'm—they were here when I got here! And if you touch me with that strap I'm runnin' away, 'cause I don't let anybody beat me but my dad!"

Alexander called the authorities on the phone and told them the whole story. When he got done telling how I wasn't "rehabilitable," and they "oughta send the little sonabitch off to prison," they told him they didn't want me either and hung up. There was nothing the fool could do. I walked out and went to bed laughin'.

The next night the three of us snuck down the fire escape again. By this time we knew that once Alexander goes to sleep he's not wakin' up. I'd decided to steal this pen full of ducks. We brought them all back in a gunny sack and turned 'em loose in the backyard. Early in the morning everybody's sitting around eating peanut butter sandwiches when Alexander finds the ducks.

"Where'd them ducks come from?"

Nobody knows. "What ducks?"

Alexander says, "Well . . . if no one don't come after 'em, it's all right."

"WHAT'LL YOU BOYS HAVE TODAY?"

"We want four of them double-decker burgers, with lotsa cheese, man, and none of them stale buns, and five orders of french fries, an' a gallon of root beer."

Buckley, Campbell and me were sitting up at the counter of the greasy corner hamburger joint. Since the pigeons were discovered in Alexander's backyard, everyone in the area knew who we were and hated us. We'd got this hamburger guy's pigeons too. So when he brought us the food and I pulled out a rusty old revolver and told him to hand over the cash, he started stuttering uncontrollably. He held the money out at arm's length, his worst fear having been realized. We grabbed the loot and took off.

The burger guy ran to Alexander, who caught up with us just as we were running out of a pie factory, where we'd stolen a rack of pies. That was it. He whipped us till he was too tired to lift his strop. Then he beat me with the buckle on his belt for a while.

After that we went on a real rampage. At night we'd take all four tires off a car and leave it up on wooden blocks. We'd do five or six cars like that in one night and sell the tires to the crooks running the local gas station. They'd give us five dollars apiece for them, repaint the rims and sell the tires back to some of the people we'd stole them from for fifteen or twenty bucks apiece.

Instead of going to school during the day, we'd check out houses where the folks both worked and the kids went to school. After we'd cased a house we'd break in, take the radios, TV's, jewelry, clothes, and sell them to the pimps and dope dealers down on Central Avenue. Alexander was sleeping while we were out rehabilitating ourselves by getting wise to the streets.

On Friday nights Alexander sent us home. What actually happened was, he turned us loose; he'd put us on the bus, but we never went home. Me and Campbell and Buckley saw a different part of L.A. every weekend, sleeping in cars and pulling little heists to pay our way around.

One Friday we rode the trolley over to USC, a real rich university right in the heart of the ghetto. When we got off, the sun had gone down but the dirty heat had stuck around. We walked down the alleys behind the fraternity houses, trying all the garage doors. Finally we found one that was open.

"Hey, lookit that!" I cried, pointing to a beer keg against the wall. "Let's see if there's anything in it." It was full.

We started drinking out of the tap. It was a lot of beer but it was also warm and flat. We were taking turns lying on our backs, the beer splashing out over our faces and clothes. There was beer all over the floor. None of us could see straight.

The next thing I remember the lights came on and some flattop frat dude with a dumb look on his face was standing in the door. The three of us ran down the alley, got back on the trolley heading uptown, and kept right on riding until we got uptown.

We were still pretty drunk when we got off and started walking down Hill Street. We were walking by the RKO theater when we saw a huge cardboard can filled with money for the March of Dimes wired to the ticket booth. We decided to take it.

"What's the cartoon?" "How much for popcorn?" I kept talking to the cashier, keeping her attention while the other two tugged at the can right under her nose. But the thing was too heavy for them to handle, so I had to help. The three of us removed this bucket of change and carried it off. If the cashier saw us, she was too shocked to do anything about it.

We dragged the can around back to the alley and dumped out the contents. It was a huge mountain of money, at least a couple hundred dollars. We started divvying it up, fives first, then ones, then coins. It was taking a lotta time just as we got down to quarters, here comes the cops. I grabbed what I had and took off as fast as I could. Buckley and Campbell were greedy, though. They tried to hide the money in a trash can before the police got 'em. Buckley got caught running with that big March of Dimes tub. I met Campbell on the way back to the home. He told me he'd hid himself in a trash can and heard Buckley get caught.

"Man, you smell like rotten eggs."

"Yeh," he laughed, "but I didn't get caught like Buckley."

"Wonder what ol' Alexander's gonna say about us comin' back so soon," I said. "We might even hafta wake him up."

Neither of us liked the prospect. But when we got there, and Alexander asked us what we were doing back so soon, I told him, "I've changed my mind Mr. Alexander, I like this place."

Alexander was a dog, but he had no sense. "Well," he says, "go on up to your room and go to bed. It's after seven o'clock."

A couple hours later there's a knock on the front door. We could hear the cop car with its engine running, doors slamming, a cop telling Buckley to shut up. We knew they'd be coming up to get us.

The cops were beating the door down. "Open up, police." They had to beat on the door with their clubs before they finally managed to wake up Alexander.

"What's the matter, officers?" Alexander croaks out.

"We caught this kid in an alley downtown. He was running with a March of Dimes collection basket that he and his buddies stole from in front of the RKO theater."

Alexander knew he was in trouble; he was supposed to *take* us home. He told the cops me and Campbell were Buckley's partners and we were right upstairs in bed.

The cops came and got us, but all they did was bawl us out. "You should be ashamed stealing from poor crippled kids." I didn't care shit about that. That was dead, didn't mean a thing to me. Alexander's whip did, though. When the cops left he nearly crippled us.

The cops' report led to a full investigation of Alexander. The pigeon incident, my robbery, and then the March of Dimes thing finally drew a flood of county people. When they found out about Alexander keeping the clothing allowance, feedin' us peanut butter, and sendin' us home on weekends, they decided *he* was an incompetent and closed him down. Since I was the one who had caused all the trouble, I got a ticket back to see Judge Reed.

I could see he had a plan for me this time. He said I needed "close parental control," which meant that he was putting me in with this fanatical, middle-aged Christian, Mrs. Richardson— a screaming believer.

Light streamed in over the big desk in the parlor. The place had a peculiar smell of aging couches, crocheted doilies, and furniture polish. Sunday morning, my first Sunday morning at Mrs. Richardson's, all dressed up in a new suit she bought me down at the secondhand store. "It's a little big," she said, "but you'll grow into it." The shoes she got me were a little big too— two sizes too big—but they didn't have my size. "You can't wear them sneakers to my church, James, and you must go the way of the Lord."

She handed me a prayer book and a hymnal across the desk. I had to say, "Yes, ma'am, thank you," every time she spoke to me or she'd break off into a lecture I couldn't stand. "No slouching, stand up straight. It's almost time to go."

She made me go to the morning services, Sunday school, and then Bible training all afternoon. There was something wrong with me, she said, and the only way for me to become a good boy was by changing my behavior completely. She made me join the choir the next Sunday, and after that when her friends came over in the evenings I had to sing solos for them while Mrs. Richardson bragged about all she was doing for me.

At first I believed Mrs. Richardson when she said there was something wrong with me, and I went along with her program. I even went so far as to get a job doing yardwork for Reverend Monroe, who grew to like me and made me an usher. The ushering was the high point of my career in the church. I greeted the people as they came in and showed them to their seats. Then I'd stand reverently at the head of an aisle while the Reverend gave his sermon. It was always the same: he'd start out slowly with some quotation or other, put in a little stack of morality, then lead up to his conversations with God—where God had inspired his teachings and told him they needed a proper place to be heard: a new church. This was the cue to start the collection; me and the other ushers would take the baskets around and the flock would dig in deep.

After a while I got tired of church and hip to the Reverend. He was the biggest crook in the neighborhood. Leading all those people on about how him and God is pals and they got to show their faith by contributing to the church fund. Shit, that old bastard had a big house and a new Cadillac every year. And later, after he'd collected over fifty-thousand dollars for the church, he just split—left L.A. with the loot and never returned.

Meanwhile, though, I got a little of the action myself. While Monroe was up there preaching, I'd slip into the cloakroom to pilfer the ladies' handbags. And after everybody left, I helped count the collection, taking ten or fifteen dollars for myself each week. But like the good Reverend, I kept up my act: always sweet and respectful. I filled in everything with "Yes, sir, yes, ma'am," until everyone at the church from Monroe on down was telling Mrs. Richardson "what a good boy your James Edward is."

I was making a good living for my age, until one Sunday this real believer kid named Jack ushered with me and saw me tuck a ten-spot up my sleeve. He told Monroe, who came running out of his house after me as I left the church and searched me down. By that time I had the money stashed in my shoe, but Jack insisted I had it, so they even made me take off my socks. That did it. When the bill dropped out, Monroe slapped me down and blackballed me from the church. Mrs. Richardson sang hymns over my body while she cried and beat me with her strap.

After that, I completely gave up thinkin' something was wrong with me. On Sundays Mrs. Richardson would make me get dressed up and send me off to church. I told her I had another church, but of course I didn't. Instead I'd blow some grass and go to all these little churches in East L.A. to listen to the music. The women singing their solos were my favorite. They had that deep Southern inflection in their voices that vibrated more feeling than any other sound I'd ever heard.

I didn't go to any one church though, and I'd stopped going to school. Every day on the way to school I'd look for something to do—practically anything seemed to be better than going to class. Down the street from Mrs. Richardson's was a mortuary where they had funerals every day. All the cars parked out in front, everybody dressed up in black—it looked good. One day I slipped inside. There he was, some old boy decked out in his finest with a bunch of flowers on his chest. The whole place was so somber it was exciting. When the mourners got in their cars after the service, I jumped in with some of them. They never noticed. I rode across town in the caravan all the way to Forest Lawn. From then on I was hooked—I went to all kinds of funerals all over town. I even got into a big military funeral of a general all dressed in his uniform. It was cold out at the cemetery. I felt really sad when they played taps and shot off the rifles. I didn't know what it meant, but I loved it. I kept going because I'd see all these people. Then someone would say what a nice guy he was. I couldn't wait to get up and walk by the coffin. I couldn't wait to look in there and see the old boy—and there he was.

TWO

FUNERAL TRIPPING. THE SMELL OF THE thing comes back to me strong: all the dime-store perfume and cigar smoke rolling around, tons of flowers, and the odor I never could figure out, that old embalming fluid.

Those dead people were a lot nicer than Mrs. Richardson. She wouldn't let me go home; she was making too much bread off my ass. "Now, James," I can hear her croak, "James, you get better and I'll let you go in six months." Fact is, she kept me there for two whole years. I was wild, crazy mad at her—but she taught me how to control it. I could look at her sweet as pie while doing nothing but plotting on her death. It was my one wish and dream to return to that house and burn the place down. Make it into a burning coffin for Mrs. Richardson—closed-box funeral. I'd even toss a bottle of perfume in there to make it right.

When I finally did get out, I couldn't go through with it; I was just too happy about leaving.

By the time I got cut loose from Mrs. R's I was thirteen and flyin' high. My mother had moved over into Watts. It was spring of 1956, and the gang activity was reaching its height. Everybody was in a gang. The gangs from Watts were raiding down in Compton and the Compton boys were raiding up into Watts.

The dominant gang in my new neighborhood was called the Farmers, headed up by Junior Terrell. Junior looked like a monkey: he was big, but his arms hung clear down to his knees, his forehead sloped out, and when he walked his feet pointed out in different directions. His hands were as big as Sonny Liston's and he could move like Sugar Ray. On the Avenue the dudes that knew him stepped aside. He talked only to other guys in the gang and never to chicks unless they were at the head of a train and he was the engineer.

I really dug the shit out of the Farmers. First of all, they dressed real sharp. That was important after my experience of wearing nothing but hand-me-downs and secondhand stuff. Then they drove a squadron of old cut-down Buicks which they lowered, chromed, and painted all kinds of wild colors. But most important, they were tough, and I always admired toughness.

Anyway, my mother had moved into their neighborhood, so I couldn't help but come into contact with them. They hung out at a place near my house and on the weekends went over to the dances the city had out in the park—Sport Night they called it—and supposedly they put it on to keep kids off the street. They had it in this broken-down hall without any windows. Most of the slats had been stripped from the walls. The most you could say for the place was that it had a roof and electricity for the bands. On Friday night, though, the place was jammed.

I remember I went down there for the first time on the Friday right after my thirteenth birthday. All the Farmers were inside with their girlfriends doing a real funky bop: just about fucking on the dance floor. Everyone was dancing hard and I wanted to get in on it bad. But being new in the neighborhood, I didn't know any of the chicks except by sight, so I just went up to the foxiest one in the room, named Katie, and asked her to dance. She said "okay" kind of sly and we danced.

I knew she was a Farmer chick but I didn't care. We danced like crazy for a long time; then she said she had to split, and I went outside. I was immediately surrounded by Farmers, mad as hell that I'd danced with their chick. The next thing I knew, some Joe Louis fires at me out of the dark and I was getting stomped on from every side. I would have been hurt bad, but just at that moment an old lowrider named Billy—one of those thirty-year-old dudes that's just always on the scene—ran down the steps to save my ass. He pulled the Farmers off and sent me home.

The next day I took my bongos down to the empty lot next to the liquor store where the Farmers hung out. I'd made the bongos at school, but I didn't have my math together and didn't know how to work the machines, so they turned out lopsided and ugly. They looked like eggs but they worked, and the Farmers all liked the way I played. I started going down every day to play my bongos, and after a couple of weeks they asked me if I wanted to become a junior Farmer—a "Future Farmer of America" they called it. Of course I did, and said so, trying to keep my cool.

Right away I had to get my shit together: my outfit and my hog. The Farmers dressed up in overalls, white shirts, homburg hats, and knobs which they'd buy two sizes too big, soak in water and bend up so the toes stuck straight up in the air. I used the good old tuck-and-roll to steal the overalls, and ran out of a shoe store with a thirty-dollar pair of knobs on. I borrowed a hat and then started working on a '37 Buick I got from my uncle's junkyard—it smoked like hell but it ran.

I was immediately taken up in the forefront of the gang warfare, the test for trust and the main reason for sticking together. The first time out I proved I could do more than play bongos good. One of the other members of the Farmers had been waylaid by a rival gang, and we were going to avenge him. We found out about a party this gang was having and decided to get them all. I had the idea to burn the place down with gas bombs, Molotov cocktails. When I was younger, we used to throw them up against the walls over in Aliso Village. It's a beautiful, decent sight to see. We did it down there just to watch them burn but now I wanted to use them for real. None of the other Farmers had done it before. When I demonstrated the way the thing worked they were all excited. We made about twenty or thirty bombs and drove off to this party, whipped 'em through the windows and burned the place to the ground. People were running out of the joint screaming, and as they ran out more cocktails covered the lawn and sidewalk with exploding gas. All the small fires soon became one huge one. We threw a few unlit cocktails into the middle of the house to finish it off; then we went to their leader's house and torched it up too.

Besides being willing to attack other gangs ferociously, we were absolutely notorious for ripping off expensive chicks. We'd cruise over on a weekend to the west side of L.A., find a party, walk in and take the thing over. We were funkier and more aggressive than these real proper dudes, and their chicks liked that. After a while, one of us would ask some sharp-looking chick if she wanted to go to the store. When she got outside and into one of the Buicks, the next thing she knew she was all the way over in hell—in the middle of Watts with a squad of Buicks behind her. We'd take her down to our clubhouse and strip her down, then we'd all fuck her, as many as twenty guys in a train.

Sex was a very minute thing. It didn't have to make any sense. It was for the minute. You did it for a while, then it became natural. Everything we did was like that—unquestioning and explosive. You can only do crazy shit when it's your routine. With sex it was the game that was routine: nearly every train started and ended with the same moves. On the street it was more the attitude—looking for openings to fuck around or fuck somebody up—so the actions themselves were diverse and spontaneous. Like the time, a couple of months after hooking up with the Farmers, when I was just walking around down on 103rd Street with four brothers. We'd been smoking some weed and were really broke and hungry when we walked by this Mexican bakery. There were all kinds of pastries and cakes in the window, just sitting there. We didn't hesitate.

We went around to the back of the place, giggling like a pack of fools, climbed up a fence and onto the roof. I broke open the ventilation system and we all slithered down it, dropping the last ten feet to the floor. What a surprise! A huge room filled with cakes and cookies. Vat upon vat of icing and cake mix, banks of stainless-steel ovens, giant sinks, and sacks of flour for days. We started eating and smearing the stuff all over the walls, throwing bowls of icing into the ovens, and ripping the sinks off the walls. I picked up a hundred-pound sack of flour and broke it over one of the dudes' heads. He came up all white and coughing, his eyes looking like two pissholes in a snowbank. Then somebody did the same to me. Another guy was breaking every dish he could find, and there was water an inch deep from the ripped-up sinks. We were sliding and skating around in the paste of flour and water, laughing hysterically, and throwing shit at each other. This went on for hours until the inside of that bakery was chaos.

At four a.m. the baking crew came in through the front door. We heard them coming and ran for it, but the back door was locked and we were laughing too hard to break it open. They stood there gazing at our handiwork in a state of total shock. Then they started yelling and swinging at us with their stirring sticks. The place was like a skating rink; it was so slippery that the bakers would fall on their asses every time they took a swing. We maneuvered around them to the front door and ran out into the street: five black kids hauling ass through the dawn with flour pouring out of our ears, a bunch of squealing bakers chasing us, waving their sticks in the air.

Four of us got away but Tony, the littlest guy, was caught and beat up by the bakers. When the cops came they tricked him into telling our names. That night they came to our houses, pulled us out of bed, and took us to the Watts police station. They questioned me for hours; I just kept saying that I'd been home all night. Tony insisted that I'd been with him. Since there was only his word against mine and none of the bakers could say for sure who was who, we were all released, except for Tony. He never came back to the neighborhood. I never saw him again.

A FEW WEEKS LATER THE JUVENILE authorities came to the conclusion that even though Tony's testimony wasn't enough to convict me of anything, it was enough to send me to "camp" for probation violation. The cops picked me up and took me in front of the Juvenile Board, a bunch of mangy old dogs who told me I'd like "camp" because it was in the hills. At the time,

I really didn't mind going; I remember thinking I was on the Way Up. It was in Los Padres National Forest and we were outdoors all day, but I got tired of that in a hurry. I wanted to get into camp with bigger, tougher kids, or else back to the streets. I hooked up with a Chicano dude and escaped by using bent forks to climb the chicken-wire fence.

I never went home. I went back to Aliso Village and shacked up with various divorcees at night. During the day I hustled and became an expert at tuck-and-roll. This suspicious-looking dude named Buster, my partner, would go into an expensive men's store downtown. I'd follow him in. All the salespeople would be paranoid watching him as I tucked-and-rolled a suit under my coat. We'd do four or five of these jobs a day for customers we'd line up at the pool hall in the Village. I was making thirty or forty dollars a day doing this, which wasn't bad money for my age.

Since I hadn't gone home, my mother had absolutely no idea where I was, and my probation officer couldn't find me either. I saw him several times in the street and dodged him. One day I came around a corner and there he was, right in front of me. I took a big gulp of air and started to turn just as he grabs me. "Hold it right there, James," he says, "you're goin' back to camp." I asked him when. He said, "Now!" I broke his hold by bringing my arms up hard from underneath, and outran him down the street. There was just no way I was going back to that camp when I was having so much fun on the streets.

After I got away, I kept seeing the guy around the ghetto more and more. I knew I was going to get caught sooner or later. Finally he saw me down on 103rd Street. When I started to run he started to scream, "Stop! Thief! Thief!" and a fat old traffic cop ran me down on his three-wheeler.

"You're not goin' back to camp now, boy," he snarled. "You're goin' back to the judge!" He was all blown out, puffin' and heavin' in like a steam shovel. I laughed in his face.

". . . A HARDENED CRIMINAL AT FOURTEEN. An example of undisciplined living, loose morals . . . " Judge Reed, his fat lips moving as if they were something separate from his immobile head, was reading the riot act, saying how the County could no longer be responsible for me. He was sending me up to higher authorities, to the California Youth Authority. I was on my way to Paso Robles, the reform school up in the Central Valley for kids twelve to sixteen.

Kids from all over California who have been delinquents all their lives finally meet each other in Paso Robles. Some, like me, are moving in for the first time, a few for the second or third.

I rode up on the bus with a dude named Wally Collins—we called him "June"—a funny-looking kid with a big wide nose. He just looked like a June. He was straight from Alabama and a crazy motherfucker with a bad attitude just like me. I mean, he liked to have his fun and never stopped giving the cops shit. On the bus trip we got bored and carved our initials on the side panel with June's nail clippers. At Paso Robles the driver told the clerks in Receive and Release that someone on the bus had done some carving. The clerks told the guard, who lined us up in a long row, handcuffed side by side.

The clerk, a little man with moles all over his face, pointed at me and June and whispered something we couldn't hear. The guard nodded and announced loudly, "We'll take care of them. We don't take that kind of crap around here."

He came walking down the line toward us, swinging all these keys he had on a long lanyard. He was walking real slow, staring all the kids down, letting everyone know he was the boss. The next thing I knew, he twirled the lanyard in the air and hit me right on top of the head with them. It hurt so bad I was paralyzed. For a minute all I could do was stand there looking at this big motherfucker, barely believing he'd hit me. Then I ran at him blindly. June helped me, but we were handcuffed together, besides being too little for the job. He knocked us both down and dragged us half a mile to the Hole.

When we got down there it was all dark and smelly. The smell was vomit. There wasn't much air to begin with, and it was deep into August. It was like hell. We figured since they gave us single cells and just threw us in, we'd lie around for a month or so. June went to sleep. I lay back on the steel bunk and tried breathing through my mouth.

At six that evening the cops got us up, yelling, "Fall in line!" Everyone stumbled out of their cells into the corridor. I was feeling weird because I didn't know any of the kids in there or what the fuck was going on. Nobody said a word. I tried asking the kid behind what was happnin' but he just looked at me like I wasn't there. It wasn't natural. These dudes looked funny. A lot of fuckin' Indians. The bull gave some kind of military order I couldn't understand and everybody turned a quarter step. Two more orders and he had the whole line marching double time down the runway and out onto the football field. "Hup, hup, hup." I thought they must be joking.

Officer Butts, a big redneck cowboy who sported a snap shirt, pointy-toed boots, and topped it off with a ten-gallon hat, was out in the middle of the field under an umbrella, sipping on some ice water. The sun was low. There wasn't any air out there either. It was just boiling.

Butts didn't say anything. He sat there like a big purple-faced mummy while the other kids made me and June fall in at the end of the line. There must have been sixty guys standing at attention when Butts shouts, "Forward! Run!"

The line moved out fast. Around the track through all that heat. After the first lap my feet were burning, my lungs were aching, and I was dizzy. After three laps, June dropped to the ground spread-eagled and passed out. Butts came up out of his chair on the dead run. "Get up you son of a bitch!" he cried, and kicked June as hard as he could. Nobody else stopped running, as if they knew some things that June and I didn't. They just kept going around that track with two Indians leading the way.

Butts was still kicking at June, so I went over, sat down under the umbrella for a rest, and had a slug of his drink. When he saw what I was doing, he went right out of his mind.

"You black bastid! What the fuck do you think you're doin'?" He was so mad he could barely talk—this huge bull with his high, funny voice. Before he could get at me with his boots I jumped up and started running again. There was no way I could keep it up, though: I had to fall out again. This time Butts got a couple of kicks in, then had me and June sent back to the Hole without a shower. We were steaming, and the mosquitos were having a ball.

THE HOLE WAS RUN BY THE Paso Robles goon squad. Butts' partner on the afternoon shift was named Martin. He looked, dressed, and acted the part of Butts' twin brother. Nasty Jack, the guard on the morning shift, was even worse. The night guard provided our only comic relief: Just Plain Williams, an ancient cop working a soft job while waiting to die.

Every morning they got us up before the birds at four thirty—to run. They had me running twelve miles a day, half of it *after* chow at night. Butts never let us stop. I couldn't possibly finish the whole distance without a rest; I'd still be out on the track while the rest of the dudes were already showering up. In the morning after we'd packed in our six miles, they had us march down a dirt road to some pits—just a bunch of holes in the ground that the cons had dug up with picks and shovels. They'd make us dig and dig till the holes were like ten feet deep, and then they had us fill them up again. Butts used to laugh, "Time for yer rehabilitations! Start diggin', boys." June didn't go for this shit at all. He'd disappear down one of the holes no one was working in, or chase everyone else away from his hole and go to sleep at the bottom in the cool shade. When Butts got wise to this he'd let June get to sleep and then have a bunch of dudes begin burying June alive.

Life was a constant battle between us and the guards. I spent six months in the Paso Robles Hole because I couldn't get enough clean time together. They had this rating system: three was excellent, two passing, one didn't mean shit. I just couldn't get my twos together. As soon as I did I broke a guy's arm in a baseball game and Butts got me transferred to Preston.

PRESTON IS AN OLD PLACE OFF Highway 99 in Ione, California. Originally the only building was a castle, and the cons did their time in there, but as the institution expanded new buildings were constructed, and the castle became the administration building.

They went through the same routine every time I got transferred: asking the same questions that they had a dozen times and writing it all down, of course. I guess they need the paper work to increase the number of jobs in the system and keep the budget high. When they asked me where I was from, I answered, "Shit, I'm from Paso Robles." Which wasn't just a wise remark: I'd moved so much that I could never exactly say where I was from. I was from everywhere.

The authorities also had a setup at Preston where the new arrivals were put into a dormitory with a bunch of older cons called COs—gorillas that the counselors themselves were afraid to deal with. They put them in charge of us in the hope that by giving them a little power they'd make them into rats. These guys at Preston loved their duty, loved doing the dirty work for the counselors.

The main activity in this dormitory was buffing the rubberized concrete floor with big hand buffers that weighed about forty or fifty pounds. They had ten of these buffers working and all the kids were supposed to take a turn. But when the guy called my name I said, "No, I won't do it. Don't even ask me." At this the COs got up from where they were playing cards in the corner and pushed me into a back room. There were three of them: Buzz Moran from the Slausons, a Chicano dude by the name of Ed Venitas and a white goon named Carey.

"Now look," said Buzz, with that you-know-you-better-cooperate look. "Our job in this house is to make *sure* you buff that floor and anything else the cops say you gotta do. Your only job here is to *do* it. We're just askin' you this one time. Now get yer ass out there and start buffin'!"

Moran had the other two hold me while he worked me over good. When he got through I was still talking crazy, so they called the cop in. He told them to beat on me some more, but they knew it wouldn't work that way and sent me back out on the floor with the other kids.

I couldn't understand how people put up with filling holes they had dug or buffing a floor that was already so shiny you could see your face in it. It was just a useless way of wasting time that didn't have any point but to let you know what would happen if you didn't take orders. I felt like this time I was letting them know right away that I wasn't putting up with their bullshit.

"They" in this case meant the COs. The authorities work it so you're one-on-one with another convict—setting you against one another. In this case, me against Buzz Moran. I knew he was out to get me after the little difference of opinion in the dormitory. I also knew he must have a lot of enemies among the other guys he'd beat up or forced to do dumb jobs.

The next day, I heard the rumors I'd already suspected to be true. This dude who used to run with the Slausons himself told me what a dog and a snitch Moran was. He also told me that Moran was gonna get me for making him look bad. Later in the morning, this same dude, Mike, slipped me a piece of pipe.

In the afternoon it was hot and humid. Nothing moved inside the prison except the prisoners and their keepers. It was one of those days when the sounds from far away made a dull thud when they hit your ears, the crawling heat got under your skin and made you feel like you're in a snake pit.

"March! Hup! Hup! Hup!" Out of the dormitory onto this black-topped yard. I was burning up and so was the rest of the company. Our boots were so hot we could hardly keep our feet in them. The cops standing in the shade joking and fucking off while the COs counted cadence, Buzz Moran playing his role of head counter.

After an hour I'd had more than enough; I pulled out of line and stood there. Moran saw me, immediately called halt, and walked down the line, followed by Venitas and Carey threatening the other dudes not to move. They came walking toward where I was standing all alone, cussing me and generally warming up to give the cops and everyone else a show with me as the victim.

Moran was about three yards away from me when I rushed him with the pipe. I let out an insane scream and hit him across the top of the head as hard as I could. He crumbled to the ground with a puzzled look on his face. Nobody else was moving now except me, and I didn't stop for a second. I kept pounding at Moran around the head and in the groin. Everyone else was too stunned to move. I was still screaming, although I can't remember what. I was trying to beat Buzz Moran to death. I would have, too, but some of the kids came unstuck, and one of the biggest dudes smashed me on the side of the neck. The cops fell into a righteous panic, blowing whistles, yelling to each other, and keeping a good distance until they could figure out what was happening. I was sobbing, laughing, begging the dudes to let me finish Moran off.

It all happened fast—within a minute—but it was a *full* minute. It filled me up. I was high as the sky. Jungle Jim brought me down hard. Jungle, a barrel-chested, jar-headed goon with hair all over his body like Mussolini, extended his notorious reputation for brutality all over my body. When I came to, my tongue was cut, I couldn't breathe, my blood was all over the place. I looked up, and there was Jungle leering down at me with a gas gun in his hand. When I started trying to yell at him I could only croak out "muhfuck." Jungle Jim made some joke about how glad he was to see me conscious again, shot the gas canister into my closed-wall cell, and slammed the door. The gas was so thick I had to keep my head in the toilet, flushing it constantly in order to get air. When the goon figured the first canister had done its job he came back and gave me another one.

After a month and a half in the Hole with Jungle Jim as my special protector, I was assigned to a company on the main-line for fourteen and fifteen-year-olds. Most of the time we had to spend in a big, bare day room that had a wood platform at one end with a few weights, some aluminum tables and chairs, and a television that was constantly on. The counselor, a sinister bastard named LeNeure, sat up front, next to the buzzer he could use to call in the goons if anything happened. LeNeure had been wiped out in a riot once, with a steel ashtray, and had a big ugly scar across his left eye. He hated us. He worked there because he hated us. His biggest thrill came from getting us to fight so he could blackjack whoever won.

Every day was the same. The chow was so terrible, I couldn't eat it, especially since I knew that the guys in the kitchen pissed and shit in it from time to time. They had me working on the farm for no wages. The rest was all fuckin' TV.

I felt like exploding. I was so full of crap I couldn't stand it. Just after dinner one night I walked into the room, took one of the chairs and smashed the television to bits, and started throwing what was left of it at LeNeure. Everyone else started throwing chairs at him too. He pressed the buzzer a bunch of times and beat it out the door. At that I grabbed the first white kid I could get my hands on and beat the shit out of him. Soon there was a miniature race riot going on. The goons were there, knocked down the door and shot the joint up with a ton of tear gas. No one could stand that for very long, and one by one we ran out the door. The goons were lined up outside waiting: as we came out coughing, they beat us with their clubs. Their favorite move was to wait until you'd just gone by and swing the club up behind you between your legs—just the second you thought you'd got by one free you get it in the nuts.

After they beat us they took all the blacks and Mexicans to the Hole. I wanted to try an escape but the place was in the middle of a lot of farmland and a black boy stood out in all that corn. Furthermore, the prison officials paid the farmers fifty bucks for every kid they caught. Even if you did get out of prison the chances of getting out of Ione were slim to none.

The only attempt I saw was pulled off by a bunch of white kids led by a little dude named Puppet. He and three other guys attacked the guard. They were pounding the shit out of old LeNeure, trying to get his keys. The COs woke up in the middle of it and went to help LeNeure. I didn't know this Puppet at all, but I jumped into the scuffle on impulse, grabbed one of the COs, and started wailin' on his ass. When the cops came I thought I was on the way to the Hole again. But in the dark and confusion the cop hadn't seen what I was doing and thought I was trying to *help* him. They actually made me a hero, gave me a special award for bravery. The company and Puppet knew the truth, though, so nobody accused me of being a rat.

I started playing football to relieve the boredom. Getting on the team meant special diet and special time to practice, plus plenty of legal contact. I was in good shape from running so goddamn much at Paso Robles, so I did very well right from the start. I scored a lot of touchdowns for the coach, and in return he had me fed some decent grub and wrote me out fine reports.

I also went to church every Sunday. The counselors always kept a careful check on who went to church since it was voluntary. They figured if you went to church you must be on the road to recovery. The services were led by a white Baptist preacher from Ione who drove up every Sunday in his black Cadillac, ahead of one of those yellow school buses filled with a choir of youngsters. Most of the dudes who went to church did it to get off on the girls. I'd go to laugh at the preacher.

He'd get to lying like old Reverend Monroe about how he'd talked to God in the woods, waving his arms around, saying God told him he was one of the Chosen Few ordained personally to spread His message. He'd go on and on misquoting the bible and comparing himself with Moses. Unable to stifle my laughs, I'd sometimes burst out right in the middle of the service. Then this hick would roll his eyes back to the other side of his head and start another lie about how the devil was right there among us.

There was a regular theater at Preston that even had seats and a balcony. Once a week they'd show a movie, usually pretty old and fucked up. One Saturday night as I was watching *Blackbeard the Pirate*, I got the idea of starting a gang called the Pirates when I hit the streets. I could relate to Blackbeard: pillaging towns, taking over ships, ripping off all the good-looking women. That stuff was right on target. I figured with a gang like that I could do whatever I pleased, which was the absolute only thing I wanted to do. In December '57 my time was up. I couldn't wait. I'd done my year.

THREE

"Poor-Devil! You black bastard! Get your ass out here! I got somethin' to talk to you about!"

A pointed head with batwing ears bounced up above the railing of the porch. Poor-Devil was trying to get his beady eyes into focus. "Mothafuckah wake a man up . . ." He groaned, then took a look at me and grinned. "Oh! Iss you, Carr! Hey, man, welcome back! Howya doin?"

"Fine, fine," I said impatiently. "Hey, Poor-Devil, you ever hear of Blackbeard the Pirate?"

"Noooo . . . What kinda shit you talkin'?" Poor-Devil hadn't heard of anything outside of Los Angeles, much less Blackbeard.

"Listen, man," I went on, "Blackbeard the Pirate is in the movies, see, an' I caught his act in the joint. He had nothin' but the boldest pirate gang of all: they robbed all these ships and got the chicks and made dudes walk the plank an' shit. You an' me, we're gonna start a pirate gang, too. We're gonna have wig ponytails with silk scarves, an' navy bell-bottoms, an' boots, an' silk blouses. And we're gonna *march* together wherever we go."

Poor-Devil had really woken up to this. "Carr, thass a bad-ass plan: I can see you now," he laughed, "BLACKASS THE PIRATE. Listen, man, I know at least ten guys'll come in right now!" Which is why I'd come to make Poor-Devil my first recruit: he was small and weak but so crafty that he was always on top of it and had plenty of tough friends.

It was about nine o'clock. Poor-Devil had obviously passed out the night before on this rickety couch, now he was hungry. "Let's get some breakfast an' then I gotta get some more wine, he said. "Then we can go over to Stan's house and get into action."

While we were inhaling some eggs and grits, Poor-Devil filled me in on the neighborhood activity since I'd been away. Nobody went to school, any more; everyone cut to Stan's. Stan was a real pretty boy with a bad gas, and all the chicks loved him. His parents both worked, so every one partied hard there all day long.

By the time we got to the house with a couple of gallons of tokay, ten people were already dancing and fucking and carrying on. Poor-Devil introduced me to Stan and his partner Gino and ran down to all the dudes what the Pirates would be like. I said the first thing we had to do was learn how to march. Everyone thought that was cool, so we ran out and started right there. I had all these dudes out on Normandy Avenue marching up and down the sidewalk, with me alongside calling the cadence, and Poor-Devil out in front.

IN A WEEK STAN'S HOUSE FILLED up with guys wanting to join. Poor-Devil helped me pick out the toughest and told the rest to go home. There were fifteen of us, marching around East L.A.

in pirate outfits, drinking wine, dropping all kinds of pills and making big plans.

The only thing we still needed were the silk blouses. We all wanted them bad but didn't have money enough to get the ruffled kind we wanted. One day when we were bullshitting as usual, I got tired of talking tough and said, "You all want those motherfuckin' shirts, don't you? Well, I know a place we can get all the money we need to buy 'em. We're goin' down to the Western Union office. They've got plenty a money in there."

The dudes thought this was just fine, so I marched them right into the place and when this old clerk asked me what we wanted I said, "Give us the money—we got guns."

When the guy gave us the bread we just split. It was about two hundred dollars. None of us had a gun.

After we got the blouses the Pirates became one of the best-known gangs in the ghetto. Membership jumped up to about forty. Whenever a guy wanted to join, we'd call him a "leathercap" or a "rumpkin bill" (our private slang for "fool") and then make him fight one of us. If he did all right, then this "new-boy" would have to rob a Helms bakery truck and give the money to the Pirates. Then he was in, and he could start to work his way up in the gang.

ONE NIGHT STAN, GINO, AND A few other Pirates went to raid a party that the Businessmen, another big L.A. gang, were putting on. These guys got their name from ripping off expensive clothes and dressing up like prosperous dudes. When the Pirates pulled up, the party was going pretty good. All the Businessmen were drunk or stoned. There was a lot of dancing in the front room, a lot of fucking going on in back, and the Pirates wanted the action. So they started to tear the place up.

They threw all the furniture through a plate-glass window in the living room and chased all kinds of naked people out of the bedrooms. It was chaos until Ralph Lynn, the toughest guy in the Businessmen, got ahold of Stan, fucked him up really bad and threw him out the window.

After that the Pirates split outside to regroup; a couple of them came over to another party to get the rest of us. We all headed back to the Businessmen's. I was really hot to fight, while ol' Poor-Devil was agitating up a storm. When we got there we saw Stan lying out on the grass in the middle of all this furniture, which got us even more pissed. We sent one of our new-boys into the house in his Pirate uniform to talk with the Businessmen. In a few minutes he came back out all beat to shit.

That gave us an excuse to go in there and finish off the pad. There were so many Pirates now they couldn't do a thing. Some of us went through the house destroying what was left of its contents while another bunch either grabbed the chicks or beat up Businessmen as they tried to run out the doors. The only woman left inside, the mother of the dude who lived there, was screaming her lungs out. The only things standing were the walls. We'd had a ball.

A MONTH LATER STAN DID A real dumb thing that served to make our little game more serious. He took a bunch of other Pirates into Slauson to a party just because there was a chick over there he wanted to fuck. I knew what that part of town was like and refused to go. The whole neighborhood was in a gang called the Slausons—hundreds of them—and they were all armed robbers with plenty of guns. Stan and the boys thought they were tough, but they didn't even make it to the party before they were beat up and robbed.

Next day Poor-Devil and I were sitting around my house. We couldn't avenge the beating Stan got head-on; there were just too many Slausons for that.

"Guns," I said. "We gotta have some guns." At the time I was the only Pirate with a piece. "If we have the guns to do the job, we can just ambush the fuckers in the park." On Friday nights all the Slausons got in a big gym to dance. "When they come out," I said, "we'll just let em have it. They'll never know what hit 'em. Now look, there's a sport shop right down on Normandy with all the guns we need. At lunch there's only one guy in there, some ol' dude with a head like a chicken and glasses thick as your finger. We'll jus' take the old boy's glasses off and stomp on 'em. He won't know *what's* happening."

We went down to the shop. Sure enough, the old dude was alone in the place. "Gimme a pack of beebees," I told him. Since they were right behind him, he had to turn his back on me. When he did I choked him around the neck. Poor-Devil threw his glasses against a wall. We took all his guns and fifty dollars in cash and ran out the back door.

On Friday night our whole gang met at the park in Slauson. I walked up to the gym and looked in the window; they were all in there, all the punks who'd beaten up Stan. When the music stopped at 9:30 they came out, heading for other parties. When more than half the crowd had come out we started shooting from the bushes. It was a stampede—people running every which way, screaming and crying. When we ran out of ammunition we came out of the bushes and found a lot of people so scared they were cowering on the ground, unable to move. We beat them up with the guns and ran to our cars. As we pulled out, the street was blocked off by cops. We couldn't get away.

In those days we still played the cops' game: they didn't come around until after the fighting was over, and you let them arrest you without resisting. But when they got us into the Firestone Station things got rougher. "You're all punks!" they yelled, and started beating us with their clubs. We ended up fighting them; they came out on top.

THEY PUT ME IN JACK DANIEL'S Boys' Home, which was just like the rest—terrible. After a few weeks, instead of going home on the weekend, I ran off back to Aliso Village. The Pirates were gone. Stan was in some federal prison in Oklahoma. Gino was at a prison camp in northern California. And Poor-Devil had just disappeared.

I moved in with Esther, a big woman about twenty-five, a divorcee with a bunch of kids and a big welfare check she spent most of on me. Me and this other dude were both living there, fucking Esther, eating her food, and lying around playing records. A lot of people hung out there because Esther was so "welfare rich." One of these dudes, the craziest, was a dope fiend by the name of Willie Ranson. He was the moldiest character I'd ever met, always talking about robberies and scoring his next hit. He kept saying how easy it was to pull a job, how he hadn't worked a day since he'd discovered divorcees and armed robbery.

I had serious doubts about "turning pro," but Willie needed a partner so he kept working on me about how easy it was till finally I said okay, let's go.

We drove over to the west side. Willie went into a gun shop and bought a twenty-two and a thirty-ought-six, which we sawed off so they'd fit under our coats. When we got the guns ready we went out, stole a Packard, and cruised around looking for a place to hit.

We walked into the first quiet-looking grocery store we passed, a Mexican market in Pico Gardens. Willie stepped right up to the cashier. I walked behind the pile of bread which was stacked up on the counter. Willie asked the dude for the money. I pushed the barrel of the thirty-ought into his face through the loaves.

While the clerk put the money into a bag, Willie started walking around getting some bottles of port wine and lemon juice. Here I am sweatin' blood behind the Wonder Bread, nervous as hell at doing my first job like this, and fucking Willie's doing his shopping! I stood there shaking with a rifle against this poor clerk's ribs waiting for Willie to come back with his goddamn groceries and get the money. When he did, I ran to the car as fast as I could, with Willie right behind. It had just rained: the wheels on the old Packard spun out; we fishtailed all over the road, heading for Esther's.

An hour later the cops came around knocking on doors asking about dudes with our descriptions. Ol' Esther went to the door in her housecoat and hairnet, looking like a class-A Aliso Village divorcee. She told them she'd been inside all day taking care of her sick children: "Bin here all week in fac', off'sahs, an' nobody done came ta see me, 'cep you." We're kicked back in the next room grinning at Esther's act, knowing we wouldn't get caught now. We split up the money, about fifty each.

After that I went crazy. Money was just sitting around alongside the streets. I carried my rifle strapped under my coat wherever I went. When the mood struck me, I'd just go in and rob a liquor store or market. My response to anyone's money problems was, "Shit, man, they's a bank on every corner," which meant the liquor store.

Me and Willie would go to Johnnie's liquor store on Friday evening and hang around the parking lot drinking wine with the pimps, burglars, pickpockets and whores. Whenever some old man would go into Johnnie's to cash his paycheck, one of us would go in the store to buy some gum so we could see how much money he was geting. If the guy had a big check we'd go over to his car just as he was getting in and start talking to him. After a few seconds I'd pull the rifle out of my coat and let him see the barrel. These old boys were so scared, they'd give the money over right away. We never did get caught doing this, even though it was right in our neighborhood because the people we robbed would never remember what we looked like; all they'd remember was the gun.

I robbed all the liquor stores in the neighborhood except Johnnie's—seven or eight altogether—just by walking in and pointing the rifle at them. At each store I'd get anywhere from a hundred and fifty to four hundred dollars. But the money never lasted very long because I was always going on shopping sprees.

I loved shoes, and Roger's Bootery had real nice ones. I started going in there almost every day, buying as many as three pairs at a time. After a week the clerk made it a point to be especially friendly to me. He'd call me by my first name and pour me a drink of Chivas Regal every time I came in. I bought more than thirty pairs of shoes there in less than two months. I liked clothes, too, so I bought a bunch of suits and shirts.

I was really showy with my money. Willie taught me the trick of carrying a lot of change and jingling it so that people'd think I was rich. And I carried a Texas roll—a wad of bills, mostly ones and fives with a few big bills on the outside and play money on the inside to make it fatter.

Willie and I hooked up occasionally for more robberies, mostly fancy liquor stores on the west side which were easy because they weren't getting robbed very often. The only problem was getting away: we stood out because there weren't any blacks living in that part of town.

At the same time, we were ripping off taxi cabs. Willie and I did this only once in a while, but our friend Jo Phillips, whom I'd known from Flats and Preston, was a taxi specialist. He got out of jail around this time and went to work right away. One night he came home with five hundred dollars—he'd held up seventeen taxi drivers!

We pulled so many robberies that it became a way of life. We weren't in school and didn't have any intention of going. We were unskilled and didn't want to work anyway. Since we were spending money so fast we had to pull jobs at least once a week. We'd spend two hundred dollars a day buying everything we wanted. You spend money like this because in the back of your mind you know that you can always get more just by pulling another job. When we bought wine we'd get six or seven half gallons for the winos and get drunk with them on the street corner.

Even though we were robbing fools, we were very careful about which liquor stores we hit. A lot of the bigger ones are death traps. One dude hides in the back and sits there looking and waiting. When somebody comes in to rob the place the clerk is very polite because, he says, he's insured and doesn't want any trouble. As the holdup man takes the money and turns to go, the clerk ducks down behind the counter and the guard steps out with a scattergun and blows you away.

I TOOK WHATEVER I WANTED, WHENEVER I wanted it. The only thing I had in mind was figuring out how to pull off a bigger job than the last one—to make a grand slam. The thought of stopping never entered my mind.

I robbed on impulse and got caught by chance in one of those "field interrogations" the cops are always pulling. One night on my way back to Flats this squad car pulls up. I knew they had me. It was one of those times I knew they'd hang something on me even if they couldn't make the right connections. All of a sudden I had that old sinking feeling: "What the fuck, I'm gonna get popped."

They took me to County Jail because I said I was eighteen; since I was so "grown up" I wanted to be in with the older dudes. When I went to the arraignment they had a big stack of robberies against me. I didn't think they were serious; I thought I'd just do a little time in reform school and then get out.

Black Dick, a dude I knew from Preston, was in County then too. When I got back to the cell block, he met me and asked what I was in for and what was I doing in County Jail at my age. When I gave him the list of property sheets on the robberies he checked them out and said, "Boy, you better tell them how old you are, or they're gonna send you to state prison for a long time."

The next day in the courtroom, all the people I'd robbed were in there staring at me with that victim look. The DA was looking smug as hell. But before they began to go through their acts, I said to the judge in my most innocent voice, "Your Honor, sir, there must be some mistake. This is a real courtroom, and I'm only sixteen." It was illegal for me to even be *in* that courtroom if I was telling the truth. The DA nearly crapped in his pants, said there must indeed be some mistake, I was lying. But the bailiff called my parole officer and confirmed my statement. They had to send me back to Juvenile Hall. Willie wasn't so lucky: They sent him right up to Quentin, where he ended up doing eight years.

Finally I was sent back to old Judge Reed. He told everyone that I was getting worse and worse, "an incorrigible criminal— he'll never change." He sent me back to Preston. In Classification I convinced them it would be good for me to be outside chopping down trees at a camp. The warden thought that was okay since I had a year to do. That's when they sent me to Mount Bullion.

Mount Bullion is a forestry camp up near Yosemite; it's run by the Forest Rangers, with only a few cops around to watch the juvies. The rangers spend the whole day worrying about clearing paths, cutting down trees, and digging post-holes. They had no idea who we were—young blacks and Mexicans from L.A. and Frisco—or what to do with us. They really didn't want us there, even though we did a lot of their shitwork, but they had no choice. The Youth Authority uses the camps as a last test to either give you one more chance to reform yourself or to "make sure" that you're fit meat for the prison system. Most of the kids who get sent there have already been in reform school, so they take advantage of the relatively lenient rangers and fuck up.

I'd known a lot of hot-dog guys before I got to Bullion, but never had I seen the likes of Maynard Farrell. Maynard was the doggie daddy, master of the homos. He always slept surrounded by two or three of them in the rear of our dormitory while he had the rest of his homos out turning tricks for money, especially with the old cons. Maynard boasted that no one in that camp could ever come without coming to him first.

Maynard was on my work crew, as was my friend Johnny Washington, who loved homosexuals but could never get one on his own. The crew worked together every day, getting up at six A.M. to start up the trail to chop trees for a firebreak on the mountain. All nine dudes on our crew were young blacks, and we were all fuck-offs. Now the rangers who assigned the crews must have had no sense at all because one noon we got back from work and there's this new, young, cute white kid waiting at our table. We couldn't believe our eyes.

"Well, well, what a brave boy!" says Maynard, sitting practically in the kid's lap. "What kinda work you in, boy? Cocksuckin' or cornholin'?"

The rest of us crowded around the kid, asking him how many of us he thought he could take at once, "since he was gonna be takin' us all out on that trail this afternoon."

"Let's eat!" yelled Maynard. "To celebrate the punk!"

The kid sat there bewildered. He didn't know how to fight back. You could see he kept hoping we were just joking, laughing along with us, then protesting, then sitting paralyzed with fear. By the time we hit the trail he didn't know whether he was coming or going.

Halfway up, in a switchback between the rocks where the trail widened out, I pulled the kid behind a rock for a little talk. "Listen," I whispered, "the guys are really gonna rip you off, that's no shit. But if you come across for me, I'll tell 'em you're all right so they won't fuck with ya. Okay?"

He stammered out something I didn't pay much attention to, since by then I had his pants down and already had my cock halfway up his ass. I pushed him up the rock and kept fucking him while he babbled how I was hurting him and he'd never been fucked before and he wished I'd hurry up and come.

Soon as I finished Johnny Washington jumped in to take my place. The kid let out a scream. Our plan was to have each guy in the crew go behind the boulder and tell the kid he wouldn't tell anyone else he'd fucked him. By the time three of us'd pulled this stunt, the kid was getting wise, but there was nothing he could do. Everyone in the crew punked this poor guy, and then Washington punked him again and took off all his clothes. The kid went running naked down the trail, his face all dirty, his body scratched up, and his ass raw and bloody. He ran down to the ranger screaming about how eight niggers had raped the shit out of him. When we saw him down there we stopped laughing and took off into the brush.

The ranger called the cops, who brought in two helicopters to look for us.

We were running madly through the manzanita brush and scrub oak without one idea in hell of which way to go to get away. We'd get separated into ones and twos, then bump into each other again, running in circles like Keystone Kops. The police could see everything that was going on from up in the air, and probably laughed their heads off as they let us run around for a while. When they decided to drop down and pick us up, they hovered just over our heads, beating us with the wash from the chopper blades. Rocks and dirt were flying so thick we couldn't see. I kept falling down and running into things until every part of my body was bruised or bleeding. I couldn't hear anything but the copters; they were so low the noise was deafening. I finally fell down behind a big boulder and put my arms over my head. A few minutes later two bulls kicked me into one of the helicopters, put a pair of handcuffs on me real tight, and flew all of us back to camp.

The head ranger, an old black we called Saw Horse, was really pissed—called us a shame to our race and had us shipped out to the jail in Mariposa.

Mariposa was a cowboy town with hitching posts and saloons—the whole Western bit. The sheriff was a real country bumpkin. He'd never seen so many black boys in one place, much less in his jail. When he came into our cell and asked us what we'd done, we told him we'd just finished fucking a white boy. His face went white; he was really scared. One of the dudes from the crew, Jerry Wilcox, was a real fool. As the sheriff backed away, he swaggered up to him and drawled, "Sher'ff, *Ah* think Ah wanna fuck *yew!*"

USUALLY NEW CONS AT TRACY ARE put in double cells. I wasn't allowed to cell with anyone. When my assignment came up the guard said, "Wait a minute. Carr here has a red tag. Gotta put this boy in a cell by hisself." That suited me fine.

They wanted to watch me. In Tracy there were lots of fifteen- and sixteen-year-olds put in side by side with old cons from Folsom and Quentin. A whole lot of youngsters got raped and turned into homos there. In fact, Tracy had the reputation for being the worst place for this sort of thing of all the prisons in California. After the Mount Bullion incident, they wanted to keep an eye on me.

They assigned me to D-unit, up on the third tier. After the guard gave me the cell, he split, leaving me alone to figure things out. I put my things away and walked out onto the yard.

"Hey, blood, over HERE!" It was Lee Mason, an older dude I'd met a few times in L.A. Juvenile Hall. You couldn't miss recognizing him cause he looked like a big black insect with bulging bug-eyes. People called him Lee-Bug. "James, how the hell you get to be so big?" Lee-Bug was three years older than me but considerably smaller. "We gonna be able to use you 'round here. Lissen, m'man, we'll take a little tour an' you can tell me about the streets while I tell you about this joint."

It was one *huge* motherfucker. Cells without end: five tiers high on either side of a corridor a mile long. And it looked like a ghost town. Evidence of destruction everywhere. Cardboard in the windows, paper blowing all over. With all of us youngsters in there, it was always at a boil, with no outlet but violence.

"We got ourselves a full-blown race war on our hands, James. You gotta be tough, you gotta stick together, and you gotta fight to stay alive."

I told Lee-Bug about what we'd done at Bullion. He loved it. That sort of shit was right up his alley. He took me back out on the yard. A crowd of his partners gathered around. Lee-Bug introduced me to Jim Howard, Chuck Greer, Hog Jaw, Robert Edwards, Cadillac, Harry Thompson, and Little Joe Jackson. I shook hands all around while Lee-Bug told them the story of Mount Bullion. They laughed like crazy and were nice to me right off. Besides, I *was* big and in good shape from running and lifting weights: they were always looking for a new dude like me to join them, a potential ally in the race warfare.

At five, recall was announced over the loudspeakers. As the cons walked back into the cell block, I was amazed at the pure *size* of the prison population. I'd just never imagined there would be so many guys.

Everyone walked in cliques, groups of from about five to thirty guys. The younger kids always walked in big bunches. Individuals or weak groups walking alone got ratpacked, pressured out of their canteen draw, or stabbed right in the hallway. A strong group wouldn't be bothered. This was called the wolf code; and the blacks' clique was the Wolf Pack, strongest group in Tracy.

After count was over I walked down from my cell on the third tier to go to chow. Lee-Bug and all these so-called notorious dudes were waiting for me. Together, the fifteen of us went down, and from then on I did everything with the Pack. I was so tough they let me in right away.

As soon as I'd joined the Wolf Pack, Lee-Bug and I got real heavy into the pressure thing, always ripping some kid for his canteen. They started calling us "the Booty Bandits"; all the other cons knew about us and were afraid.

When a new kid named Abernathy arrived, a real fat kid, we decided to rip him off right away. As we were walking across the yard we passed a carpenter's cart; I grabbed a hammer off it and stuck it under my coat. We sat down in the bleachers with the Pack. This fool Abernathy comes over to talk to us thinking he was going to join our group. You could just *look* at him and tell he was never going to make it. Immediately nervous and scared, he started making small talk: "Hiya, fellas, m' name's A-bernathy. I just got . . . here from . . . Preston . . . yes-terday . . ."

Lee-Bug looked Abernathy up and down, then went right to work "This here's a helluva joint, boy." He rolled his tongue around his mouth, grinned, and went on: "Hey boy, ain't I seen you some before?"—ten seconds here to let him suffer—"Yeah! YOU was the kid who got punked by all those dudes at Paso Robles. I was jus' old enough to watch then, but I could tell you give some sweet head."

Abernathy shrunk back in horror. "I-I-I don' know what you talkin' about! I ain't no homosexual an' I ain' never been in Paso Robles, an' all I can say, you mus' be thinkin a some other Ab'nathy, heh-heh-heh . . . " Meanwhile, everyone in the Wolf Pack was jiving his ass saying how queer he looked and how his ass could take care of everybody and with his lips he *must* give good head.

Right in the middle of all this I jumped up, pulled out the hammer, and yelled, "*Punk*, you a fuckin' liar! I know you're a punk! Heard about you even before you got here, an' I been waitin' for you."

Abernathy looked at that hammer, then at Lee-Bug, then at me, and he knew he was going to get punked, so he said, "Yeh, it's true."

Just then they called lockup. Lee-Bug grabbed the kid by the back of his coat, took him to his cell, and raped him. When the cops opened the cell Abernathy went stone crazy, ran across the yard over to Custody, and told them he'd been raped. The cops dragged him over to Captain Hocker's office, where he told the captain that some guy named Lee-Bug had fucked him with the help of some big guy with a hammer. Hocker figured this had to be me.

The Wolf Pack was back sitting out on the bleachers, talking about how we were all gonna fuck this kid in the shower that night, We were always getting trains going where ten or twenty guys would punk the same kid.

Just as we were working out our "game plan," five police came walking on the yard with Abernathy in tow. We knew he'd told. They came over and called out, "Mason, Thompson, Carr, Greer—to the captain's office." I started fat-mouthing, saying "Whatchyou talkin' about?" because I really hadn't fucked the kid. But I still had the hammer under my coat.

When we got to Hocker's office they called Lee-Bug in first, knowing he was the protagonist. During the five minutes he was in there we heard Lee-Bug calling Hocker a bunch of motherfuckers and then we heard Hocker tell the guard to take old Lee-Bug to the Hole.

Hocker was the head of Custody, a short, stocky Southerner with a thick neck and a big bald head. He was an absolute dog, a manipulator, and one-hundred percent racist; he didn't like white cons too much either. I'd seen Hocker only once before, but when I got in there he started raw-jawing me about my "notorious reputation for this kinda shit."

Lieutenant Edwards, called "Twitchy" because of his nervous tic, was sitting next to Hocker. When he greeted me warmly— calling me "Jimmy"—I knew something was wrong. He was obviously trying to play on my youth in an attempt to divide me from my friends. "So you've come under the influence of Lee Mason, eh, my boy?" he asked rhetorically.

"I don't know what you're talkin' about,—I replied. "I ain't done nothin'. I want outta here right now I'm hungry."

Edwards tried to hold back the twitch as he stammered out, "You're not gettin' outta here—you're gonna spend a *month* in the Hole and then you're going to AC! We brought you here from Mount Bullion to better yourself, but you're only getting worse! So you're going to AC and get back in a program, and if you show you can function there, we'll put you out on the mainline again."

I asked him if that was final. When he said yes, I bent over and spat right in his face.

That was the dumbest thing I'd ever done. Twitchy went twitching right out of his chair. Three giant bulls grabbed me and dragged me out of the room, through the Hole, and into my new home—the Black Hole.

I was squirming and protesting the whole way—"Man, lighten up, I didn't hurt nobody"—but the bulls just laughed and twisted my arm and legs till I thought they'd fall off. When we got to the Black Hole they opened the door and threw me head first against the far wall. They ran in and started kicking, stomping on my nuts whenever they had the chance. Then they marched out laughing, slammed the the door, and left me there to rot in the dark.

FOUR

THE FIFTEEN DAYS I SPENT IN the Black Hole, recalling my life up to that point and dreaming about the streets, were followed by another fifteen days in the main Hole.

I had a single cell with a broken window. I slept on a steel strip awakened each morning by a gust of cold Valley fog. Made a mirror out of broken glass fixed to a piece of canvas torn from a tennis shoe to see what was happening on the tier: nothing. Fed twice a day. Tiny portions of mainline food without dessert or butter. Nothing to do in there, no comic books to read and no conversation except yelling at the cops. Just lie there all day long. Make noise at night to pass the time.

LEE-BUG GOT SENT TO THE ADJUSTMENT Center with me. All the fuckups from the mainline were in there, mostly young blacks in for riots, pressure, and rip offs. The authorities, in accord with their characteristic idea of planned chaos, put all the weak cons who need protective custody in AC, in a separate section.

They put you in there and give you a program to go through, after which you're eligible to go back to the mainline. It always takes you longer than the program, though, because it takes a while to "adjust." The program demands involvement in some school, occupational therapy, crafts, and recreation.

The main difference between AC and the mainline is less freedom of movement (more time in cells) and fewer privileges (no weightlifting or movies). We were separated from the rest of the prison, but we were all together as a group since everyone in the Pack had been put in together following the Abernathy affair.

Recreation consisted of boxing. There was a small AC yard with a pile of gloves, and we were all supposed to spar for a few minutes a day. We mainly used the gloves to cover up fights that occurred without them: you'd beat and kick the shit out of some dude, then put gloves on him and call the police to take him to the hospital.

The real recreation, though, was at night, and was simply raising hell. Most of us slept all day and rose at nine thirty p.m., just after the guard had made his evening rounds. The "head cheerleader," a Chicano from L.A. named PeeWee who'd been in AC a year and a half, would kick things off, yelling, "Hepa! Hepa!" Everyone would get up and start rattling the doors of the cells, swearing at the cops and making as much noise as possible, both to let out steam and let the mainline know we were still alive.

When we'd built the yelling up to a frenzy, we'd start lighting fires. The cells face each other across the tier, so you work in teams with the guy across from you. You take a sheet, shred it up, and tie it together to make a line. On the end of the line you tie a bar of soap which slides real good. You slide the bar across the hall and under your partner's door (there's a six-inch-wide space there). He then ties the line to a stack of newspapers, which you pull from his door to the middle of the tier. After cutting this line, leaving the paper in the middle, you throw another line across. Your partner douses the soap with lighter fluid and gets the soap burning good; then you pull it into the tier, setting the stack of papers on fire. Everyone does this at the same time right after night rounds, so there's fires all up and down the tier. When the prison fire department arrives, they have to walk through the burning bags of shit we've also thrown out on the tier. Next to the noise, fires were the greatest tradition in AC. The walls, which had once been yellow, were completely blackened, and the place smelled like an incinerator all the time.

Third on the list was flooding, which we only did about twice a week. We'd stuff T-shirts down our toilets and flush them over and over until the water covered the entire tier, turning it into a no man's land. The drawback of flooding was that when the floor was covered with water the guards wouldn't bring us any food. It was nice not to see them, but we'd get too hungry to keep it up.

We'd keep this madness up all night, every night, urged on by PeeWee to make bigger fires and enough noise to keep the whole institution awake. The arrival of the guards with our breakfast at six a.m. marked the end of our workday; after breakfast PeeWee'd call out, "Okay, boys, let's get some sleep."

Hocker was fiendish. He'd put us in AC for ripping off Abernathy, yet he threw Abernathy in too. And right in with the rest of us, not in protective custody, thereby setting us all up for a repeat performance.

Abernathy never came out of his cell, but a week after we arrived we discovered he was right down the tier from us. Most everyone started harassing him right away, calling him "girl" and "punk" and yelling how they'd kill him, but I wrote him a real nice letter about how it's cold-blooded what had happened, and what we're gonna do is clear it all up since it's no use us fighting among ourselves. *Come to the yard tomorrow*, I told him, *and we'll resolve it.*

Abernathy found us at the domino table. I slapped him on the back in greeting. Lee-Bug told him he wanted to talk things over in the latrine. When they got there, Lee-Bug slapped him around and raped him. Then we ran a train of twenty guys through there. By the time we were done it was time for lockup.

Abernathy came out of the latrine looking highly confused. Spotting the cop on yard duty, he ran over and hugged him, crying that he'd been raped. The cop freaked out, yelling, "Let go of me!" Only after he'd peeled Abernathy off did he ask what'd happened.

"They RAPED me!" the kid sobbed. The cop asked where. Abernathy replied that it was in the latrine. But the cop wouldn't go for that, because if it got reported it would mean he wasn't doing his job. So he told Abernathy to shut up and go to his cell.

Lee-Bug smiled and said to the cop, "I don't know what's wrong with that kid, boss."

Abernathy never came out of his cell again, and gradually went out of his head. He never saw a soul—people just took out their frustrations by yelling down the tier at him. Pretty soon he was shitting on the floor and pissing in his pants. The shrink examined him and had him shipped off to Atascadero.

AC was boring the shit out of me, and I wanted to get out. I went before the AC committee, which Hocker sits on. He told me I hadn't done anything bad recently, but I hadn't done anything good, either. He wouldn't let me out until I got involved in the programs.

I went back and enrolled in school, which wasn't school at all. The teacher, a college student preparing for his exams, just sat behind his desk studying. There were some spelling books scattered around, but all the students just sat there and talked. The teacher gave us all decent reports, and we let him study in peace.

Then there was occupational therapy, where you get your hands covered with clay and get good reports. The therapist plays games and shows you how to make pots. His name was Harris, and he was an ex-boxer who was punch-drunk from getting beat so bad. Right in the middle of pottery lessons he'd start sparring. Or sometimes you'd be talking to him and he'd put his fists in front of his face. The dude was a real cluck.

BY THE TIME I GOT BACK to the committee Hocker'd been transferred to Quentin. The new captain, a young guy named Stevens, was part of the new breed of dogs. He had ideas about pacifying Tracy and all its hardasses by being a Real Good Guy and getting everyone Involved. He started right off saying how it looks like I'm getting real involved in the programs. I say yes, sir, I've decided to do something with myself.

Twitchy, who also sat on the committee, asked me my plans. I told him the first thing that entered my mind, which was that I wanted to learn the shoemaking trade.

They said that was excellent, but I couldn't be running around with Lee Mason if and when they let him out of AC. I lied to them that Lee and I had fallen out and that I'd already decided to quit hanging out with him.

Stevens gave me one of those white-evangelist smiles and said, "James, I want you to go out there and pitch. I know you can make it."

"Yes, sir," I replied fervently, "I'll hang right in there."

I'd finally learned the song and dance. Guys who'd been in and out of AC ten times had told me I had to look like a future shopkeeper to get along with the authorities. They'll eat it up every time.

I WAS BACK OUT ON THE mainline, right inside a three-way shooting gallery: blacks against whites against Mexicans. We had our law—the convict code—which said you were loyal to your friends to the death; didn't snitch, even against a dangerous enemy; and you always avenged a partner's death. If a white dude killed your friend, you wouldn't tell the cops a thing even when they asked you about it. You resolved the killing yourself—*always*. The code recognized that the convict was in direct opposition to the prison officials. We were all incarcerated by the same enemy: the cops. Even at moments of great racial stress it was still clear who the real enemy was. And although we fought among ourselves like vicious dogs, we were united in our common hatred for our guards and torturers.

At San Quentin or Folsom a dude would be murdered on the main yard where five hundred cons could see it, and nobody'd say a thing . . . nobody even saw it happen. The code was a living thing that everyone inside instinctively obeyed in those days.

In the early '50s, liberal penologists, people with Ph.D.s and so forth, had begun to talk about "rehabilitating" cons instead of just caging them up. They started using the word "inmate" instead of convict, as if we were on some fucking ship or something. The guys who went for this rehabilitation shit—the dudes that really believed the authorities were giving them a chance to improve—were called "inmates" by the cons. Inmates didn't follow the code. They believed in the prison officials, not the cons, so if they saw something they'd report it.

But at Tracy in 1959, an inmate was a hard bird to find.

About this same time (1959, early 1960) the Chicanos started the "Mexican Mafia." They took a group oath of absolute loyalty to share everything, stick together, and avenge each other. It created a powerful pack based on fanatical nationalism. Everyone who took the oath was initiated with an "M" tattoo inside his right wrist. Once a Mexican took that oath, he was in for life.

What really fucked the Mexicans up was being considered "between" black and white. The whites kept them that way by alternately accepting and rejecting them. This was the favorite trick of the prison authorities and to some degree of the white cons as well. The increased confusion among the Mexicans made for strange attempts to create a sort of negative racial identity. For example, they'd tell any Mexican who had a black or white lover to break up with him. If the Mexican refused, they'd enforce the demand by killing him.

The Mafia did have its positive side, though. The sharing broke down a lot of petty property hoarding, and their clannish sticking together alleviated to some extent the uncertainty of their position. But their extreme, nearly hysterical brand of nationalism did them more harm than good. They merged their personalities with this nationalism much more than the blacks ever did, and tried to build up both at the same time. A lot of senseless murders occurred due to "macho madness"; the younger Mexicans out to prove themselves by committing extremely absurd acts in order to outdo the older dudes.

But they could never do enough—their identity was based on unreachable goals of power. Along with their "middle" racial position, this impossible desire for power made the Mexicans very easy to manipulate. They were constantly incited to destroy either themselves or the blacks or the whites, depending on the mood and calculations of the authorities; and they never really caught on to what was happening.

THE CHOW HALL SEATS EVERYONE IN the pen in four partitioned sections. At Tracy, the food was okay because they had a farm there and the meat and dairy products were fresh. The food was very important to the cons: it was one of the few things they had to look forward to. A guard stood at the end of the chow line to see that no one took too much; anyone who did would be given a disciplinary infraction—a CDC-115—and would have to appear before a court and get a warning or get sent to the Hole.

The food was good at Tracy not only because of the farm, but because of the YAs. These juveniles used to fuck up the place all the time, much more than the A-numbers (adults, who had indeterminate sentences), because they knew they were going home on a certain date and could therefore raise hell without fear of extending their sentences. So good food was provided to keep the kids quiet.

WHEN I ASKED THE DUDES IN my clique, they explained to me that there were only a few good places to work—anything outside of these was pure labor. They couldn't define wage labor, they just hated work and wouldn't do it. You find this throughout the penal system. That's why we were there, because we'd found alternative ways to support ourselves. And in prison, where all our labor was designed to help the authorities, we were always looking for ways to facilitate our own needs rather than theirs.

My friends told me that I had to go to Classification, where the officials were going to tell me what job I would work according to the psychological and aptitude tests they'd given me. They were going to tell me what I could and couldn't do, all determined by these graphs. (Years later, one of these counselors told me I didn't have an aptitude for arithmetic, though I was doing calculus at the time.) The only other choice I had was to throw for no-control. This meant I would refuse to do anything they told me I was qualified to do: You tell them you know you won't like it, then explain to them just what it is you can do best.

The cops in Classification were real friendly to me in order to find out what I was like. They said they'd looked through my chart and found out that I'd make a good painter. Now, this was just bullshit. They needed another painter; if they'd had an opening in the auto shop they'd have said I was destined to be a mechanic. They were just juggling paper.

I hated to paint. As a matter of fact, I didn't want to do a fucking thing; but I took the job because I had no intentions of painting.

When I came out of Classification, Lee-Bug was waiting for me. He was a tier tender, which meant that he'd sweep the corridors in the morning for forty minutes and was free to raise hell the rest of the time. When I told him I was going to the paint shop, he said, "I *told* ya not to take *nothin'*. You're not gonna like it, you have to spend the whole day there." I didn't give a shit, though. To me it was just like school— regulated and channeled—but I *knew* that they weren't going to make me work.

First day at paint shop, the instructor explained to me what it was about and how nice it was to paint. I wasn't even slightly interested, but I said that I was going to try hard because I wanted to go out and get a job.

The free man assigned me to a black con who was supposed to instruct me. The dude was Ernie Matson, a big guy about five years older than me, and he just liked to paint; that was his game. I didn't tell him what I thought of painting right away, but I never did any work—just laid back and sniffed paint thinner. After a couple days Ernie came up and asked me if I wanted to mix some paint. I told him then that I wasn't at all interested; he just smiled and kept on turning in good reports on me. He was a real nice dude.

Every day I'd sit over in a corner and sniff thinner with a bunch of Mexicans. The blacks and whites were really into learning how to paint, thinking they were gonna get out and make a grand slam and get rich. After they were in there a while they were given the honor of painting the institution. But I was like the Mexicans—didn't give a shit. Finally I just stopped going to the paint shop.

Two dudes from the Wolf Pack, Thompson and Greer, worked on the trash detail and were always telling me how great it was. So I put in a job-change application with this cop named Chandler, who was head of garbage. We started talking, and it turned out we were both from Oklahoma. Chandler liked me because of that, and recommended that I be put on the detail.

When Captain Stevens called me into his office he asked why I hadn't been in paint shop.

Stevens didn't give a fuck about the paint shop; he was asking all these questions so he could pick my brain and find out if I was going to give him any shit. After making the most of his chance to give me a general grilling, he finally approved my assignment to the trash detail.

The thing that made the job so good was that we could go anywhere, because we had to pick up trash for the whole institution. We wore special uniforms which identified us as being on the trash detail; these and our special IDs opened every door in the pen except the one leading to the street. I saw all of Tracy for the first time. It's actually a big factory with time clocks; the cons punch in and out, just like guys on the streets. The pay scale isn't quite as good, though—like three cents an hour working for the third largest manufacturing concern in the state of California.

Everything the prisons and state hospitals need is produced by prisoners. Everything from mattresses to ventilation systems. California cons make all the state's license plates, and those for Oregon and Nevada as well. In addition, the prisons produce commodities on contract to commercial manufacturers, like Thrill soap and Mattel toys.

Naturally, with all this stuff being made, the cons want to get their hands on some of it—and they always do. We trashmen were the middlemen, the Teamsters for the whole joint. We pushed around a big cart, called the "Cadillac," filled with six big trash barrels. Underneath a shallow cover of trash, the cadillac carried a contraband general store. We carried everything from banana oil to specially made clothing to weapons. We made at least two cartons of cigarettes on every deal, one from the guy who wanted something and one from the guy who had the stuff. No sentiments about it—we even sold knives to our enemies. The only real consideration was "How much?" Just a nice knife for a fair price.

Among the three of us everything we made got shared out equally since we all took the same risk of going to the Hole or getting a five-to-life for peddling knives. Greer was the brains of the outfit. He'd been on the detail the longest and carried a little tablet around—his office, he called it—where he kept track of all the deals, of who got what for how much.

In the kitchen we worked with Monty Pearson, who brewed up barrels of wine in the garbage cans out back. He had every kind the kitchen made possible: raisin wine, berry wine, orange special. We took the stuff out in doubled-over can liners. The fucking stuff was potent—dudes'd buy some from us and be drunk before we left. Some guys carried tubes of toothpaste with them so their breath wouldn't stink. If a guard caught them staggering around, they'd just say they'd had a hard day's work.

George Jackson worked the butcher shop to death. When we came by he'd have every different kind of meat and cheese wrapped up and labeled just like a delicatessen, stashed and ready for us to deliver. The cons cooked the meat in their cells. They'd take a gallon can, put holes around the bottom, and weld legs for it to stand on. Then they'd put a smaller can packed with milk cartons under it so it burned like a candle. The flame goes up and the smoke goes out the holes. One guy watches for the cop while the other fans the smoke out the window.

The sandwich man who was working for us would walk real fast up and down the tiers so the guards didn't notice, hawking the stuff. He had bonneroo rolls and cookies which were better than the ones at the canteen for half the price, steak sandwiches with different kinds of garnishes, and just a whole lot of food. He'd take orders the first trip and then come back to deliver, and after that return to my cell. I'd be kicked back on the bed smoking a red dot cigar (they were the thing at the time), listening to the radio with my special cushion earphones. He'd dump all the cigarettes on the bed and I'd give him 20 percent. (Since they were the only commodity of any value available in large quantities, cigarettes had become the everyday medium of exchange in the prison.)

Thompson and Greer had the tailors make them special jackets several sizes too large with big pockets lining the entire inside back. They'd walk along the honor unit (which was open all the time; the other units had restricted movement) collecting cigarettes and filling their jackets with them. They'd have as many as ten cartons stashed in there, of which eight would be contraband: at that time you could have as many cartons in your cell as you wanted, but only two at a time on your person. Finally we accumulated so many cigarettes—eight hundred cartons or more—that it was ridiculous, and there began to be a limitation on what you could have in your cell, too.

Trash was the lifeline for the entire convict population. All the other cons loved us, and we loved them as long as they paid up. It was the only kind of work I could ever get into.

After work we often did a little moonlighting on a pressure crew. We'd catch the new kids in the Guidance Center, where they were put for three weeks of orientation. I'd spot one who hadn't been around the horn and start talking to him, assessing the situation. If he was really weak I'd just flat out threaten to kill him if he didn't give me half his canteen draw each month. But sometimes we had to use more subtle schemes, like the nice guy/tough guy game.

I was the tough guy 'cause I looked so mean. I'd walk up to a fish and ask what he was in for. No matter what he replied, I'd say, "You a lyin' motherfucker! I saw in the paper where some dude raped my sister and they caught him and you look just like the dude. I think it's you." Automatically the dude would try to defend himself, but I'd say "Bullshit!" and run off to get my knife.

Then the nice guy—usually Harry Thompson since he was the littlest—would slide up and say how crazy I was and how I'd already killed a couple of dudes. The fish'd be real upset: he'd never been in jail, he didn't know he was supposed to fight, he probably didn't want to. So he'd go for the pig—swallow the line. The nice guy'd say he might be able to get this shit squashed, since the goon is a friend of his. So he'd come over to me and we'd pretend to be having a conference. Then I'd start after the fish and reach in my coat like I was going to pull out a knife. The kid'd be ready to piss on himself.

Harry'd grab my arm and pretend to cool me off. Then he'd walk back and tell the kid that I was real mad but that I could be bought off for half his canteen draw. He'd add that he, Harry, would pay me off for the first three months, and the kid could pay it back later.

That afternoon I'd tell the poor kid that he really had a good friend in Harry—there weren't many guys who'd do that for another dude in jail. I'd add that I still thought he was the one who raped my sister, but I was willing to forget about it.

Three months later the guy would pay the original debt and think he was finished owing. Harry'd go up to him and say he still owed since the interest on the loan was two-for-one. This interest game was really vicious. Every pen had a few guys loaning cigarettes to dudes who needed to pay back debts immediately. They charged three-for-two packs if the guy was a regular customer or two-for-one if he was a fish. The thing is, the interest was compounded so that one carton at three-for-two increased after two weeks to twenty-three packs, and so on every two weeks. So dudes got stuck so far in debt that they couldn't get out unless they got money sent in from the outside. I always left them a little for toothpaste and took the rest of their canteen draw plus whatever they could get sent in. I'd get money through the mail all the time. This one dude, Mark Harris, owed me a lot of money, and his mother sent me thirty dollars a month. She knew what was going on but couldn't do anything about it.

ME AND MY FRIENDS WEREN'T THE only ones trying to live comfortably. Lots of dudes had good hustles going, often connected with their prison jobs. Brown, for example, was the convict head of the pharmacy—a real businessman with a bonneroo suit and watch, a tall clean-cut dude who was properly spoken. He peddled pills all over the institution, and sold pHisoHex, hand and face lotion and cologne to the homosexuals.

Brown was the punk man: he had about six homos working for him selling pills, and he had three top-notch holes, homos who looked like beautiful women, whom he was pimping. He sold them to the old dudes who came from Folsom. Brown'd send them down to the honor unit where the doors were kept unlocked. He turned the place into a whorehouse, had these homos jumping in and out of there at fifteen dollars a trick. Some dudes would pay their whole draw for one of Brown's "girls" like Jackie Hinton.

Jackie was real beautiful, but a mercenary bitch. He was in for check forging and was real intelligent—even the captain liked him, and made him his clerk. He knew he looked good and that all the old men wanted him, so he'd tease the shit out of them unless they were rich. He'd get panties and bras from the laundry, where they did clothes from the state hospitals. He had his cell fixed up like a boudoir with pink cotton blankets and lace, and he even wore perfume.

Brown had only top notch holes. There were all kinds of intrigues going on to try to get these punks away from him, but they weren't leaving Brown 'cause he had the pills.

SOME DUDES HAD SOFT JOBS GARDENING the homes of the highranking police. This black guy, Dupree Roland, gardened for a lieutenant who was one of the biggest racists at Tracy.

The lieutenant's wife stayed home all day while her husband was at work, and somehow she and Dupree became intimately involved and started sleeping together. Dupree'd stay at her house all day and go back to the prison before the lieutenant came home.

This had been going on for a couple of years when Dupree got his discharge. He'd served all his time—five years—so he was released unconditionally rather than paroled. When the cop took him to the bus station he told Dupree to buy a ticket somewhere, but Dupree showed him his discharge papers and told him he wanted to hang around for a few hours. Just then the lieutenant's wife came in, walked over to Dupree and kissed him. The two of them got into her station wagon and drove off. She'd withdrawn all the money from her and her husband's joint account, and had taken all the valuables.

The cop who'd brought Dupree to the station started talking about what he'd seen. The guards all hate their superiors, and take advantage of any opportunity to embarrass them. The police told the cons, who thought it was the funniest story they'd ever heard.

The lieutenant went crazy. He'd be walking on the yard and five cons'd yell out, "Hey, lieutenant, where's your wife?" He'd go berserk and have everyone near him thrown in the Hole.

Our clique lifted weights together every day out on the yard. We had a fad going to see who could get the biggest arms. One day four friends and I went out to the weight pile right under the gun tower. After a couple of sets, Joey Aaron said that we didn't have enough weight. Now, Joey was a beast; he was five-ten, two hundred pounds, with a fifty-inch chest and a twenty-eight-inch waist. He could flex his chest and set two water glasses on it, and he liked to throw his weight around. So he went over to George Jackson, who was doing curls. George was a loner: I'd seen him every day in the butcher shop, but had never spoken to him outside of business. He weighed only about one-seventy, and his rosy cheeks made him look weak.

Joey growled, "I want that bar, you pretty little punk."

"If you want it," George said softly, "you'll have to take it."

Joey huffed and shouted, "I'll take it, an' I'll kick your ass too!"

George, acting real calm even though he was obviously no match for Joey, told him that he'd fight but not underneath the gun tower. We were all staring at George, unable to *believe* that he would talk this way to Joey.

As the two of them started to walk into the wing to fight, a big crowd gathered. More and more people came from all over the yard, and before you knew it there was a caravan of dudes streaming in, eager to see someone get fucked up. George and Joey walked into the shower—but George *still* didn't look scared!

After waiting for the spectators to arrive, Joey charged at George like a lumbering bull, swinging his fists madly. George tattooed him with a couple of quick jabs and danced out of his way untouched. This set the pattern for the fight: Each time Joey went after him, George got a few little hits in, savage but fast. Not one of them did too much damage to the big man, but gradually they wore him down.

Now it was George's turn to charge. With a tremendous yell he jumped on Joey, knocked him to the ground, and began biting his jugular vein. Since Joey was barely conscious and couldn't offer much assistance, Jim Howard and some other guy ran in and pulled George off—Joey was really a mess by this time: both his eyes were swollen shut and his lips were bleeding. Nobody could believe it. Joey believed it; he knew he'd been beaten fair, and told George he was willing to forget it. George agreed to leave him alone. They both walked away and went on about their business.

I GOT TO KNOW GEORGE A little better after this fight. One evening in the chow line he motioned me over. Somehow George had managed to steal a cream pie from the kitchen and had concealed it under his coat. He enlisted me to run interference for him in order to avoid the cops who policed the dining hall.

We moved quickly toward the door. George had a habit of walking rapidly whenever he'd done something, so he got ahead of me. I increased my speed to catch him; when we got to the exit both of us were running so fast we collided and George fell. The pie was jarred out from under his arm, and the filling ran down his leg.

George turned red—he knew he was caught—looked up at the ceiling, gritting his teeth, and handed the bull his ID card. I excused myself and walked around the two of them, but the cop had seen me running with George and called me back to search my coat. He didn't find anything, but gave me a one-fifteen anyway. When we got to Disciplinary committee, they just laughed at us and let us off with a warning.

I WENT ALONG EASY, SNIFFING GLUE in the shoe shop, until my CYA Board appearance. They asked me what I'd do if I got out, and when I gave the right answer—"live with my mother and work in a shoe shop"—they gave me a sixty-day date. Two uneventful months later I went home.

FIVE

I WENT TO LIVE WITH MY mother on 47th Street, but the first night home I fell out with her and got so mad I had to break all the windows in the house to avoid doing something to her.

The next day I saw my parole officer and explained that I couldn't live with my mother and had nowhere else to go. When this happens to a juvenile in Los Angeles (I was sixteen at the time) they give you a room in a flophouse and a meal ticket at Simon's, the number one chain restaurant on skid row. The PO gave me a little pat on the back and told me not to fuck up. I was on my own.

THE EAGLE ROCK HOTEL, ON FIRST and Hill in downtown L.A., is what you'd call a real shady place. It's populated by homos working the streets, dope fiends and pushers, a few prostitutes, and a number of ex-cons on parole like me.

As soon as I arrived I saw all these dudes I knew lurking around the lobby, waiting for some hustle to materialize. There in the corner was my old friend Maynard Farrell. Transferred with me from Mount Bullion to Tracy, he'd put on a real good song-and-dance there and had been released in a few months. Maynard told me about all the hustles here—he's playing on a well-off homo—and told me there were plenty around who'd pay fifteen dollars to get fucked (which turned out to be bullshit: most of the homos there were hookers).

Maynard and I walked up to the fourth floor to my room. A brass bed, a washbasin, and a chair, looking out on the rooftops of skid row. Then he took me on a grand tour of the Eagle Rock: past people cooking up dope in the hallways, past rooms called "shooting galleries,"—where some poor junkie would let the others use his room in exchange for the cotton which caught the residue from boiling dope. Sounds of fucking emerged from a few rooms, moaning and crying from others. Everybody in the Eagle Rock lived hand to mouth, with the ex-cons (and their Simon's meal tickets) by far the healthiest.

Maynard wanted to do burglaries together, but his plans—such as stealing clothes from a cleaners were ridiculous, and he was afraid to go for anything bigger. When it came time a couple days later for me to "go to work," I said good-bye to Maynard and went to check out Aliso Village.

Flats hadn't changed a bit, except that everything was more deteriorated and the number of rats had risen noticeably. The first few times down there I didn't get into any crime; I just picked up on the divorcees who were always drinking, popping pills and looking for big young guys to fuck. I guess I made them feel alive again for a few minutes. Then I met a knock-out fifteen-year-old chick named Henrietta who loved to fuck almost as much as I did. I'd pick her up in Flats nearly every day; then we'd go back to the Eagle Rock to screw.

On the way to get Henrietta one day, I was walking past an old jalopy when this dude gets out looking sharper than a broke dick dog. "Look here, cool," he said to me, "I know you, don't I." I'd known Slick, too, by sight and by reputation, since I was a kid. The old boy was still pulling robberies at forty and not getting caught. We decided right on the spot to join forces.

Slick wanted to pull a liquor store job in West L.A. "Naw," I told him, "those liquor stores are no good any more. I got a better idea—it's on the West Side too. A big fuckin' market on Adams and Hauser." I hadn't even cased this place; all I knew was that there was a supermarket on that corner, and I knew some people two blocks away where we might be able to run and hide. I told Slick there was two thousand dollars—I had no idea how much there'd be—and his eyes lit up.

We were off. I was really tired of eating at Simon's. We got in Slick's hog (a chopped-down '56 Buick), picked up his two .38s at a chick's house, and drove over to the market.

I didn't know a thing about the place. We started walking around, filling a shopping basket while I stalled, trying to figure out who to put the gun to. Slick finally whispered, "Where's the manager?" I told him the manager was on his break, but he'd be back in a minute.

As we turned down the next aisle I saw a guy who might be the manager, 'cause he wasn't doing anything, so I asked him where the coffee was.

"Over there." He pointed.

"Hey, man," I said, "you must be the manager, you really know your way around."

"No," he says, "I'm not the manager, he's—"

"Well, you *take* me to the manager," I said, pulling my gun.

He led me back to the office, where after a brief conversation the manager handed over two sacks of money.

"What's in that safe?" I demanded.

"Nothing."

"You lyin' motherfucker! Open it!"

There was nothing inside.

Out in the front of the store Slick was waving his gun around. All the customers and bag boys were lying face down on the floor. I showed him the two big sacks of dough and we got out fast; around the corner and into the car.

We drove to my friends' house like nothing had happened, had some beers and listened to Ray Charles for a couple of hours as the sirens went by. Split back to Aliso Village with eleven hundred dollars between us.

It was the most money I'd had in a long time. The next day I spent five hundred of it on clothes. It felt good to step into the First Street Pool Hall with my sharp new suit. I was already thinking of pulling more jobs. I still really wanted a grand slam; what I ended up doing, though, was liquor stores.

In one week I pulled three jobs in a row, six hundred dollars' worth, just to get a hog like my partner had. Unfortunately, Slick got pulled down on another beef and one of the liquor store owners spotted him on the lineup. The cops dealt him into ratting on me.

There I was, up in the Eagle Rock in bed with Henrietta, a thousand miles from any liquor store, when there was a knock on the door. The only other way out was four stories down, so I politely opened the door and let the gentlemen in.

They'd got me good, I was committed without trial or hearing this time. The Classification Committee at Chino gave me all their fucking tests again and then, figuring I was too fast for Tracy, assigned me to Soledad North Facility. They gave me a year's continuance besides, which meant I had no possibility of parole until then.

Soledad North is the medium-security extension of Soledad Central, completely separated from the main institution. Like Tracy, its population is composed of both YAs and A-numbers.

I hated the place immediately: there was *nothing* going on. No cliques, no hustles. Since it's an extension of Soledad Central, the North Facility is not at all self-sufficient—even the food is prepared and brought in from Central. Therefore, it has no economy. There was a little gambling and two-for-three going on, but real puny. I was dying to get back to Tracy.

After about a week I was going stir-crazy and broke, so it was time to get a couple canteen punks. I hooked up with a dude named Miller, who had a parole date to get out in a month, Miller and I zoomed in on this kid Reynolds, a real young fish who'd never been busted before. We ran the game on him—the main game, good guy/bad guy—and ripped off his canteen.

Reynolds ran to the cops, and they came to us. Since there was no Hole or AC in the North Facility, they took us to O-Wing of Soledad Central and left us there for a week. Miller's in the cell next to mine, sniveling for days about how he was gonna get out in a month and now he's screwed. I couldn't take all his crying, so I told him I'd take the whole beef and clear him when we got to the Disciplinary Committee.

When we got there I told them Miller hadn't done anything. They were satisfied with this and sent Miller back to North Facility, but they wouldn't send me there 'cause there's no Hole. I was referred to the Tracy Adjustment Center and shipped off a few days later.

AFTER TWO WEEKS OF NIGHT LIFE in AC, I went back to the Tracy Disciplinary Committee. They complained about how I'm up to my old tricks again and asked what in the hell they should do with me.

Questions like that are always a trap, so I just ignored it and told them how I'd taken the rap for Miller because he was getting out. Furthermore, I told them, I never wanted to go to Soledad in the first place; I wanted to come back to the Tracy mainline and learn a trade.

When some gray-suit asked me which trade, I replied "butchery," because butchers make a lot of money and are always in demand, and I knew someone whose uncle'd give me a job. This just took them on a trip: they said okay, they'd give me a break and put me on the mainline and on the waiting list for butchery. In the meantime, Captain Stevens said, I'd have to take another job; what job did I want?

"Why don't you put me on trash detail?"

Stevens looked in my record and saw all the great reports Chandler had written me, so he assigned me to work on the detail and live in D-wing.

The two guys who were working on the trash detail, Rock and A.C., were pretty new and hadn't got much hustling going. Pretty soon, though, I helped them to develop more of the job's potential. We got to be friends, and I started talking to them about recruiting a clique. All the old crew had gone home, and no one had really taken their place. Since Rock and A.C. knew all the new dudes and I knew how to agitate and recruit, we combined our talents and quickly began building a strong group.

ABOUT THIS TIME, MY FRIEND W. L. Nolen—who later was murdered by the guards at Soledad—got interested in boxing, and pretty soon we all took it up. Julius Grant, who used to be light-heavyweight champion of California, was training us. There was a big fight card coming up in April ('60), when boxers from the Marine Corps and athletic clubs would be coming in, and everyone's attention was focused on that.

Naturally, rumors began that the main event was going to be a riot. I didn't know whether the cons or the cops had started the rumor, but I liked the idea: nothing much was going on and the place needed a little action. So I redoubled my efforts at agitation.

By the day of the fight card, we had a lot of dudes riled up and quite a few knives and pipes. Early that morning we went out to the Rec shack and checked out all the baseball bats. Our plan was to start the riot as soon as the bell rang for the first fight.

The ring was set up in the middle of the yard, with all the boxers around the edge and a little guy with a bullhorn in the middle. A big crowd had gathered by two o'clock, when the first match was, scheduled to begin.

The announcer, a fat little dude from an athletic club, was standing there yelling all this crap, "In this corner . . . and in this corner . . . ," guessing how much the cons weighed.

When the bell rang, it was nothing but a deluge of heads headed toward the ground. All these guys getting crowned "King for a Day." Guys got piped, shanked, and everything else, though somehow no one got killed. The police couldn't shoot from the towers because there's all these YAs here (not to mention the Marines and the announcer), so they just filled the yard with tear gas. Dust flying, whistles blowing, cons running into the blocks. Marines hopping around in the ring, wanting to come fight the niggers but afraid of being shot at by the guards.

When we'd been driven inside we all thought the shit was over, but it had just begun. It had started out just as a regular race riot, cons fighting cons. But when all this pandemonium began, the dudes in the Adjustment Center took the opportunity to vault the fence into the main yard. These dudes—mostly what was becoming the Mexican Mafia—had no interest in beating up cons, but were after the guards. They picked up the bats we'd left behind, went after a knot of guards, and fucked them up bad.

Finally the cops got reinforcements and herded the Mexicans back to A.C. Meanwhile we'd all been locked in our cells, except for the guys who were caught in the act and who were now in the Hole. They started their investigation with these dudes in the Hole and found out that I'd been the main agitator.

About ten that night I was kicked back in my cell when six cops opened the door and called me out on the tier. I asked them what it was, and they said I knew damn well what it was and they were gonna beat my goddamned ass. I went on denying any part in the riot as they led me off to the Hole.

When they got me there they told me to take off my clothes.

"Look man," I said, "I wanna know why I'm here, cause I haven't did a thing. I *didn't*—"

And they rat-packed me. Grabbed both my legs and my nuts—one guy's squeezing my nuts as hard as he could—pulled and twisted my arms, choked me around the neck. After beating me up they threw me in the Black Hole.

I was in there for a week on isolation diet. It wasn't so weird this time, though, because the noise was so great: the whole institution was locked up and hollering. The chaos was so intense I could feel it even in there.

I went before the Disciplinary Committee, and Twitchy's so fucked up over the place falling apart that he's twitching every second. He jumped all over as he told me, "L-look . . . we don't need any crusaders here. You, somewhere, have developed a leadership ability, and we don't want this here. So we're gonna refer you to a full board with the recommendation that you be transferred to San Quentin."

Twitchy's looking at me, trying to figure out my reaction. I felt so good about going to Quentin I didn't know what to do, but I just said, "I don't give a fuck about going to San Quentin. I haven't did anything, though."

"You're a goddamned liar," he said. "You masterminded this shit and touched off all this chaos. We can't have your type here. We're sending you to the Board, and that's all there is to it."

I figured he was bullshitting, because I couldn't believe that they'd send me to Quentin. I'd never heard of a single YA getting sent there.

A few days later we went to the Board. They told us beforehand that they'd referred everybody in the Hole to Quentin, so we all went to the Board together determined to call their bluff. I was the only black dude there; the rest were mostly Mexicans, with a few whites, including Puppet. Pelon was sent not to the Board but to outside court: he had broken Chandler's arm with a bat.

The Board had its full membership there, looking very somber. This only increased our impression that they were bluffing us about the Quentin thing, that they wanted to give us a good scare. In addition, we'd heard in the Hole—in that vague way that cons communicate some inkling of their legal rights—that it was completely illegal to send a juvenile to state prison. (In California the only pens officially referred to as "state prisons" are Folsom and San Quentin.)

The Board told me that I'd been recommended to Quentin, and asked me what I thought about that. "Fine with me," I shot back. "I'd rather go up there than stay here, cause I'm sick of AC and you don't seem to wanna leave me alone on the mainline."

"Boy," some fat Valley rancher drawled, "we're gonna send you on a trip you'll never forget. And after one day in San Quentin, the Adjustment Center here is gonna seem like bein' in your black mama's arms."

One of the more bureaucratic types shuffled some papers and told me that would be all, they'd see what they could do about granting my wish to go to Quentin. That night in the Hole, I found out everyone else had acted like I had and gotten the same response.

But we still didn't believe it; we knew they were bluffing. Two days later we were all lying in our cells when we heard chains rattling. The door opened, and Grumpy cried, "We're goin!"

Still we figured we were going to Soledad. When the bus started north, we figured Vacaville. We were yelling out the windows and playing games, and when the bus driver told us to quiet down we told him to get fucked. "Well, yell now, boys," he cracked, "'cause when you get where you're goin' you're gonna get your asses beat, 'cause it ain't like Tracy."

The closer we got the quieter we became. We finally began to believe them. Most of us had never been this far north, so we had to rely on the dudes from Oakland to tell us where we were headed. Anywhere but Quentin.

When we turned toward Richmond there was no chance for Vacaville.

"Yep," one of the Oakland dudes said, "we're goin' to Quentin," and no one else said a word. As we got on the San Rafael Bridge, everyone started thinking about what it'd be like. Nobody was proud about graduating anymore—we just thought about all the cons we heard had been killed there.

Out of the fog on our left loomed this mustard-colored turd, the ugliest hulk I'd ever seen.

SIX

As our bus pulled inside the prison gates, I felt the whole world closing in on me. When I climbed out of the bus, the first thing I saw was Captain Hocker, who'd left Tracy a year before; behind him stood the Quentin goon squad: six giants in green overalls with three-foot clubs hanging at their sides. Hocker was playing the tough cop all the way, with his trench coat, black gloves, and blue captain's cap trimmed with lots of gold braid.

His voice cut through the cold Bay fog as he gave us his welcoming speech: "Uh-huh, uh-huh, you finally made it. Well, this is a lot different than where you just came from. Now you're in San Quentin."

As if we didn't know it—the thirty of us on the bus that day. The graduating class of '58. We didn't exactly have a bright future. During the next dozen years, a third of the class was murdered, nearly a third turned into homos, while the rest of us survived relatively unharmed. None of us hit the streets in less than ten years, and most of the survivors are still inside fourteen years later.

After they took our pictures we were escorted into Hocker's office for a personal audience. When I got in there I couldn't believe it. This dude was so unsubtle it was unreal. His walls were covered with the most gruesome drawings of starving Indians rotting in the early California prisons, and for bookends he had replicas of the shackles they used to keep them locked up in. I suppose the idea was to show how the modern prisons were more humane, but Hocker's sneers indicated that he liked the tradition these photographs suggested.

Hocker stared at us for a full five minutes before he drew himself up: "I'm going to give you boys a little advice. You're young. People get killed out on this yard for less than stepping on another guy's toes, get it? So I advise you not to step on anybody's shoes. The best thing you can do is drink a lot of water and walk real slow. My advice to you is to get out there on the yard. There are a lot of people out there. Get lost. Get lost as fast as you can."

I didn't feel quite as tough when I walked out of there as when we went in. The fog, the size and shape of Quentin, the way the cops acted, and Hocker's crazy speeches added up to make me a little uneasy. I wasn't afraid of dying; it was the unknown that had me worried.

The authorities had already broken the law just by bringing us there. They'd taken all of us juvenile commitments and made us into adults just by changing the letters on our ID numbers. That justified putting sixteen-year-old kids in the pen.

The cops escorting us to our cell blocks went the long, long way to give us some idea about the size of the prison we were in. They wanted to awe us with the place where over five thousand cons live and work, with the buildings made out of granite blocks thick enough to stop the H-bomb. And, of course, there were the gun towers everywhere, equipped with every kind of weapon.

When we got to the reception center, the place was filled with cons wanting to give us tough young kids a hard time. A few dudes had come to welcome us, though. Iron Man was there. He asked me who had won the riot. When I told him the blacks, he whooped and slapped me on the back. Then a guard pushed me into some clerk's office to get my cell assignment.

I was sent into the maximum security wing along with the other new arrivals. It was a very difficult place to live since we had hourly check-ins with a guard on the yard and confinement to our cells after three o'clock in the afternoon. They served us dinner an hour and a half after we ate our lunch. Hocker wanted to isolate us from the mainline prison population while he figured out what to do with us. We were the first kids they'd ever had to deal with in Q.

Next day out on the tier, I came across Jo Phillips, the infamous taxi-cab bandit of Watts. When they'd finally run Jo down they'd hung him with no less than forty counts of armed robbery. I hadn't known him too well outside, but he was still glad to see me. He was already homesick after only a few months in prison. To make him feel better, he had me tell him about the activities of all the dudes he used to know.

In return, Jo told me about his prison hustle. He had had himself assigned to the textile factory, keeping the looms stocked with bobbins. All he had to do in terms of labor was walk around for five minutes every two hours and fill the machines. "The rest of the time," he said, "I just go down to the shoe shop to get the good glue, sniff it up and float away." He closed his eyes and rolled his head back to show how he felt working out with the glue.

This sounded fine with me. I went to Classification and told them I wanted to work in the textile mill. They were so surprised I had volunteered that they assigned me there and ordered me to report the next day.

Jo really did have the scene worked out. The first day I came on we made the job even easier. I discovered how to overload the machines so we had to refill them only every four hours.

After finishing our first rounds we walked over to the shoe shop. There are only a couple of guards for this huge industrial area and they don't do much walking around. On the way down Jo told me about this dude Pierce that ran the shoe shop. He was a homosexual, one of the most notorious in all of Quentin, plus he was a vicious knife-fighter to boot, with a face twisted up by big red scars of proud flesh from straight-razor slashes. His favorite pastime was finding youngsters and seducing them with little gifts, then paying the tier tender to get them moved into the cell with him. If they resisted his advances he pulled his knife and raped them.

Even though this guy was a savage, Jo had me convinced we could rip him off together. The two of us walked in and asked Pierce to give us some glue. He immediately realized I was a new kid and started acting real friendly. "You can have all the glue you want," and he got us a gallon of stuff. We asked him about his famous bonneroo boots—how he made 'em and how much they cost. The dude was still smiling, staring at me like I was a spring lamb. "I'll make you boys boots for free, just give me your sizes." That we did, and split.

The glue was fine. We spent all our time sitting out behind the textile factory dipping rags and sniffing up some high. We were so far gone most of the time that we weren't even there. Glue is good but it gives you a horrible headache the next day. I burped and pissed glue for two weeks. When we ran out we switched to carbon tet which we got free from the dry-cleaning plant. We didn't want to even see old-dog Pierce again.

We managed to avoid him for a few weeks until one Sunday Jo and I were looking in the library for a young homo to suck our dicks. We ran smack into Pierce, who was righteously pissed off that we had been avoiding him. He tried to hide his anger by acting sweet. Without hesitating much, though, he asked me to move into his cell. I told him I wanted to but I couldn't even buy my way off max row. Pierce didn't believe it, and wasn't taking no for an answer. "Listen," he mumbled, I gave you a whole gallon of glue and I'm making you a pair of boots—you haven't done shit for me. Why don't you let me suck yer dick? A little suck ain't gonna hurt you none."

I had no intention of letting Pierce get anywhere near me. I agreed to meet him in an hour behind the gym just to get rid of him. Jo knew Pierce was mad as hell at me for not coming around right, and he knew what old scar-face could do. "You'd better fuck him up before he gets a chance at you," he said as Pierce walked away. "The dude is sinister, James." Jo had anticipated that something like this might happen. He was prepared with a long butcher knife he pulled out of his pants and handed to me. The blade was so sharp it cut my shirt when I slipped it down inside my denims.

I took the knife, not really intending to use it. I thought I could just beat him up and that would be the end of it, so I asked Jo if it was really necessary to slice the con. It seemed too petty a situation to knife someone.

Jo insisted. "James, if you don't stick him he's gonna kill you the next time you aren't looking. This dude is an animal, man, he just don't understand anything but force."

We went over to the gym. By the time we got to the back, Pierce was all upset because I was late. I told him that I would make up for it by letting him suck my dick, and Jo's too. He said that was fine with him. When we got to turning the trick I went for my belt like I was going to take down my pants, pulled out Jo's knife, and cut Pierce across the gut. "There you are, old man, satisfied now?" He was standing there looking at me and holding his guts in his hands. We left him lying there.

Jo and I went out on the yard over to where the blacks were hanging out and told them what we'd done. All the dudes thought that it was fine I had stuck Pierce—it meant I was tough enough to run with them. In fact, the whole thing had been arranged by Jo as my initiation. He knew what Pierce did to kids that ripped him off, and he wanted to see how I'd react. It was manipulation, and it was cold, but dudes didn't want to be running with guys who hadn't proven themselves in battle. Nobody thought about trying to resolve disagreements peacefully.

JUNIOR GRAY WAS RECOGNIZED BY THE blacks as the baddest dude among us: a superb knife fighter and good with his fists. On his way to dinner one night, Junior got in a hot argument with some Indian named Reese. The two of them started fighting and then Junior was jumped by a bunch of whites and Indians.

The blacks were sitting out on the bleachers in the yard having their after-dinner rap when the word came out that Junior Gray had been rat-packed. Homer, a skinny little guy with a gift for rabblerousing, got up and started shouting at the dudes: "Now things have gone on like this long enough! These grayboys and Indians have been taking advantage of us for too long. If we let them get away with this, the color black won't be worth shit. We'll be on the bottom and that's where we'll stay. There ain't nothin' for it but to wipe a few of those dudes out permanently!"

Homer's speech was met with wildness. Everyone started blowing hard and getting organized for the coming battle. Iron Man was sent to get weapons; I took on the job of "inviting" the Indians and the grayboys to the battlefield. Iron Man went down next morning to the athletic field. He jumped over the door to the equipment office, knocked out the attendant, grabbed all the baseball bats in the place, and split.

I found Reese kicked back in his cell drinking the local brand of white lightning. When he saw me he leaned up on an elbow and said, "Hiya, nigger, have a drink." He was a bold dude; I respected Reese as much as I hated him. I took a paper cup full of his alcohol and gulped it. It burned a line down my gut.

"Just fine, Indian. Good booze you savages are swillin' here. You think you got what it takes to settle what you started?" He nodded. "Fine, all you gotta do is show up on the lower field at two. Bring any equipment you punks want."

"Hope you're ready to die, nigger!" he coughed out. I told him that he was a little confused and split back to the upper yard to tell the boys the good news.

At two, thirty of us went down to the lower yard together, hiding the Louisville Sluggers up under our coats.

Reese's boys were already lined up ready to go, just like a Wild West shootout. We spread out across the yard waiting for Jo to give the signal to attack. As the guard on the walk above turned his back, Jo let out a whistle and we rushed them. When they saw our bats they tried to split but we'd blocked the entrance. They had only knives and knew their chances were slim. We charged them, swinging our bats high in the air. Sickening thuds echoed on the yard as the Sluggers came down hard on redskin skulls.

Six of them died right there with split heads leaking all over the ground. The ones that escaped death got away being fucked up bad. Reese had stood his ground. He was courageous but he didn't have a chance. He was the first to die.

By the time the guard had completed his circuit we were sitting back at the bleachers jiving and jawing like nothing at all had happened.

The cop saw all those bodies and all that blood and started firing his carbine to bring the other police. They ran past us as we sat there grinning. When the ambulances went by we acted curious, like we were trying to figure out just what exactly had happened down there.

The authorities knew the reason for Little Big Horn. They knew how popular Junior Gray was—but they still didn't know exactly who did the job. So they locked all the blacks under twenty-five, all the YAs, and all the Indians in the Adjustment Center.

I was lying back on my bed in there wondering what the cons did to pass the time, when a couple of dudes starting calling, "Smitty, Smitty, tell us a lie." They were answered by a black dude with a silky smooth voice, the kind they put all night on a big-town jazz station. Smitty began a monologue about fucking a chick: the smell of her sweat, the taste of her pussy, the texture of her skin. Smitty could *lie*.

"Smitty, we know you're lying! Don't just sit there and lie like that." The dudes encouraged him by using a little negative psychology on him, just at the point where he was getting into her hot ass. He described each thrust, each move. By the time he was ready, I was rooting for him to come, along with everyone else. When he did, I damned near joined him. It was that real.

Every night Smitty would get called on and lie. One night it would be Iwo Jima and Japs, the next about the biggest coke deal in history, and every night cunt the world over. The dude had imagination. He might have made it big on the stage if he'd ever made it back to the streets.

AFTER TWO WEEKS IN THE AC, Jo Phillips and I were put back out on the mainline. Homer was charged with murder and taken to outside court, but there wasn't enough evidence. All the witnesses were either dead or smart enough not to talk. The case was never solved.

In retaliation, the Indians threw a Molotov into the cell of a black who had nothing to do with the incident. They just wanted to kill a black to even part of the score. He happened to be in the first cell that they passed. The black didn't die, though: the gas exploded on the wall and only burned part of his face off. He smothered it quickly. In a couple of months he just looked a little bit different, but he was alive.

Iron Man, who had his nickname because he was just five seven and could lift plenty of iron, confessed to killing Reese, though, because he was madly in love with a punk. The cops had wanted to get rid of him because he was always ripping kids off for their canteen; they'd given him an early parole date to facilitate matters. But Iron Man didn't want to be separated from his homo, so he confessed to Captain Hocker that he had killed Reese. Hocker didn't believe him and insisted he was going to send Iron Man back to the streets. Iron Man went out on the yard the next day and slugged a cop; Hocker had no choice but to extend his sentence by five years.

But where Iron Man was crazy for love, his cell-mate was love crazy. Billy Joe Davis was the "treetop raper." He was busted for raping seven women in Echo Park in Los Angeles. He caught each of them the same way, by jumping out of the trees. As soon as he was put into the pen, he raped a young kid who was his cell partner and was sent to the Hole.

When he got out of there they ordered him to work in the bakery. Davis was charcoal black and used to sleep on top of the flour sacks. The dude refused to shower; he wouldn't wash, so that his skin took on this gray coloration. The cops had to hold a pistol on him to make him put water on his body. He thought that taking a wash would make him weak. He never cut or combed his hair.

Davis was a superstitious wild man. The one thing Billy Joe could do was play the guitar and sing the blues. When Jimmy Reed came to Q, Davis was one of the cons on the bill. He got more applause than Reed—a standing ovation after each one of his songs.

Since there weren't any trees in Quentin, Davis would leap from the second or third tier onto the first and land on some poor dude's back. We all called him the "fiendish Dracula." Finally the pigs put him in solitary—he was uncontrollable.

I was what the police called an "incorrigible." I did two weeks clean time on the mainline and then got busted for taking an extra steak at dinner when I was given one small piece of meat.

The day I was sent back to the Hole, the Muslims put on a convention in the lower yard. They'd give their racist rap, then split when a riot started. They excused their cowardly behavior by saying that the white devil wanted them to fight and they weren't falling for the trap.

The Nazis and the Muslims usually got along. Their philosophies complimented each other; each group was certain of its own racial supremacy and neither was overly aggressive. They left each other alone; each group had its own turf to look out for. This one time, though, some Nazis happened to be standing nearby when a Muslim gave his rap about the white man being the incarnation of evil. The Nazis were forced to move or risk losing face.

The cops watched the whole thing from the catwalk. Their strategy in this case was to let things go until it looked like the Muslims might get the upper hand, then move in, round up the blacks, and take them all to the Hole.

So there I was down in the Hole, kicked back with nothing but Muslims around me raving at each other like storefront preachers. What I didn't know was that this sermonizing was all put on for my benefit; they were trying to convert me.

When I didn't respond to their analysis of the white race, Lamar Rivers, their leader, called over to me and asked me my name. Rivers knew the Muslim ideology better than anyone else. He had a gifted tongue: he could stay up all night running down the teachings of Elijah Muhammad.

Lamar looked like the man on the Hills Brothers coffee can: he was tall and very skinny because he fasted all the time. The dude thought he had the gift of prophecy—that everything he said was the word of the Messenger of Allah. Lamar asked me a bunch of questions about myself, like how old I was and where I came from. When I told him I was seventeen, all of a sudden he got serious. He said I should have someone outside find me a lawyer to file a suit against the state for putting me in the pen illegally. He said I could be on the streets and rich if I took legal action. But that legal stuff didn't mean shit to me; the only lawyers I knew were crooks. I ignored what Rivers said.

He asked me if I ate pork. I answered that I ate it at every opportunity, because it was my favorite meat. Lamar became extremely agitated. "Don't you know Muhammad forbid us to eat pork?" (I didn't know it at the time, but Red Nelson, the associate superintendent, was attempting to destroy the Muslim organization. He had all the Muslims down there in the Hole and was starving them by feeding them nothing but pork three times a day. Lamar had ordered his disciples to fast and none of them had eaten for nearly two weeks.)

I was sitting there watching and getting fat because the guards gave me all I could eat from what the Muslims refused. Every day Rivers would ask me to give up the hog. I didn't even hear the dude. It gave me a chuckle to think that I had been put down in the Hole for eating too much and here I was stuffing myself while I was being punished.

A few days after I got down there, one of Lamar's newer recruits broke and asked a guard for something to eat. The guard immediately went and told Nelson, who came down to the Hole in person.

Nelson asked the kid if he was hungry. It was obvious the kid was starving to death—skinny as a rail and losing his mind from hunger. He looked up at Nelson and whispered, "Yeah," but in a way the other Muslims couldn't see what he said. The cops took him out of his cell and around the corner and gave him pigs' feet, ham hocks, and beans, and let him eat his fill. The kid must have been relieved thinking that he was going to be able to eat without Lamar finding out about it. But Nelson wasn't through with his little sideshow. Before he put the kid back in his cell he pulled him up short in front of Lamar, practically lifting him off the floor by the back of his collar. "Tell them what you had to eat, boy."

Lamar Rivers cried, "What did you have to eat?" and the kid stammered out, "Pork."

Nelson wasn't satisfied with that, he wanted the kid to tell them exactly what it was. "Tell them *what* you had to eat," he repeated.

"Pigs' feet and ham hocks."

Nelson grinned at the half-starved dudes looking back at him with sunken eyes through the steel: "Any of the rest of you care to dine, there's plenty left."

I had never seen Nelson before; but I couldn't believe what a dog he was. When he was gone, Lamar started preaching: "Allah is gonna take that motherfucker and run him off the planet!"

When Lamar went to the Disciplinary Committee and saw Nelson sitting there grinning, he went berserk. He jumped right up on the table, yelling "Beasts! Beasts!" and kicked Nelson in the mouth. The cops dragged him out still screaming and kicking. They sent Lamar Rivers to Vacaville and gave him shock treatments until he forgot all about Allah.

The cops didn't break the Muslims. Their starvation tactic stopped after a couple of weeks because Hocker was afraid it might get to the outside. Then he switched over to more direct tactics.

Besides Lamar Rivers, Booker North was the most important Muslim leader in San Quentin. He was a fantastically effective proselytizer out on the mainline. Every month he would convert ten or fifteen dudes to Islam. They put him in the Adjustment Center on permanent status. But Booker went right on rapping, usually in the exercise yard.

There were quite a few Nazis in there who had no great love for either Booker or the Muslims. A couple of the more aggressive white supremacists were told by some guards, "Look, we want to get rid of North. If you guys start a fight with him down on the AC yard, we're gonna reach down and kill him."

The next time Booker started his sermon, the Nazis got around him and started insulting him. When he ran after them to beat them up, the Nazis split in all directions so the cops up in the buildings would have a clear shot. Booker was hit in the head two or three times by high-power rifles and died instantly.

The mood was getting so intense that even dudes in the same clique turned insane against each other. Lobo, a tall handsome Chicano whom everyone wanted to sleep with but nobody dared mess with because of his quick temper, and Bobby Lopez, who was also in the Mafia, were just talking peacefully one day. Bobby kiddingly called Lobo a punk, and suddenly the big guy stomped off with Bobby running after him to try and cool him out.

When he couldn't catch the dude, Bobby forgot about it and went back out on the yard. As he was walking across he heard someone behind him call his name. Three feet away from him stood Lobo with a big metal file sharpened to a point in his hand. As Bobby turned to run, Lobo jumped him, stabbed him eleven times, threw the file in the air and ran. The knife hit the catwalk and came down next to Bobby, who was on his knees in a pool of blood. He managed to stagger to his feet and stumble a few steps before he fell down and died. Lobo disappeared into the crowd which had gathered, and got away. They never caught him.

This incident accelerated the madness. Lobo became a blood-thirsty killer: He fell in love with murder, it was his passion. There were always dudes who wanted other dudes murdered, and Lobo turned his passion into a profitable business. For ten cartons of cigarettes, Lobo or one of the other Mafia dudes would kill anyone.

The situation deteriorated to the point where even the prison officials, who were themselves manipulating the chaos, lost control. The madness didn't have any limits. The feeling was that you might be killed at any moment. The police didn't really care about that, but they didn't want one of the juvenile commitments to get offed, and they didn't want to transfer us either. That would seem like a concession and a sign of weakness.

But it happened. One of the YAs who had been transferred with me from Tracy was murdered. The prison officials kept the story out of the papers, but his mother found out. She went screaming to Sacramento. She didn't even know her son was in Quentin until she found out about how he died.

All of us kids had high hopes that she'd make a big enough stink to have some government committee or something investigate. Some of us even thought we'd get out to the streets. We spent a week dreaming. I went to bed every night plotting on ripe supermarkets and sharp clothes.

When they came by and told us to roll up our shit we thought we were on our way back to Tracy. But when we got on the bus, the driver told us our next stop was going to be Soledad Central.

SEVEN

I WAS UNAFFECTED BY THE TRANSFER; it hardly mattered to me where I did time. As for the authorities' decision to transfer us, it meant getting us out of "prison" and into a "correctional" institution. There are only two legally defined prisons in California—Quentin and Folsom. The rest are called this and that; of course, they are all prisons. But it was legal for them to shuffle us to Soledad, so there we were. The only plus about my new assignment was that George Jackson was in Soledad and that meant we would be partners once again.

After clearing the reception center, I went out looking for George, and found him on the yard near the weight pile. George was angry at the way he had landed back in prison, and he almost lost control of himself as he started to tell me the story: "After I got out of Tracy, I hooked up with Michael Wright. We started pulling a lot of robberies—you know, mostly liquor stores. Well, one night Wright went in to do the job while I stayed outside in the car. I waited a long, long time but decided against going in because I didn't want to leave the car running. After what seemed like five fuckin' minutes, Wright runs out with a sack full of money, but he'd taken too long. Somebody in the back of the store must have seen what was going on, and called the cops, because they got there just as we were about to drive off. That was it.

"When I got to court the DA offered me a deal, saying that he was going to be lenient with me because I hadn't pulled the gun: if I copped a guilty plea he'd make sure I'd only hafta do a year of county jail time. It sounded too good to be true. I took it because I knew the alternative was a long stretch in the pen. When I went up to get sentenced I found out that the judge had other ideas. He gave us both one-to-life in Soledad!"

George was upset and frustrated. While he was telling his story, we had wandered over to the weight pile and started working out with a big stack of iron. We didn't pay any attention to the fact that the weight was reserved. The cons reserve the weights by putting their name on a tag which they attach to the bar. Sometimes the tag stays on all day if the dude who reserved it is bad enough. After we'd been talking and pushing for about fifteen minutes, a con came over and told us that the weight belonged to Big Jake Lewis and we'd better cool it. George had been in Soledad for a couple of months and didn't know who this dude was, and anyway, we didn't care.

Half an hour later, a giant came out on the yard. It was Big Jake Lewis—six-foot-seven and wide as a door. He had a thin face, sharp features, and never smiled. Jake had a flute in his hand as he walked over to where we were working out. "Hey, you weak motherfuckers," he shouted, "don't you know that's my weight?"

"Well, if its your weight, it's just too fuckin' bad," I said, while George put more iron on the bar. "We'll be done in an hour and you can come by and use it then."

The big man stared at us for a full minute. "When I catch you out from under these guns I'm going to crack your heads together so hard even you won't know which of you niggers is which!"

"You just go right ahead and do that whenever your heart feels the need," George replied. Jake stormed off.

That night at dinner, there was Jake working in the kitchen serving food in the chow line. When we first glanced over at him he was glaring at us, and he didn't stop until we got to where he was serving. Without saying shit, he slopped gravy all over our plates.

George said he'd never seen Jake work the chow line before. We sat down next to a dude named Harper, who'd caught what Jake had done to us and started talking about him. According to Harper, Jake had beaten the entire Quentin goon squad of seven men in 1958: they all had pick handles and he used his hands. George didn't believe it. He whispered that he was going to have to kill this dude because he was such an animal.

We looked up to see Big Jake coming toward our table with a steel pitcher in his hand. He was trembling with rage: "I told you not to fool with my weights. Now I'm gonna teach you punks a lesson!" He poured the contents of the pitcher he was carrying all over George and me. It was scalding hot coffee, so hot I thought the shirt sticking to my chest was going to brand me forever. I jumped up and Jake hit me on the chin. I went down and damn near out. As he went for George the cops rushed the three of us and took us over to Control.

The lieutenant walked in and asked us what the problem was. George and I were still burning from the coffee but we were cons and had no intention of helping the police, so we told him that there wasn' any problem, it was just a misunderstanding, Jake came in though and told the cop exactly what had happened. He was blunt; he said whatever was on his mind. The cops were just afraid of him. The lieutenant merely told us he didn't want any killing. We all assured him that nothing like that was going to happen and he sent us back out on the mainline.

George and I were plotting how we were gonna put this dude under before he got back to his cell. George wanted to sneak up on him on the tier and stab him in the back of the neck. But before we could execute the plan we ran into Jake on the yard. The dude was so bold—he just walked up and asked us if we wanted to fight.

George was still ready to do anything, so they went into the shower room near the athletic field. Big Jake picked George up and threw him against the tile wall, knocked him stone cold. "Okay, punk, you're next." I didn't move. "If you want, you can run get a knife. I'll be waiting." I still didn't move.

I carried George half-conscious back to his cell. I thought that George would have realized that Jake was just too tough to mess with. But when he came to, he was still talking in a whisper, since that was all he could manage, about killing the bastard.

I was real surprised when a few days later I saw the two of them, Jake and George, out on the yard at the card table playing cooncan. I sat down and watched Jake finish trimming George out of his canteen draw. George got up, extremely anguished, and walked back to his cell without saving a word. Being an arrogant dude, Big Jake arrived five minutes later to collect. But instead of asking for all of George's draw he only took half of it and shook hands with us when he left. After that the three of us became friends and we started to work together.

DOC HARRISON WAS FORTY-FIVE, WITH A lot of gray hairs and a worn face that had seen lots of hard time. He always wore a long gray coat. He had done time for murder in Huntsville prison in Texas, where he had murdered a dude, and later at Folsom he had killed two other cons.

Doc owned a homo named Bobby. The kid looked like a beautiful woman, with a thin, shapely figure and big dark eyes that he made up to look bigger. He was sexy and all the dudes wanted to fuck him. Doc guarded him jealously even though he didn't sleep with the punk. It was a status symbol for Doc.

One night when I was watching television, Doc came over to me and asked if I wanted a job. I was hurting financially at the time, so I asked him what he had in mind. Harrison offered me five packs a day to watch Bobby while he was at work, to make sure that the other cons wouldn't punk his homo. That was a lot of money so I accepted the offer.

Soledad was loose; you didn't have to work if you didn't want to. I was free to guard Doc's punk all day. I took him to lunch and everywhere else I went.

I'd been working for Doc about two weeks when one night he asked me to go back in the shower with him. Just as we got back in there, he pulled out a knife. I stepped back, not really knowing what to expect. I knew Doc acted like he trusted me, but I thought he might have gotten paranoid thinking I'd been fucking his Bobby. Then he handed me the knife and said, "This is yours. You know how to use it?"

"I've stuck some meat," I told him, "but I've never fought with one.

Well, Doc started to give me lessons. Every night after work he'd spend a couple of hours with me. It took about a month before he had built up enough confidence in my ability to spring his scheme on me. Doc asked me if I was interested in setting up a little gambling business. He knew I was open to any way of making easy money, and I'd proven myself to him by keeping good track of his homo and learning how to handle a blade.

Doc brought out some dice and explained how these were house dice—honeycombs, they called them. In the center of each is a little bit of honey which gets hot as the dice are used, making the dice stick on four and seven. He had another set of "six-ace flats," too, which were weighted so that seven would come up frequently. If the game lasted long enough the house had to win. He also showed me how to use a marked deck and how to signal what kind of cards you had when using a straight deck.

When the lessons were over and Doc was sure that I was ready, he went around and got a lot of dudes blacks, Mexicans and whites—to play in a big game. It was legitimate, because he paid off the police. Before the game Doc came into my cell to give me some final instructions: "Don't go feeling bad about cheating these dudes—they'd do the same to you if they knew how. James, if you do like I taught you, we'll have all the cartons on this wing within a week!"

The first night we won thirteen cartons, and the second we did even better. By the fifth night we had won all the cigarettes on the wing. The dudes were all mad because they knew we had cheated them even though they didn't know how. Since we had all the cigarettes, dudes were forced to come to me to borrow; they didn't even bother talking to Doc, because they knew he was such a cold dog. I told them I had to get the okay from the good Doc. He didn't want any part of it. He was vicious, and enjoyed making those cons suffer.

THERE WEREN'T ANY MORE CIGARETTES. DUDES were getting desperate. One night our friend Joe Larson got the usual package of food and butts from home. As he was walking back from the post office, Malo Sanchez and some other Mexican Mafias saw him with his goodies. They rat-packed Joe, took his package, and left his head looking like the butcher had slapped five pounds of ground round alongside it. They ate his cookies, dropped the crumbs on him, and left him lying unconscious.

I was angry that this dude had been beaten without provocation. I was right up front yelling for immediate revenge, putting in my two cents without initiating anything. We were on the way to battle when Doc walked in.

"Wait a minute, youngsters. There's a right way to do everything. We know these dudes are tough; the only way we're gonna fuck them up is by catching them flat, like when they walk into the day room after wake-up still half asleep."

Actually Doc wanted it so that he wasn't on the wing when the shit started, because he knew the cops were looking for an excuse to get rid of him permanently. All the boys agreed with Doc's idea and we sat down and planned the assault, assigned dudes to get weapons, and mapped out the day room so we would all know where to attack from.

The next morning we had a meeting after breakfast. Each of us took a knife and a man to deal with. We were supposed to kill him or have an awfully good reason why not.

As the Mexicans came back into the day room, we took them. They were caught moving slow and unarmed. It was a slaughter. There were slashed stomachs and intestines spilling out all over the floor. The French toast they'd had for breakfast poured out along with a lot of blood. In just a couple of minutes we were standing ankle deep in human waste. It was more violence than I'd ever seen before. The concentration was too much. I just managed to stagger out of there.

Just before I made the door I was met by the tier cop who took one look at the scene and flipped out. He was looking me right in the eye, and he saw everyone who was there, but he was so frightened, all he could do was stand there helplessly blowing on his whistle. I pushed past him and got out onto the tier. The lieutenant ran right past me, but he didn't notice I was covered with blood. When he looked into the day room he started giving orders getting anyone around to help carry the wounded Mexicans to the infirmary. He even asked some of the cons standing around watching, including me, to carry the wounded to the hospital.

I went straight back from the hospital to my cell. By this time the guards were coming around checking for blood on people's clothing. When the cops saw me they got all hopped up. I was fuckin' drenched in blood. I pleaded with them to talk to the lieutenant, but they wouldn't listen to my story about helping the lieutenant like a good scout. They dragged me down to the Hole thinking they had themselves a murderer.

The next day the DA from Salinas came to interrogate the suspects. When it was my turn I walked in, sat down, and the fool said, "Mr. Carr, it's my job to find out what happened here yesterday and so far I'm having a hard time getting any information at all."

"Well, here's the facts," I said, looking the hick in the eye, "I don't know anything about what happened other than that the lieutenant had me carry this dude to the hospital and now I'm in here. Furthermore, I don't give a fuck about your job. So just leave me alone." I got up and walked out on him without turning around.

In all the confusion that had followed the massacre, the lieutenant didn't discover that I was being held as one of the suspects until he finally got around to visiting the Hole. I reminded him of what had happened and he had the guards release me back to the mainline.

Soon as I got on the tier again, George and Big Jake pulled me into the shower and told me that Hank Sanchez had a cousin in Soledad who was convinced that I had killed Hank in the massacre. George said that I had best be on guard because this guy intended to kill me. Jake gave me a straight razor and a knife which I taped to my arms so I could carry them with me wherever I went.

I got more and more paranoid as the days went on. I'd be walking down the tier and turn around to find four or five of the Mafia staring at me. Finally I couldn't stand it any more. I had Hank Sanchez's cousin pointed out to me, and walked up to him.

"I hear you think that I killed your cousin. Well, I was there but I didn't do it and I don't know who did. If you feel like you have something to settle with me, go right ahead, right here and now."

The cousin stared at me a second; he said he didn't want to do nothin'. "It's bad enough that there's already one Sanchez dead. If anything happened to any of the rest of us, our mothers would kill themselves. So let's just forget about it." After that they left me alone and that was the end of it. They transferred Doc Harrison to Folsom, though. They just couldn't believe that he hadn't masterminded all those executions.

OUR CLIQUE AVOIDED DEFENDING BLACK DUDES who didn't run with us. There were just too many guys who acted tough, got into shit, and then ran for help. One of these "tough" guys was a young kid from Sacramento named Johnson, who thought he was Mr. Cool. He was a little different from the usual cardboard tough guy who gets in over his head—underneath his bullshit, Johnson was a likeable dude.

That's why we got upset when we heard a rumor that he had been rat-packed for no reason by six white dudes. Actually, it turned out, he had been in a hassle with a white over a homo and had ended up stabbed in the ensuing conflict. But we were pissed, especially Jake, who was fuming already after having just been turned down by the parole board again for the umpteenth time. The speechmaking was just beginning when suddenly Jake's elephant voice stopped the show.

"Look. Let's just go in there and take the whole fuckin' wing over!"

None of us could tell if he was serious or not. We didn't have any plan at all; we got behind it because it was different.

About twelve of us, including George Jackson and me, stormed onto the wing. We knocked the cop out, took his keys and locked the wing down. But we didn't have the keys to the cells. The rest of the cons had to stay locked. They yelled out a bunch of encouragements and we yelled back, but that was about all we could do.

The D-wing cops went to Control for reinforcements. While they were gone we tore up the tables so we could use the legs for clubs. By the time we'd finished that, the lieutenant unlocked the door, stuck his head in, and cried, "What the hell do you boys think you're doing in there?"

Jake answered, "Not a motherfucking thing . . . you boys want to fight?" The lieutenant thought we were crazy. He had no intention of trying to get us out of there with the force at his command. The week before the Mexicans had whipped them good so they weren't anxious to do it again.

But we figured if they fought the Mexicans they'd fight us. The lieutenant called out again, "You boys are gonna have to move out of this wing." We told him we weren't about to leave. "Well, then, we'll just have to move you."

That was too much for Jake, who wanted some action. He went up to the cop, said, "You'll what?" and slapped him in the mouth. He hurt him pretty bad and made him look like a fool—but he wouldn't dare fight Jake, so the cops all split, locking the door behind them.

Half an hour later the captain called on the phone and Smitty, a fake Muslim and a real raw-jaw artist, answered. He screamed into the phone, "Captain, there's only one thing we got to say to you: go fuck yourself!" Then he ripped the cord out of the wall.

Next it was the warden's turn. He came down and asked us if were going to come out. We all yelled together, "No! You ass-lickers are gonna have to come in and get us!" Then we smashed the television and all the windows.

The cops were up on the roof, breaking out glass so they could put riot guns in and shoot tear gas. They fired a couple of canisters, but the gas floated up and got the boys in the cells without touching us. We were sitting there laughing. We thought that once they'd shot some gas they would come charging in. But they still had no intentions of coming in there.

After thirty more minutes the cops reappeared on the roof. This time they had rifles instead of riot guns. All the cops were pointing at me. I didn't know why at the time; later I found out it was because I was a juvenile and they didn't want to shoot me. They yelled in through a bullhorn that we had one more chance to come out. Jake reaffirmed that they could all go get fucked. We weren't coming. The cop then yelled down that Jake should let me and Smitty out because we were juveniles; but we didn't want to come out—we told the cops to go to hell. If we had left they would have killed all those dudes, although we didn't understand this at the time, either.

The sound of a shot ricocheted off the walls. Then another. It got mighty hot mighty fast. We turned over the sheet-metal tables to hide behind, and pulled them up against the wall at the end of the corridor. Bullets were smashing against the steel and sending bits of stone and shards of plaster all around us. We backed the tables up, trying to keep them pointed up toward the rifle fire while moving under them to make it to the shower way down at the other end of the corridor, right under where most of the cops were firing from. They saw us coming and opened the front door. Everyone except four of us—George Jackson, Big Jake, Smitty and me—ran for it; they'd had enough.

Jake jumped up and started hollering at them for deserting us. He still thought that the cops were going to come in there and fight us, and he figured the dudes that split would be necessary for the brawl.

Then the cops started blasting away, shooting all the tiles off the wall. We were covered with cement dust and dried blood. We were scraped and bruised from moving the tables, and Jake had a couple of nicks, but none of us had been shot.

At the height of the gunfire, when it was impossible to hear your own voice, George started rapping. We all huddled close together to hear George take us on a trip about the streets. He talked about all the girls he was going to fuck and all the good food he was going to eat. He talked about East L.A. till I got homesick and told him to cool it. We were so far into it that we lost track of what was happening until Jake noticed that the cops had stopped firing for the first time in six hours.

Some cop was blowing through the bullhorn. There was a mumble and a few squeaks; then the voice of the lieutenant came over: "Now, you boys have had your fun. This is your last chance to come out of there walking. The Salinas National Guard is here and they aren't going to waste their ammunition. You've got five minutes to make up your minds." Click. The bullhorn went dead and there was silence.

Before we could say anything, a dozen shotguns burped, spraying the place with buckshot, just to show us they meant business. None of us had any intention of dying cornered like dogs, so we came out from under the benches. Jake, still not wanting to give up, said he thought that we should have them execute us right there. "They ain't never gonna let us out of these prisons alive. It's better to die like a man."

I wasn't saying anything, but Smitty blurted out, "I don't believe that this is the way Allah intended for me to die."

Jake screamed, "Shut up, punk, there ain't no motherfuckin' Allah! We're gonna have a vote here."

George had been thinking the situation over. "Frankly speaking, I'm ready to leave," he said to Jake, "but if you're gonna stay here and be executed, I'll stay and die with you." I told Jake the same thing, putting the burden on his shoulders. Jake told Smitty that he didn't have a say because he was a fool. He thought for a second, then called out to the cop: "All right, punks, we're coming out." They ordered us to come out backward with our hands over our heads.

When we reached the door, we turned around and confronted the cops. Until that moment we didn't know how afraid they were. All the cops from all the shifts were outside the wing and behind them stood twenty guardsmen in full battle gear. It looked like the last Germans surrendering at the end of World War II. We were just four unarmed blacks against this multitude of military, but they still hadn't defeated us. Jake looked at me and George, and he had fire in his eyes.

With a scream that would have startled a deaf man, he leaped at the police and started swinging, downing six or seven with his first blows. At the same time George and I cut down a few more. We fought like devils but there were too many of them. They swarmed over us, swinging their rifle butts and clubs, hitting each other in their frenzy.

When we were subdued, they chained us together by our feet. Then they led us through a line of club-swinging cops who beat us around the head and groin as we hobbled past. When they'd had enough of getting even, they chained us to a post and went off to wire Sacramento for instructions.

Two hours later we were on a bus headed for San Quentin. When we got there we were taken to the Disciplinary Committee, Red Nelson and Captain Hocker in charge.

Jake went in first. A couple minutes later he was out with twenty-nine days in the Hole and a transfer to Folsom. We all went in and came out with twenty-nine days.

They brought everyone who was involved in the takeover at Soledad. We were all down there together. Jake was still fuming about how all these other dudes had deserted us. He would call each of them by name and insult the dude for an hour, and then move on to the next one. He did this every day all day until his voice gave out. We could still hear him in his cell rumbling in a hoarse whisper. The dude had endurance.

THEY HAD TO GET ME OUT of there after my time in the Hole because I was still a juvenile commitment. They sent me back to Tracy, which is where I wanted to be anyway. I was taken immediately to Twitchy.

"You been mighty busy since you left here," he said. "We don't need any riots in this institution. We don't need people like you here at all. When we sent you away we thought we were getting rid of you. We got a nice place here and we want to keep it that way, so you're going to the Adjustment Center."

They put me into Segregation where you can come out of the cell only once a week to take a shower. The minimum time in Segregation is ninety days, *if* you don't get a beef in the meantime.

The same madness was still going on: lighting fires, throwing food at the cops. I got right in with all of it. But as my time kept getting extended, I realized I might never get out of there . . . especially with Twitchy at the controls.

I'd been down there seven months when Twitchy's wife died. I was so happy I didn't know what to do. I wrote him a letter with a tombstone on it that said: "The old bitch is dead! How sweet it is!" I was going to mail it, but before I did I had a dude named Tyrone check it out for spelling errors and shit. He told me that if I sent it I was never going to get out. He suggested that I send Twitchy a sympathy card. I ordered a card from the canteen, wrote a little "I'm so sorry" note, and sent the thing off.

Two days later the cops came and took me to Twitchy. He greeted me with a twitch and said, "This place must have been good for you. You've really changed." I told him how I had been reading books and doing a lot of thinking about myself. Twitchy said that he would let me out if I went to see the psychiatrist. I had refused before, but I was tired of total lockdown, so I said sure, I'd go.

I walked to the shrink smoking my pipe. When I got to his office, he was sitting back in his chair with his feet up on the desk smoking his pipe. I sat down and neither of us said a word. We both just sat there puffing and ignoring each other.

"There's nothing wrong with you."

"I know."

"I don't know why they sent you here."

"Neither do I."

Then he told me he'd write a good recommendation for me. I thanked him and walked out.

When I saw Twitchy a week later he was acting real surprised. He said that the psychiatrist had written a damn favorable report on me and that he was putting me back out on the mainline.

A couple of months later I went to the Board. The warden asked me if I thought I could make it on the streets. I told him, "I'm sure I can. I've learned how to control myself. I'm going to college as soon as I get out—my aunt has agreed to pay for it." I said it all nice and humble, the way they always like it in the end. They believed me, or else didn't care what I said and just wanted to rid of me.

"You can go," the warden said, "as soon as you can get on the bus."

EIGHT

I REMEMBER ON THE BUS RIDE home thinking that I had just done my last stretch in the pen. Every smell of exhaust from the cars on the highway reinforced that feeling: I was on the streets for good; nothing could stop me this time. All the little obstacles that got in my way before were conquerable; another opportunity was always around the corner. I was flying—tough, smart, and clean.

My first hurdle was the parole authorities. They thought they could trip me up by isolating me from my friends. I was given a room and a meal ticket in an old-folks' home called the Carmel Hotel out in Santa Monica. It was one of those sand-colored buildings with grubby looking palm trees here and there, and the smell of age all over the place. I guess they thought the senior citizens would have a sobering effect on me.

The second day I was in the place, I spent the whole day smoking weed and thinking up ways to get out. I finally gave up and just decided to make it expensive. I invited ten of my old friends out to a party and charged the whole bill to the county. My parole officer was kind of amused. Instead of disciplining me, he saw how impossible it was for a kid like me to live in an old folks' home, and allowed me to move in with my Aunt Harriet.

Harriet was the only member of the family who hadn't given up on me. I visited her every time I was on the streets, and she wrote me encouraging letters when I was in prison. She was a pretty, thin, middle-aged woman with a wide smile and a good sense of humor. I had gone to see her the first night I hit the streets, even though my parole officer had insisted that I stay out of that part of town. We had a happy reunion, staying up drinking and talking about old times until early the next morning.

While I'd been in prison, her husband Gino had been murdered in an argument in one of the night spots he managed. The dude had been in Quentin himself previous to this for a bunch of gambling beefs. In the morning over breakfast she asked me if I wanted to move into the spare bedroom in her apartment. I liked the idea. My plans called for getting into a situation where I could operate, and I knew nothing was happening for me in the way of hustles over in Santa Monica.

Before the parole officer made my transfer formal he insisted on visiting Harriet in her apartment. She told me about it later. He was impressed—her pad was well furnished, which meant that she had money and I wouldn't be needing to steal and, besides that, Harriet was very sophisticated. She talked about her plans to pay for my college education and all the strict rules she was going to make me live up to. I hadn't asked her to do any of this; she was smart enough to say what the dude wanted to hear and clever enough to present it in a way that was believable. Harriet was a fox!

I moved in with her the next Monday. Actually, moving wasn't much of a job—I didn't have hardly any clothes. Maynard Farrell had taken all of my clothes out of the Eagle Rock when I was arrested.

I started running with a bunch of the ex-Pirates that were still around, like John Buckley and Poor-Devil. They still knew how to party all right—lots of pills, juice, and chicks—but they were pulling penny-ante stickups. That was a sure way to go back to the pen: it meant you had to be constantly robbing, and you were bound to get caught if the jobs were frequent and poorly planned as they almost always were. I liked these dudes. I hung out with them and did shit but refused to do any jobs with them. I wanted an opportunity to get into the big time, not knowing where it would come from or how, but confident nonetheless that I would have my chance.

Harriet and I got along great. She left me alone, didn't make me go to school or work. When I wasn't partying I just lay around her pad, got fat, and listened to her hi-fi.

Harriet owned the building, a duplex, and she rented the downstairs apartment to a dude named Maurice. There were always good sounds coming from Maurice's pad. I figured the dude was rich from the size of his hi-fi and the few glimpses I had caught of him going into the place; he wore real fine rags.

I asked Harriet to introduce us, thinking that the dude must be into a good hustle. The day after, she talked to him, and that night he invited me down. He had a fancy pad all right: leather furniture, fat carpets that went wall to wall, and a huge collection of records. He poured us a couple of glasses of Chivas Regal and we got to talking.

Maurice told me that he was a bookie. He worked all over the city picking up bets and paying dudes, using the wire service he bought from the dagos. The dude was prospering, making three hundred and fifty to five hundred dollars a week. He looked like he spent every penny of it. His closet was filled with custom-tailored clothes; even his khaki fatigues were fitted. Maurice had his hair done in a marcel, a process in a Caesar style, and he had manicured fingernails. The dude had a personality to match his wardrobe: smooth and together, always in control.

I saw Maurice as someone to emulate. He had everything that I wanted. I wanted to know who he was working for, hoping that he would cut me in on some of his action. When he told me he was working for my Aunt Harriet, I nearly dropped my load. I knew that she was sly. I never figured that she was into being that kind of a businesswoman. But Maurice told me that she had been doing business a long time before she met her husband, Gino. She had started taking bets years before while working with the heavy-betting women of the garment district.

Maurice had been talking slow over the top of several drinks for the last hour. The clock hit eight and Maurice got up, telling me he was sorry but business came first. I didn't want to miss the opportunity to watch the dude go into action, so I asked him up-front if I could go along for the ride. He said it was fine with him, and we left.

Maurice had two cars, a beat-up gray 1940 Dodge and a brand new Buick Riviera. I went strutting up to the Buick and started to get in but Maurice shook his head. He was getting into the jalopy. I couldn't figure the thing out. Actually, he was just being cool: he didn't want any of his customers to know how successful he was, so he drove the Buick only when he went out partying.

We drove down to Central Avenue where all you can smell from downtown to the beach is barbecue. The street was lined with old wood-frame buildings in various states of disrepair. They went from just barely habitable to completely devastated. Trash filled the gutters and all the vacant lots. Broken glass covered everything else—the streets, sidewalks, the crumbling porches attached to the worn buildings.

The stores lining the streets covered the needs of the neighborhood—mostly beauty parlors, cleaners, pool halls, restaurants, and innumerable bars called "buckets-of-blood." There were so many fights in them the management saved money on cleanup by covering the floor with sawdust.

The first joint we went into was empty except for a couple of old dudes drinking at the bar and a young-looking blues singer sitting over on a bench in the corner cutting a few licks on a guitar. Maurice walked up to the bar and said a few words to the bartender, who nodded and pulled out a wad of bills. Then he went over to the old dudes, paying off one and collecting from the other. Then he waved goodbye and walked out.

We worked every bar on that desolate strip, Maurice collecting and paying out—mostly just collecting a whole lot of cash.

When we had covered Central, Maurice drove out of the ghetto into the wealthy black suburb of Baldwin Hills. The homes were like the homes that whites with similar incomes lived in—gaudy-looking tract houses. And like all middle-class people, the owners tried to disguise the fact that all the houses were sprung from the same design. They always furnished them with so-called original furniture that made them even uglier. Whereas Maurice was himself with the people down on the Avenue, he acted like a page with these bourgeois blacks, who liked to imagine they were some kind of royalty.

The first house we went to had a cocktail party going on. People were dressed in conservative clothes, dark suits and long dresses, with quiet music and pleasant conversation.

Maurice circulated quickly, masterfully flattering this woman about her dress and telling that black businessman what a nice store he had. They loved him, never figured he was bullshitting to get them to bet more. A lot of money changed hands. Nearly everyone there was one of Maurice's customers. They bet heavy; it was a status thing with them. They were bragging about who made the highest wagers.

When Maurice walked out of there he had more than a thousand dollars in his pocket. It wasn't all profit, but even after paying off the few winners and the wire service there was still a handsome amount left. For my efforts (he was actually using me as a bodyguard though he didn't tell me so), Maurice gave me fifty dollars. I knew then that I'd found my calling.

As soon as we got back to the house, I went upstairs and told Harriet about my night with Maurice. Without waiting for her reaction I asked her if I could become a bookie. She wasn't a bit surprised; being street-wise, she knew the appeal that the sight of a lot of money had on a youngster like me. Instead, she gave me a little talk about what a good business it was and told me if I really wanted to be a bookie I would have to work hard at it. Then she called Maurice up and told him that I had her permission to learn the trade.

Maurice became my teacher. He told me that every new bookie has to go out and find his own customers. I thought I knew just the place to start. I had arrived on the scene at the right time: Maurice told me that the police had recently arrested a number of the local dope pushers, most of whom also kept book. There were a lot of people looking for someone to bet with. He also pointed out that most of the people who bet were women, especially divorcees and single women in the projects who get big support checks and don't have anything to do all day but watch their kids.

Aliso Village was solid full of that kind of woman. I went back there to scout around for clients. I hung out at the pool hall down the street from the Eagle Rock Hotel where I knew a lot of people. I started keeping book, selling pills and weed, and hustling pool.

Word got around that I was taking bets and people started coming to me. I had a table in the corner of the place and treated it like it was my office. Customers would line up while I ran from my table in the corner to the pay phone, calling in the bets to Maurice, who still retained the wire service. I paid him about half my profits for his trouble.

I was a petty hustler making about a hundred and fifty a week, acting like the coolest dude in the world. I spent all the money I made on clothes, and had my hair done up in a fancy process, dyed red. At night all I could dream about was making more money than Maurice. I was really small-time.

I made enough money to go into debt. I put down a couple hundred dollars on a new Buick Riviera that I got my aunt to co-sign for. I started running with Robert Mack, who had gotten out of prison a couple of weeks earlier. His parents helped him get a new Chevrolet, and the two of us started cruising. I lost interest in working—couldn't see the point of sitting around a pool hall when I had a new car. Robert and I did some heavy partying.

When the first payment came due neither of us had enough money, so we ignored the bills and kept fuckin' around. But the second notice made it clear that the loan companies were going to repossess immediately if we didn't make a payment.

We were really getting into a tight situation. If we didn't come up with the money within ten days we were going to lose our cars, which was like losing a leg. We got to talking about some way to get the money *fast*. It was impossible to get that much cash by working—we had to pull a robbery.

We needed a third dude for the heist, and got our friend Wally who had been with us in Tracy. He was working all night as a baker to save money to get married to this chick who had six kids. He was tired of working. When we told him our idea, he was hot for it.

I still hadn't lost sight of my idea of making big money, even though I was in money trouble already. I took charge of the job to make sure that it wouldn't turn into another nickel-dime liquor store stickup. I insisted that every move be planned carefully. This was something new for the other dudes, who were used to doing things impulsively. We drove all over Watts and West L.A., looking for a store that would have a big take and be in a neighborhood where we could easily get away. It took a couple of days of driving around to find what we wanted: a Ralph's Market and Rexall drugstore in the same building over on Avalon.

Robert and Wally wanted to get some guns and rob it that same afternoon. I put the plug on that shit—we were gonna wait until Friday evening when the till would be busting. We inspected the store to figure out where each of us would stand and where we would park the getaway car. That was Thursday afternoon.

Friday morning Robert and I went over to a fancy gun store on the West Side. Robert asked the dude for a box of shells. As he bent down under the counter, I leaped over and jumped him. Robert pulled two custom twelve-gauge shotguns from the rack. The dude was hurting, trying to scream, forcing me to choke him more and more. We had his best guns. I told him to lie on the floor and keep quiet for five minutes or we would blast him. Robert grabbed a couple of boxes of double-0 and we ran out.

We drove over to Wally's house, talking about how fine the shotguns were. The stocks were high-grade wood and the barrels had all kinds of inlays with fancy designs. Wally took one look at them and said he wanted one too, but he had to settle for an old double-barreled job that Robert had kicking around in his garage. We spent the rest of the afternoon sitting around Wally's, talking to his girl and getting high. We took a couple of bennies apiece and drank a half gallon of white wine.

When we were good and loaded, the sun was down. We drove over to the market in Wally's car. I had to restrain Robert from pulling out his gun right then and there in the parking lot. He was drunk and crazy. I wanted to check the place out one last time—make sure there weren't any armed guards. I walked in there and found everything in nice order.

We parked Wally's car three blocks from the market and walked back to the parking lot with the shotguns under our coats. We hot-wired one of the cars and drove it around front. The three of us walked in with our guns still hidden, acting like we were going to do our weekend shopping. Wally went into the drugstore and stood in front of the magazine rack while I took a position near the cash registers in the market. Robert took out his shotgun and fired a round at the ceiling to get everyone's attention. The whole place hit the floor. As Wally and I were collecting the cash from the registers, some fool got up and Robert cracked him over the head with the butt of his gun. The dude went to sleep. We filled three big grocery sacks with bills and change, then split out to the car.

The streets were on fire—sirens were coming from every direction. Wally didn't lose his cool; he drove slowly to where we had parked the other car. The sirens were getting closer. Robert freaked and started to run. Wally and I pushed Robert into the back seat and told him not to move. In his nervousness he forgot that all we had to do to escape was make the car change without drawing attention. I drove Wally's car slowly out of the neighborhood, past several loads of oncoming cops, and out onto the freeway's anonymous safety.

The money was good: forty-five hundred dollars. It looked like a fortune spilled out all over the back seat. Robert, who had acted like this was the last job he ever wanted to do, started talking about pulling another one before Wally had finished counting the money. He was a fool. We had to let things cool out for a while.

When we got back to the neighborhood, I drove over to Robert's place where we divided up the money. Wally and I went home grinning. I put my share under the house and went up to sleep, happier than a motherfucker. I had sweet dreams. Just as I was sailing away with this beautiful chick, a bright light was put in my face. Behind it was a big ugly cop holding a .38 Special to my head. It took me a minute to wake up enough to realize that I wasn't dreaming. Two more cops came into the room, pulled me out of bed, and told me to put my clothes on.

When I got out to the car, Robert Mack was in the backseat, handcuffed. I didn't want to say anything to him until we got down to the jail. Down at L.A. city jail the police questioned me first, asking me whether I had been with Robert. I denied it. The lieutenant told me that he knew I had committed the robbery but if I helped them convict Robert he'd let me go. I knew he was lying.

"I don't know what you're talking about, Boss," I said. "I wish I could help you, but I haven't did a thing,".

They let me put a phone call through to Harriet to ask her to get me an attorney, but she said she wouldn't do it unless I was innocent, and she didn't think I was. After she hung up on me, I kept on talking for five minutes, making it sound like she was going to find me a hot lawyer. But the police didn't care if I had ten attorneys—they knew I was guilty.

When Robert Mack and I got back to the cell, I asked him what had happened. He took me on a trip about how his father was stopped driving his car and told the police that Mack had been out when the robbery took place. I knew he was taking me for a trip because the police hadn't seen our car. I just thought he was trying to cover up some stupid mistake. I still trusted him.

The next morning the cops brought Wally in. His clothes were torn to shreds and he had blood and mud caked all over him. He had come home late from his woman's house and the police were waiting in front of his house in an unmarked car. When he got to the door his father told him the police were there and he ran off. They caught him after a few blocks, knocked him on the ground with a tackle, and beat him up with their pistol butts.

Wally was mad. He was deeply in love with this chick, had his nose wide open about her, and couldn't stand being separated from her. He asked me what had happened and I told him, "Ask Robert. I don't have any idea." He glared at Robert sitting quietly in the corner of his cell, and then went over to a corner himself and put his head on his knees.

Just then the doors started opening and closing, and the police came and got me. I thought maybe I was going home. (You just can't accept the fact that you're going to prison again. You think there's some way you're gonna get out of it.) I was sick of being a con and I didn't want to do any more time.

The lieutenant was smiling when I walked in. He offered me a cup of coffee and a cigarette, and told me to have a chair. He started talking to me like I was his best friend.

"I'm gonna tell you something, James," he goes, "this Robert Mack is a punk. We've dealt with him before and he's a rat. In fact, he's the one who ratted on you!"

I kept my expression the same, but I was getting curious about this quiz and even more curious about Mr. Mack.

"Mack went to a restaurant," the lieutenant continued, pausing here and there for effect, "pulled out a big sack of change, ended up buying dinner for everyone in the place. Someone got suspicious about this joker carrying around a grocery sack full of silver and called us. When we picked him up he was in a very talkative mood. Denied that he had pulled the robbery but said that he was out with you and Wally. Now, we know that three black boys robbed Ralph's and you all have records. You're dead unless you cooperate with us and help us send Mack up for good."

I was drove up by this shit, but I still didn't let on.

"Sure wish I could help, but I don't know a thing about this. I hadn't seen that dude Mack for two days until last night in the police car."

I knew I'd get Robert, but I wasn't about to help the police.

The lieutenant pounded his desk and sneered, "You're a goddamned liar! You were at Mack's house last night after the robbery. His mother saw you and his brother drove you home."

I said, "I ain't got nothing else to say."

The lieutenant stood up. "You're going to state prison. Get the fuck out of here!"

When they brought Wally in for questioning he got in a fight with the cops. He was crazy with love. They dragged him back to the cell screaming at Mack that he was going to kill him.

AFTER A WEEKEND IN CITY JAIL, they transferred us to County Jail. Since it was Monday morning, there were so many people waiting to be booked that we had to stand in line for eight hours.

I was assigned to a tank (cell block) and went there to get my cell assignment. The trustee and his aides occupied the first few cells; the rest was called "skid row." These cells were completely filthy and so overcrowded that guys would put their mattresses under the bunks in the cells during the day and drag them out into the corridor (which everyone called the "freeway") at night.

I knew the trustee, Skip, from my Aliso Village days, so I got a pretty good cell. The dudes in there were about to tell me to get out when Skip came by and said I was his friend. Skip wasn't a trustee by accident—he was the biggest, meanest guy in the tank. He got his position by beating all comers, and until he was beaten he had whatever he wanted: the best clothes, food, and cigarettes. And since the trustees can leave the tank, he was free to go out and buy candy bars and matches and sell them at fantastic prices. Unlike the penitentiary, dudes had their own money in County, so cash transactions were going on all the time: you could buy anything in there that you could get on the streets.

The L.A. County Jail was the finest place to sell dope. The money was right there and you didn't stand a chance of getting busted. The cops never came into the cell blocks. Guys got rich on the trade, especially the "weekenders," dudes busted on a petty beef, with steady jobs and families, who served their time on weekends. They'd bring heroin in balloons stuffed up their assholes. Naturally, they got twice the street price for the stuff. Dudes used to say that County Jail was the best place to sell shit, 'cause there weren't any cops.

After I'd been there about a week I met a guy I'd been hearing about all the time I was living in Watts. Alvin West was supposed to be the most diabolic dude in the world. He didn't give a shit about anybody other than his personal friends; he could've been trustee but he didn't want to work. Besides, he got everything he wanted anyway, just by taking it. Alvin lived in the cleanest cell and had all kinds of booty.

This guy comes down the hall one day, shuffling his feet and looking around with big beady eyes. They called him the "Chinaman" but he was as black as night. I just knew it was Alvin. I could see just by looking at him that we'd get along because I was just as big a motherfucker as he was. Skip introduced us and we started to talk. It was love at first sight. Al told me how he would lie around his cell playing cards and occasionally pull a robbery. He had a felony robbery beef right there in County Jail.

As time went on we got more and more friendly. We gambled together and played in a lot of different games. One night we got in a game with a real slick little white dude who was taking everyone's money. He had all his cash hung around his neck in a tobacco pouch. By the end of the night, both of us had lost all our money to the white dude.

We weren't angry that this slick had taken us for our bread; we had been looking for an excuse to rip him off. So we sent Al's cellmate Gus back into the game with a few dollars. Just as he was about to lose his ass again we walked into the cell. Al asked to see the cards. He turned his back and replaced them with a marked deck he had brought with him, then yelled that this dude was a cheat. Alvin showed Gus the deck. They were marked all right. West grabbed the little guy and pulled his money from around his neck. Then he told everyone else in the game to put all their money out. Their first reaction was to refuse because there were a lot of them, but they saw we were strong enough to beat the bunch and get the money besides. They emptied out and slid away.

All the next day dudes kept coming to us asking for their money back. Some of them had stories about their families and rent payments. I was getting ready to do some refunding when old Alvin came along. He started telling whoever cared to listen that he was going to fuck up the next dude that came down there.

Gus came down and asked Alvin how much money we'd got. Al answered, "I haven't counted it yet. Now, go down to the trustee and get me some boiled eggs." When Gus left, Al turned to me. "There's just not enough money here for the three of us, it's only three hundred bucks." That was fine as far as I was concerned. When Gus came back with the eggs, Al told him, "You know what, Gus, I sure hate to tell you this, but there's just not enough money here for three people."

Gus said, "Would you do me like that, Al?"

"You know I hate to," Al replied, "but I'm just not into splitting money ways it won't go, and you ain't getting any."

Just to finish him off, Alvin told him to move his stuff out of the cell and over to tank seventeen. West even threw his clothes out in the freeway. After that, I moved into his cell.

BY THE TIME OUR ARRAIGNMENT DATE came up, Wally was hurting gracious. As we were getting ready to go to court, he managed to get in line behind me. "When we get Mack in there I'm gonna beat his ass so bad he won't know who's in the fuckin' mirror!"

Before court begins they put all the cons in a holding cell called the "bullpen." There were about thirty of us in there when Mack walked in. He saw me and came over to shake my hand. I smiled, put my right hand up like I was gonna reciprocate, and then hit him with the left. Wally caught him as he fell, stood him up, and hit him with a right. He hit the ground and we went to work till his nose was broken, both his eyes were swollen shut, and his lips were all mashed. We left him in a big ball of meat over in the corner. This dude got a class ass-whipping.

The police came in and started reading off the first group of names. When they got to "Mack," some dude said that he was over in the corner lyin' down. The cop took one look at him and had him hauled off to the infirmary. We walked into the courtroom and Mack's mama was there, wondering where her Robert was.

When our case came up the DA called the names of a bunch of people who stood up in the back. They had all the people who worked in that Ralph's pointing their fingers at us. I knew then that we'd be convicted for sure. We got our trial date and went upstairs.

Back in my cell, I had to do something to take my mind off the pen. With lighted wads of paper, I started attacking the roaches that were crawling all over the place. I put the fiery balls in the cracks where they laid their eggs, and Al swatted them as they ran out. Suddenly a cop came up. "What the fuck is going on here? Carr, you're going to the Hole for starting a fire." The boys in the tank gave the cop a lot of verbal shit for busting me, but it didn't matter to that toe-headed asshole—I had to go. I rolled up my shit and he pushed me downstairs.

THE CONS CALL THE HOLE IN L.A. County Jail "Siberia" because it's so cold down there. The cells are tiny. They had eight dudes in each one when I moved in. The aisle between the cells was only wide enough for a food cart to pass through.

The first two cells were for homos who had fucked up. And lo and behold, there was Iron Man right there in Number One. He'd been in jail most of his life, loved the homos, and schemed to get put in with them. There he was with six punks. One was trimming his nails, one was giving him a haircut, and one was sucking his dick. Plus they were bringing him steaks. Iron Man was in heaven.

They threw me in with Jesse Chicago Barnes, who thought he was the world's greatest blues singer even though he couldn't sing a note. Jesse had been in Siberia for four months; there was no limit in County Jail on how long they could keep you in the Hole. They gave you so damn little food that dudes were always reaching out of their cells to grab stuff off the food cart. You got an extra day each time you did this, and Jesse did it every day. I was doing it too until I learned a little self control. I have never gotten used to hunger.

I got out of there after three weeks and immediately heard that Mack was spreading bullshit about Wally being the one who got us busted. I had Skip transfer me into Mack's cell, just to have a little talk with the boy. "You know what, Wally's going to kill you. You're hanging a jacket on him. You've already fucked him up once." Mack pleaded with me not to tell Wally. I told him to go fuck himself.

Wally and I had given all the money we'd had left from the robbery to Mack's mother to hire each of us a lawyer. It wasn't too logical under the circumstances, but Harriet wouldn't do it, and we didn't know anyone else. She took the whole bundle and hired Earle C. Brody, but she hired him just to defend Mack! Brody was black, and he was the last man in the world I would have hired. He took frustration crimes and charged huge sums. He had started out as a cop in the County Jail and studied law at night. Now he's a Superior Court judge in Los Angeles.

When Brody came down to see Robert, we asked him where our attorneys were; of course, he didn't know a thing about it. We set him straight and sent him back with some advice to talk to Mrs. Mack. Brody came back to say he'd defend all three of us, but wanted to work especially on Robert's case because he had the best chance of getting off. There was nothing we could do about the dude.

About two weeks later Brody returned and said that he had it all fixed. He had arranged with Judge Jefferson, a black judge, for us to go to court trial and be found guilty. He assured us the most we would get was a year on the farm; we wouldn't have to go to the penitentiary. We thought that was fine. When we went down to Jefferson's court. He was so nice to us we were sure of getting out.

But when our trial date came up, Jefferson's calendar was full. We were assigned to the court of Judge Burton Noble. Noble was an old dude who should have been retired a long, long time ago. He looked like a turkey, with a skinny, desolate face, hollowed-out cheeks, and all this loose skin under his neck. He looked at us through beady eyes, like he was just waiting to strike. I took one look at him and knew I was going to state prison.

None of the witnesses could identify Wally, and Noble dismissed his case. He really hated doing that. Brody tried to show how Robert and I couldn't have done it, but Noble and the jury didn't agree: we were convicted and Noble did the sentencing.

His face turned red, I mean took on some color. "It gives me pleasure to be able to take you hoodlums off the streets for good. I'm going to give you five-to-life, but I'm sure it will be a lot longer than five years before you cause anyone any more trouble." It was a bitch. There I was, headed back to the pen—forever!

IRON MAN, AL WEST, ROBERT, AND I all got sent, the next Monday, to Chino. Chino is the reception center for all the state prisons. They evaluate your case there and decide where to send you. It's a good idea to be on your best behavior when you're there so the cops will put you in a nice, quiet facility. But I wasn't into that shit. Our little Wolf Pack, brought together in County Jail, took over all the hustles at Chino.

One of the guys who ran with us, Tony Brewer, cleaned up the counseling rooms in the evening. He got the idea that it would be a perfect place to take the homos, since nobody came in there at night. The first time we went in there with this cute young kid we really got down to it. At one point, Tony was fucking him in the ass, Iron Man was being sucked, and I was getting a hand job.

The next day when I had to piss, it burned something awful. Without thinking about it I went to the infirmary. I had the fucking clap. When I got down there I was met by the police and the little homosexual who identified me as one of the assailants. The police had been waiting there all day for us to come in. I was the last to make it. The three of us were taken straight to the Hole.

Contradictory rumors filtered down to solitary. One dude was certain that I was going to Vacaville, while the tier tender insisted that I was being sent to Quentin. I got a little drove up in the middle of the week, thinking about it—the two places were so different I couldn't prepare myself for either one. Finally, on Friday I heard the chains rattling down the hall. I knew that the bus had arrived. The cell next to me opened up and Iron Man was called out. I could hear the cop say, "Tough luck, old man, you're going to Folsom." He locked the cell door and started to come get me.

NINE

THEY SENT ME TO QUENTIN. WHEN I got there, we had a full-blown race war on our hands, and things were heading toward a showdown. I was immediately assigned to close-custody, but since George Jackson had heard I was coming, he managed to walk by and say a few things. He told me he was going to see the Board soon and thought he might get paroled. We agreed to meet the next day, and the cops hustled me off to a cell.

George was still my partner. We'd been writing letters to each other, but the dude was genuinely pleased to see me; he was bursting with plans and stories that he hadn't been able to write through the prison mails.

Since that time in the Hole at Soledad, George had been deepening his political philosophy. He had become convinced that there would never be any social change in this country—that everyone, blacks included, had been too brainwashed. He believed that our only hope lay in going back to Africa to participate in the political struggles going on there. George had studied Pan-Africanism and thoroughly mastered African history while I was away. According to George, the new black man was being formed in the struggles for national liberation going on in the Portuguese colonies of Angola, Guinea, and Mozambique. That was where the highest principles of justice and equality were being put into practice. He planned to pull a bunch of bank robberies when he got out to the streets to buy guns and ammunition—machine guns and bazookas—which we would transport to Africa on a boat that we would pirate. This'd be after George got a bunch of us out of prison.

To promote his ideas, George had started giving political education classes to the Pack; each dude had to read a certain amount of material by Garvey and other nationalists and different things from Pan-African magazines George had collected. All of his plans were based on getting us together and getting released. The officials had been stringing him along, hinting that he might be paroled sometime soon, which made George even more intent on action.

Africa was on our minds, but we had plenty to worry about right where we were, too. The three main groups—ours, the Nazis, and the Mexican Mafia—were on a collision course. You could feel the tension every time you walked out on the yard; everyone was nervous and wired up whenever the groups were in the same place. There was a constant series of petty harassments and minor antagonisms, with a major outbreak every few months.

Each time a riot happened somebody got killed. If the whites won, they'd be on top until we killed one of them to even the score. The side that was "behind" would initiate a surprise attack to get out of the red. If you caught somebody taking a shit, so much the better. Since the thing broke racially it didn't matter if the guy you killed was in a group or not, just so long as he was the right color. In fact, most of the dudes who got killed weren't in groups. Some guy would get transferred from another prison and be at Quentin for a few days, not knowing anything about what was going on, and suddenly he'd get stabbed. The only motivation was to get even. The poor dude was just in the wrong place at the wrong time. We called this "stealing a life"; a guy got his life stolen. This made the groups stay together; if you weren't in one you didn't last long. The guards used to tell you to "do your own time." That was fine for them to say, but the situation just wouldn't allow it.

The prison officials were experts at keeping the races at each other's throats. Anytime the prisoners started to get together for a food strike or a work strike, Captain Hocker would call in the most notorious big-mouths and have them start rumors. Hocker was sly. He would never come right out and say anything, just drop hints. To some black guy he'd say, "We've heard that the whites are going to get you in the movie. Of course, this is just a rumor, we're just telling you so you can keep us informed if you see anything suspicious." And he would call in a white fink and tell him that the blacks were going to start trouble. Predictably, there'd be a fight and a murder, and the strike would be forgotten.

One way or another, you're gonna get killed as long as you stay in prison. You can't run and you can't hide; there's no place to go. Ours was a philosophy of desperation—all we were trying to do was stay alive. You don't even think about tomorrow. If you get there, fine, you deal with it. To imagine that you're going to do so much good time and then get out—that's dead. Dudes are getting shot down right and left, and if you don't get ripped off the chances of compounding your time are considerable. If you join a group, that's more time. If you get caught with a knife, five-to-life, and if you kill somebody and get caught—Death Row. You've reached the end of the world. I've talked with a lot of dudes out on the yard, and they say that's just what they felt like all the time. This is it—you can't go another step farther. Conditions can get no worse. The worst it can get is that they up and shoot you like a dog. They've already beaten and humiliated the shit out of you. You don't give a fuck any more. You don't even care if you get out.

Our group had more than a hundred and twenty blacks in it. Besides George, I ran mostly with a huge guy named Alberto who wore glasses so thick he looked like a mole; Larry Green, a former middleweight boxer; and Harry Thompson, a tiny dude who was a karate expert. Once in the group you were in for life. You couldn't get out, first of all because you were needed for the battles with the other groups. If you do quit and don't get killed, you at least get blackballed and life becomes miserable. And when the other groups find out you're unprotected they're gonna kill you; they've been waiting to do it anyway. Each group held together because of this and their nationalism—besides the struggle to control the hustles and the jobs that make up the prison economy.

THE RACE WAR CAME TO A head with the brutal murder of Hodges, a black from our clique. George told me how the thing had built up over a couple years: It happened that Hodges and Pablo Blanco of the Mexican Mafia were in love with the same homo, a young Mexican. And they both worked in the kitchen.

Pablo Blanco was five feet tall, with a withered arm and a terrible limp caused by a knife wound. He'd killed two guys with knives himself since he'd been in the penitentiary. Hodges was a big, strong dude who loved to box. He would get into at least one fight a week and knock somebody out. George said he warned Hodges more than once to stop acting the fool because if he didn't somebody was going to slip him some steel. But he didn't pay any attention.

Pablo told the homo he couldn't sleep with anyone who wasn't Mex. The kid ran to Hodges with the story and asked him for protection. The next day Hodges cornered Blanco in the washroom of the kitchen, beat him up, and practically drowned him in one of the big sinks. When Pablo recovered he did a strange thing—he told Hodges he was going to forget it, and that he wouldn't tell the Mafia brothers about it as long as Hodges kept clear. "If you ever cause me any more trouble, though, my friend, I am going to kill you." Hodges called Pablo a punk, said he was going to beat the shit out of him again, and walked off.

A couple of weeks later Pablo Blanco and a punk of his named Lippo walked into the shoe shop and asked Tommy Barnes for a pair of his romeos. Barnes was a little fat dude, a slob, but he could really make shoes; especially romeos—the high-topped loafers that all the Mexicans liked. When Barnes brought out the shoes to show them to Pablo, Pablo took the shoes and walked off without paying for them.

Hodges heard about it. He was always on somebody else's case, helping out some weak dude just for the fight. And he decided to defend Barnes. He went to Pablo and told him to return the shoes or else. Pablo Blanco said "I told you not to mess with me again; now you leave me no choice—I'm gonna have to kill you." Hodges' fists went into action. He knocked the little guy down in one blow and kicked him square in the mouth.

That evening after dinner Hodges was standing outside his cell by himself. As he turned, Pablo leaped out and stabbed him in the carotid artery, the big one running from the groin to the leg. Pablo dropped the huge butcher knife over the railing and ran down to the next tier. Hodges tried to catch him by jumping over the railing down to the third tier, but he'd already lost too much blood. He fell down four tiers, cracked his skull open, and died.

Pablo Blanco knew that he couldn't stay on the mainline because Hodges was more or less in our clique. He ran to turn himself in and was locked up in protective custody.

When I heard about Hodges getting ripped off through the grapevine the next morning, I knew this was it. There were more than a hundred dudes sitting in the bleachers by the time George and I got there. The agitators had already started giving pep talks, making out like Hodges was just about the greatest guy who ever lived. How we couldn't let them get away with killing Hodges because any sign of weakness would be interpreted as a signal to move on all of us. The dude was right. The one thing the clique did was allow us to survive. It was necessary to assert that or get trampled.

When the speech ended the talking was over. The entire mass of dudes got up and moved across the yard. I was carried along, heading for the other side of the yard where the Mexicans stood talking. There wasn't any plan, nobody said what we were going to do, it just happened. The outnumbered Mexicans saw us coming but it was too late. We engulfed them—none escaped. We had no weapons but our fists and feet, but those boys suffered. There were so many of us that each Mexican got worked over by four or five dudes. I hit dudes without seeing their faces; kicked whoever was lying on the ground.

I went berserk, lost control of myself, even forgot where I was. I remembered when the police in the towers opened up with their shotguns. Everyone started running at once. I was running blind, the air was so full of dust. Dudes all around me were going down under the buckshot. A Mex dropped right in front of me, hit in the back. He flipped over from the impact. I got tangled in his legs as I tried to jump over him, and we went down together with him on top. Double-O was falling like hail. The dude on top of me caught another pellet in the thigh. I managed to pick him up, carrying him perched over my back and head like a shield. I dropped the dude off in the yard and slid my ass into a building, out of the chaos.

There was George, grinning. We embraced, happy that we had escaped without getting hit. A lot of dudes weren't so lucky; several were completely paralyzed from being hit in the spine.

Hocker locked up all the blacks and Mexicans under thirty. And put all of us together in B-section. He had four of us in cells made for two. He put everybody in together. Usually when Hocker made cell assignments he was careful not to put weak dudes who were not involved in the racial strife in the same cell with fuck-ups. He threw that out the window.

This trip I got put in with two young black kids who didn't even know a war was going on. One was a country boy doing his first stretch in the pen. Henry Carver had a good outlook but it just wasn't realistic given the impending circumstances. He didn't want any part in a race war. Said he had nothing against any color just so long as people left him alone. The kid was simpleminded but solid. He gave me something to work on.

"Listen," I said, "I don't like this race thing any more than you do. I'd do anything I could to get out of it. You can't do it. Why the fuck you think you're in here with me now? You'll end up dead and not even know why. The only way to protect yourself is to find out what's happening and get with the clique before you get killed."

The other kid in the cell was a fish who weighed three hundred pounds. There was nothing I could do for him.

Finally, after nine days of misery, the guards came and walked me over to the East Block. I thought they were putting me back on the mainline. But when they put me in a cell I noticed that the shelves for personal property and the stools had been taken out. There was nothing there but the bunks and the shithole. I was confused and yelled out the door to see if anyone else had been put in this section. Sure enough, there was a bunch of other guys from the Pack scattered throughout the wing. We were all trying to figure out what Hocker had in mind.

A few minutes later they brought in Larry Green, an old friend of mine from Aliso Village—my new cellmate. Green was about five years older than me. He talked like he had a cigar in his mouth even though he didn't smoke "Hocker must have lost his mind at last," he lisped, "I can't understand what's goin' on here."

Then two cons came up with a portable acetylene torch and cut a hole in the door, a hole they said was for food trays. That made us even more confused. The cops didn't just go around altering the cells like that. When the work crew had finished cutting the hole and started to move on to the next cell, the tier tender ran up and told them to stay because Captain Hocker was coming down himself with more instructions.

When Hocker got there he stood looking at me out of the corner of his eye—the profile of evil. "Boy, I told you I wasn't going to take any more of this shit. You're going to be the first to find out just how I feel about all these murders." Hocker didn't care anything about murders; he loved them.

He told the dudes to weld a noose on the door, one big enough for a big lock. They worked the rest of the afternoon and all night until they had nooses on all the cells Hocker wanted. At midnight the captain came down again, this time with a box of strong fuckin' locks made by the cons at Joliet. He put the first lock on our cell. "Now you're in; you're in and you're not getting out. Hyah, ha ha!"

He took our earphones and books—left us nothing—and told us if he caught us with a newspaper we'd be in deep trouble. The dudes on the mainline who got the San Francisco paper were as scared of sending us one as we were of having one; if they'd got caught sending us anything, they'd get sent right in with us.

At first Green and I got along real well. We had both been studying mathematics so we worked together learning calculus. (A lot of cons you wouldn't suspect of being studious took up some academic discipline as a kind of recreation. I'd been tripping on math since Tracy.) Dudes who had gone to college would help us with formulas we couldn't work out ourselves. We worked as a team—each of us doing half the problems and explaining it to the other, who would try to find the mistakes. We had been making a lot of progress with our math, but after a while Green got tired of the math problems and he didn't give a fuck about anything else either. He got real drove up. Every day he started an argument over some insignificant point.

We used to trade off cooking the meat that we bought from the tier tenders. He would do it one day and me the next, but soon he got tired of cooking. For a while I didn't mind, 'cause it took some time out from just doing time, but after a couple of weeks I was bored with it so I started cooking just for myself. Green got real upset. He tried to explain to me that I should cook for him since I liked to cook and if it was him he'd do the same for me. This didn't sound right to me. I kept on cooking for myself, while he drifted off mouthin' his nonsense.

I liked Larry Green, but I didn't like that arguing. I told him he'd better stop or there were going to be some serious problems. But he wouldn't stop; he kept working on me. He got me to the point where I was ready to cut his head off. Then he started taking pills. He took Thorazine four times a day, he was off in the twilight zone and eating like a horse. His jaw swelled up till he looked like a bear, one who growled all the time about how terrible it was being in there. They weren't about to let us out.

I was doing everything I could to restrain myself. I had known Larry for eleven years and we had gotten along. Now he was banking on our friendship. I couldn't hurt him, but I had to do something, so I put him on shine status—on absolute zero. It made no difference what he did or said, I wouldn't talk to him. Since he was bent on going crazy, I decided to let him go alone. When they put me in there I was thinking, "I don't care if they keep me in here for fifty years, I'll still be me, I won't let them destroy me." And no matter how they fucked me up and how Hocker was never gonna let me out, I held on to resisting. You have to or you flip out. Now Larry's defeatist attitude was an assault on my morale. I had to fight it off.

I stayed as far away from him as a body could in an eight-by-eight cell. When he got on the floor I stayed on my bed, and he got the message that he had to reciprocate. I gave him the most respect I could: I left him absolutely alone. He was really hurting. I wasn't even in that cell; I was off in a world of my own working on math problems.

Green couldn't get to me, so he started to work on the cops, spitting in their faces when they came around for count. The first time he did it, he coughed up a big yellow goober and scored a ringer. The guard stopped and looked at Larry with death in his eyes, mulling over the various ways cops have of killing cons.

I still didn't talk to him. Every day I got some kicks watching this dude go to work, though I never let him know it. He never even knew I saw the act. There are only two things you do with a cop—kill him or let him alone.

The cop came back with a lieutenant. "Boy, you're in trouble if I get the key," he said. Larry whipped up another goober and hit the lieutenant right in the eye. By then the cops wanted the key so bad they didn't know what to do. But they weren't gonna get it: Hocker had the key, and he didn't trust any of his guards, so he took it home with him. They couldn't get us out of those cells.

The cops wanted Green out of there so bad they lost control. "You know, boy, you're a lucky black motherfucker." Green started cussing and spitting. He was fucking with the good Lieutenant Jameson, an expert at beating people with sticks to the edge of death.

"We'll get you tomorrow," Jameson promised, "Hocker's coming back with the key."

Captain Hocker, however, had this idea that it made no difference what we did in those cells—nobody got killed unless they wanted to live with a body or unless Hocker wanted it done proper. He used violence only when he needed a bigger budget. When Hocker came by the next day, he announced that the lieutenant wasn't getting in and we weren't getting out—in fact, the dude didn't even bring the key to work with him.

So Larry Green kept spitting and cussing, getting worse each day. By this time he was the main topic of the guards' conversation. They all wanted to kill him. They'd stand just out of spitting range and discuss various ways. Larry knew if he ever got out he'd have to go to Folsom or die.

Finally they sent Lieutenant Hardeman down. Hardeman was a black, and they figured maybe he could calm Green down. Old Hardeman tried his best to be a nice guy; I knew he was a bastard. He asked Larry how he was doing and Larry went livid: "How the fuck do you think I'm doing locked up in here like this?" Hardeman told him he better play it cool. But Larry kept right on whining in front of this black asshole, thinking the dude was there to do him some good.

Hardeman looked at me—I had known him ever since Tracy—and asked me how I was doing. I looked up from a math problem like I hadn't even known he was there until he spoke to me, "Oh, hello, Lieutenant," I said, real surprised— He couldn't believe I was still lost in math. He asked me how long I'd been in there and what for. I told him I had nothing to do with it, I was just watching. I didn't try to explain. It's honor among theives and they're thieves too. No one's to blame. He liked my answers and said he'd recommend they let me out.

As Hardeman walked away Larry Green yelled after him, "Let me out too, Hardeman! I been in here long as Carr!" Now, this dude didn't have a bear's chance of shitting in a swinging jug of getting out of there, and he was really pissed that I was going to. And sure enough, old Hardeman talked to the upstairs cops and the next day they came and let me out and left Green in there all alone.

TEN

WHEN I GOT BACK ON THE mainline, only my friend Alberto was there as always. During all this shit, Alberto never got locked up. He had the sweetest job, the best cover of anybody in the joint: he worked in the library. He had a reputation of being simply "Ol' Al" and no one knew what he was doing. The Nazis loved him and the Mexicans loved him, because he'd get them any racist, nationalist books they wanted. Even the cops liked him—he was the most efficient clerk they had going.

But they didn't like George and had him tucked away in one of the nice dark corners of B-section. They made him hard to get at. When I was able to, I slipped up over the roof, down a drainpipe and dropped onto the second door of B. I found George sitting alone in his cell, ready to go as always.

"James," said George, "we're going to become the richest cons in the penitentiary." He gave me a list of supplies he needed. "I've been checking things out, seeing where all the money is in this place we got here. The white boys have all the bread, and the dude with the most is Ben Falk. So he's the dude we have to beat." George never stopped scheming and setting goals.

He told me the story of how Falk made his fortune: He had a homo who liked him who also had a sexual relationship going with a guard. By getting this guard in love with him, the homo convinced him to bring in *Playboy* and every other hot-dog magazine imaginable. The homo would sell them for five dollars a month and he had them going all over the institution; three-quarters of the dudes in Quentin were coming up with *Playboy*, and the homo was getting rich. When the punk got a release date, he turned the hustle over to Ben Falk. Ben had to give the guard a sizable cut, but he had still accumulated more than ten thousand dollars cash.

"One thing Falk isn't into is making booze," George went on, "So that's what we start off into first. That way we won't run into him until we're strong. We're gonna turn this dark little cell into the biggest distillery in California."

I went to work right away getting the supplies we needed to get the thing going: an inner tube, tubing, yeast, vegetables, a five-gallon can to make a stove. In each section there's an overseer who gets $1,500 a month from the state for doing nothing, plus a bonus from the hustlers for doing less. I could get anything I wanted. I got a huge truck inner tube over in the motor pool, rubber hose from the gardeners, five matchboxes of yeast and vegetables from the kitchen. Like in any other black market, anyone who has the money could get this stuff and plenty more. I concealed the stuff in my clothing and fastened the inner tube around my body, and got back to George's cell.

George got to work: made a furnace out of the can, then cut the air nozzle out of the inner tube, and stuck one end of the hose in the inner tube and one end in the toilet. "Now you see," George said, "we can get all kinds of wine in this thing." So he and his cellmate got it cooking and coming out with all this wine, and the fumes went right down the toilet. They never got caught. With the sediment from the wine they boiled up white-lightnin' moonshine and sold it by the Jergens Lotion bottle for five dollars a taste. We were soon making an average of twenty-five cartons a week, and by the time George got back out on the mainline we had hundreds of cartons stacked up.

When George got out of B-section he started working in the kitchen, and I got transferred from my job in the gym to be with him. We had "bowl jobs." All we had to do was take the bowls when they were stacked up after breakfast, wheel them in barrels into the scullery, and wheel out an empty barrel to get more. The administrator who made up the job thought that bowls were used at every meal—so it was rated an eight-hour day. But they used bowls only at breakfast.

We got so busy making money that we had to "pay a boy," as George said, to push our bowls for us. We had four hundred cartons to work with before we decided to move into a bigger business: gambling.

Up to that point gambling had been handled completely by the dagos. Every black who wanted to gamble had to do it with them, because no black had enough money to back the games—until we took all the capital from the distillery and set up domino and domino poker games. The blacks immediately came over and started playing in our games, and pretty soon other dudes came over, because George always gave a little bit better deal than any other game. The thing the guys liked best was that George never sat on his money: he let them know that if they lost they'd have to pay, but if they won their shit would be delivered to their cells as fast as they could get there, 'cause we had so many guys delivering.

George hired a white professional dealer from Nevada named Smitty to run the main game, and paid him 25 percent instead of the usual 5 percent. Smitty did the same thing with a deck of cards that a monkey did with a tree. He was a real cowboy—looked like one of those range riders who'd lynch you in a second, but he wasn't racist; it was weird to see someone who looked like that act so nice. And he was wise besides; he'd been in every gambling hall in Nevada and damn near every jail. He'd gotten pretty slick.

Johnny Doro was Smitty's cell partner. That was a hell of a match. Doro was a mob organizer from Frisco who got two-to-twenty-five for pistol-whipping a guy who didn't want protection. It was funny, this sophisticated dago with a good education and property up the ass, sharing a cell with a cowboy. They got along, though, because they both liked the long green. Old Doro had his finger in every pie. Every key position in the pen, if it wanted to function, had to pay Johnny Doro. His game was simple: everything that was his was his, and everything else was negotiable. Everyone in the joint paid protection to Doro and he had the Mexican Mafia enforcing. His desire to get into every deal was nearly maniacal. He was in on every investment and never touched a thing.

Since George never invested any of our money, he could always get to all the capital right away. Cigarettes are the main medium of exchange, and they're worth more than their cash value, especially for big transactions. Most cons stockpile cigarettes rather than money. But when a shipment of smack comes into the pen, all dealing is strictly cash since the outside men have to be paid. The value of hard cash went way up just for the two or three days dope was around. George would try to get the inside line on when a dope run was on, then turn all our cigarettes into cash. He'd sell the cash for cigarettes to dudes who wanted the dope and turn the cigarettes back into cash before the next run. By setting up an incredible exchange rate we'd make a profit of from 200 to 1,000 percent.

We lived for these fantastic sums of jack. We had built the games up to the point where we controlled all the gambling in the pen; all the other games dried up. They couldn't deliver.

When the big dope came it was always handled by Doro. Anyone else would just get pieces, or get burned. If anyone got more than a piece, they'd end up having to sell to Doro at his price. When this happened Doro would need cash, lots of it. Since his was always invested, he'd come to us. Pretty soon we had a steady business relationship with the dude. He knew he could come and get three or four hundred dollars any time he needed it, and he always paid back two-for-one without any bickering. Doro didn't like riots. He had a section over in the corner of the kitchen where he ate. This table had a lot to do with keeping things cool. He just wanted to make money. All his friends ate Death Row food: four different kinds of meat a day, and fresh vegetables and anything else—and any of his friends could come over and eat. He arranged nice quiet banquets with us and the Mexican Mafia. That along with the police payoffs, helped keep the place together.

THE POSTMAN BROUGHT THE DOPE IN every month. He was always on time. He had the best reputation of all the runners in the whole penitentiary. Naturally, everybody liked him. He never saw a thing. He was a crook down to the heart; he just happened to work in Quentin.

Angelo Delgado and Jack Fox were both using the Postman for a nice thing. Angelo was a dago, and real tight with George and me, but Fox was a pure inverted asshole. We hated him. He took red devils and thought he was big shit. Angelo hated Jack Fox too—he just lived with him to keep an eye on the guy and to figure a good time to get rid of him.

Angelo would talk to us about his situation with Fox, complain about how hard life was living with the dude. Finally one day he was running it down again and said, "You know, that Jack Fox is beginning to cause me too much trouble. I don't think I can live around him any more. Do you know anyone who would be interested in making a hundred and fifty cartons to see that Jack has to live in the hospital for a while?" Angelo was a businessman talking to George and me as fellow businessmen, figuring none of us would directly dirty our hands on such a job; he just thought we could tell him the name of the right man to hire.

George didn't say anything for a while, then replied in his casual way, "Angelo, I'd be pleased to see that Mr. Fox is out of your hair, but when I'm through with him I don't know if the doctors will be able to do anything for him." But Angelo said he didn't want Jack killed, just so fucked up that the cops wouldn't let him back on the mainline for fear that someone'd kill him. In other words, he said, "almost dead."

Jack Fox worked in the scullery cleaning the dishwashing machines. He was always in the kitchen by himself, up under those machines. We thought it would be easy to catch him in there alone and waylay him. I went down there with a hammer the next night, but just as I was going to smash his head in another guy turned up and I had to split. Everyday I'd try to figure out someway to get him, but it just seemed I could never catch him alone.

A week later Jack got caught out in back of the kitchen by two of the Mexican Mafia. They told him they wanted cigarettes and Jack said, "Man, I ain't got a pack"—that's a dude's favorite phrase when he's rich. But they weren't taking any of that. They told Jack they needed forty cartons to pay back a debt, and he'd better come up with them right away. Jack had to pay, but he was tight, real tight, and mad as hell at getting ripped for all that bread. So he got in George's card game the next day to try to recover his losses. Instead, he lost the bottom part of his ass—a thousand cartons of cigarettes in twelve hours—and Smitty let him do it 'cause he knew Jack had the Postman. When Fox had lost all that, he backed out and said he had no intentions of paying.

I was sitting there trying to figure out what was wrong with him. He knew George always paid and always collected. I went around to George and told him our boy had lost. When I told him how much, George laughed, calling me a motherfucking liar; nobody had ever lost a thousand cartons before. I told him the story of how Smitty had worked the dude, and how Fox was backing out on the payment. George got himself up and we went on down to the game. Jack Fox was sitting there with all these guys around, and George asked him if he was gonna pay. "I got no intention of paying you a motherfuckin' thing."

George licked his lips and said, "Look, man, it's not necessary for you to pay. As a matter of fact, just to show you what I think about it, I'm gonna pay it myself, 'cause it's worth that much to me," and he patted Jack on the back. Jack Fox couldn't figure it out, but he had to know he had no business talking like that to George. Angelo was so happy he didn't know whether to laugh or cry. He was sitting back under his shades, grinning. He knew he was finally going to get rid of Jack. George walked off, and Jack fell for it.

That night, Jack Fox was taking his shower in the facilities above the kitchen, and we were downstairs. George pulled out a tiny knife about five inches long and started talking about how he was gonna go upstairs and carve up Jack Fox. I was telling him I wouldn't ever stick something like that in anybody, much less do it in the shower with twenty people standing around. I didn't like this carving bit; I wanted to kill him quick. There isn't anything more dangerous than trying to kill a con and not doing it, 'cause some day he's gonna see you again, and he's not gonna shake your hand. I never got into those fighting games; when I decide to kill, someone's gonna die. That's the way I like to kill people—permanent. It's easier on them, and on me too. I had this big twenty-inch file ground down to a knife. It weighed two pounds and would go right through Jack Fox. But George was a romantic—he had read too many pirate stories, and the Arabian Nights, and Shakespeare. He had a romantic idea of killing someone right. He wants to take this little knife and cut Jack's throat. There we were, standing in the kitchen arguing about how to kill this dude upstairs. Finally George said, "It's my man and I'm gonna drop him right. If you wanna help, just stand at the bottom of the stairs and point, and old George will cut him from behind."

George hid at the top of the stairs; I stood at the bottom and waited. When Jack Fox started down I looked up and said, "Hey Jack, howya doing?"

Jack shot back, "Ah, fuck, how the fuck do you think I'm doing?"

I pushed Jack back up the stairs and George ran down and grabbed the dude from behind, reached around and cut his throat—but he didn't cut deep enough. Jack started to run. George grabbed him by the coat and kept on sticking him. Jack was yelling his head off and everybody in the kitchen was looking up, everybody in the shower was looking down. By the time George finally downed him, Jack had tumbled down the stairs and out the door, covered with blood. There must have been thirty people looking at Jack and no one seeing a thing. I stood there looking too until the police came.

The lieutenant just took a piece of chalk out of his pocket and drew a circle around Jack, and then they wheeled him off to the hospital. I thought for sure he was dead. They even put a sheet over his head. But they got him into the hospital and they saved Jack Fox from the chill. Jack was lying in the hospital with all these tubes in him, and Angelo was still trying to find somebody to get rid of the dude.

That night in his cell George was worried. I assured him no one would talk, and I told him the police weren't that interested in helping Jack anyway. The cops hated him. When Fox was in Soledad originally, he thought he could whip the world. He got in a hassle with a cop when he was working in the kitchen there, and he took a huge industrial can opener (this tool is L-shaped, about two by three feet, weighing about twenty pounds) and laid into him. He didn't kill the cop, just disabled him for the rest of his life. The state had to pay all this disability. They took Fox to outside court to really squeeze him, and somehow—I don't know how—he beat the beef, and the authorities were mad. Jack's getting cut didn't really concern the police; they'd shipped him into Quentin hoping for something to happen. (Six months later I was working on the ground crew, and I had a little smuggling operation going. I was pushing a wheelbarrow full of contraband covered with grass trimmings when out of the thick fog come Captain Hocker and Lieutenant Boynpressure. They're in their trenchcoats, doing their George Raft bit. When Hocker stopped me with all this contraband I thought I was cooked, but he just walked up and said, "Y'know, I never did say anything to yuh, but you and Jackson sure did a good job on Jack Fox." And I said, "Captain, I don't know what the fuck you're talkin' about." Hocker just laughed, Boynpressure smiled and shook his head, and they drifted off again into the fog.)

TWO WEEKS AFTER WE'D CUT FOX, Hocker had me assigned to ground crew N. Most of the ground crews worked outside the gate, but N works right inside the main gate near the main arsenal. They've got a fifty-caliber machine gun set up on the wall there which looks right down on where we worked. Hocker let me know I wasn't under that gun by accident.

And it wasn't any accident that I was put on a crew with Sheik Thomas, the most dangerous dude inside. Sheik was legendary. He was about forty-five years old, five foot six and a hundred and sixty-five pounds, and about as immobile as Alcatraz in a light breeze. He looked like the devil's father. He had once fought a homosexual in Folsom with his fists for an hour without ever stopping for breath. They fought from the kitchen, all the way through the blocks, and out into the yard. This homo bit Sheik all over his face and bit both his ear lobes off, so they went down to points. Then the cops shot Sheik in the side, in both legs, shot his balls off, and still he didn't stop. He was on his knees pouring out blood and hitting the homo so hard the cops are afraid to pull him off. When they took him to the hospital, after he'd passed out from loss of blood, the doctors said he'd never walk again. Four months later Sheik was walking, and by the time I met him the dude could run around a football field with a hundred-pound sack of sand on his back.

Sheik's original beef shows what kind of guy he was. He was working for a fight promoter in Frisco as a trainer, and one night he's coaching a boxer who was supposed to be throwing the fight. But once this kid got in there he changed his mind and started winning. Sheik screamed, jumped up in the ring, and in front of the whole crowd pulled a gun out of his belt and shot this fighter.

Besides being one crazy motherfucker he was a rat, an informer. He'd rat on you right in front of your face. If you didn't like that, he'd spit on you. And if you didn't like that he'd beat you back into hamburger.

I didn't meet Sheik for a couple days. He worked the outer-most area, a sunken patch of land right next to the arsenal which he doted on like he owned it. The rest of us took it real easy, but Sheik spent most of every day out there, manicuring the grass and flowers and tending his prize fig tree. Like everyone else I had my own strip of grass and flowers, and like everyone else but Sheik I would just turn on the water (if it wasn't raining) and go sit in the shack and bullshit. The shack was situated between the East Block and Death Row; we changed clothes and stored tools in it, and it offered shelter from the dreary atmosphere of cement walls on four sides, fog and a machine gun above.

It was a soft job though, and I had a good steady hustle going right away. My first day out on the ground crew, Tom Davis, who worked in the snack bar, asked me if I'd like to make some money. He'd been in for six years of a ten-to-life murder-robbery and had settled down to try and live comfort-ably there. Tom would steal anything he could get his hands on. He would get crab, shrimp, ham and baloney from the snack bar, wrap it in plastic bags, and throw it in the trash. Then I'd go and have a snack, parking my wheelbarrow filled with grass trimmings out back. While I was eating, Tom would fill the barrow up and cover the food with grass; then I'd wheel it under the gun tower, around the corner of the East Block. Here, on the third floor, an old man named Shotgun was tier tender. Every morning at ten thirty and every afternoon at three, Shotgun would lower a basket down from his window, and I'd fill it up with food. Then at night we'd make sandwiches and sell them for a pack apiece. I was making eight cartons a night.

One day when I went over to the snack bar, Tom had unexpectedly got hold of a big box of juice. Since Shotgun didn't know about it and wouldn't be waiting, I had to go inside and tell him. I took the juice to the shed and asked a big old slow-thinker named Mule to watch it for me.

When I got back and checked it out, there were two cans missing. I thought Mule had taken them, which was all right with me, since he was watching them, so I said, "You drink some juice, brother?"

"No, I ain't drank 'em . . . Sheik came in here and drank 'em."

I tore out, with Mule running behind me scared to death trying to explain things away. When I got over to Sheik's little kingdom, I just walked down and started eating some of his figs.

Sheik went into shock when he saw what I was doing, and came over like a crab—he hobbled, but he could move: "What you doin'? Get out from down there!" Like he owned the land. Then he started working on his flowers right next to me while he kept on yelling at me to get out.

I said, "Don't lose your head old man, I been hearing about you for a number of years, how bad you are. In fact, I been hearing about you since I was a kid. Now, I don't want you to beat me up . . . cause if you do I'm goin' to have to kill you."

I was sure no one ever talked to him that way, but I let him know I wasn't going to take an ass whipping (and I'm sure he could have beat me up). Sheik was still yelling, "Get out from down here," as he's trimming his flowers, but I didn't move.

"And furthermore," I said, "you know that was my juice you drank there."

He didn't meet anything I said head-on, but he heard every word. He turned and yelled, "Who tole you I drank that juice?" (He always veiled everything, like a man who's seen a ghost and can't decide whether to kill it or run. For Sheik that decision would turn on whether or not the ghost had a knife.) I told Sheik that wasn't important—the fact was he'd drunk it and it was mine—but before I finished Sheik tore up the hill and ran to the shack, burst in with "Who's the motherfucker that tole?" and started yelling about everybody's mother and what he'd do to them, and then he spit on everyone in there.

Finally Mule confessed, "I did it, Sheik. . . I was watching it for him."

Sheik shrieked, "You're a sorry specimen for watchin' another man's juice and lettin' me drink it." He turned on me, saying, "You're a young fool for lettin' this farmer watch it. I'll pay you for your juice tomorrow."

"Okay, Sheik," I said, smiling. "It costs two packs a can."

"What?" cried the Sheik. "All I ever got for it was a pack a can!"

"Yeah, Sheik, but the price just went up."

Sheik ran out cussing his head off because he knew he had to pay. The next day Sheik paid me and beat dogshit out of Mule. After that we got to be friends. He'd come over with a hatful of figs and talk about odd times or about books. He was well-read for such a mean old dog.

A month later Sheik got a transfer to Folsom. He got a good loan business going, two-for-one, and whenever someone couldn't pay Sheik would go to work on them. One day he tried to collect from two guys who said they couldn't pay up. He spit on both of them and told them to get the stuff quick or he'd break their backs. They said they'd be right back.

Sheik was standing near the wall where the guard walked, never straying more than ten feet from the guard. He'd gotten into this habit because there'd been nearly fifty attempts on his life. Knowing all this, the two guys he'd just threatened went and got two knives and two bats. Sheik felt safe because he was so close to a cop. At Folsom they'll shoot if you slap a friend on the back. But these two guys were crazy. They ran up behind Sheik, right in front of this cop, broke both his knees so he couldn't run and beat his head into a soft-boiled egg. The cop froze. To make sure, they stabbed Sheik in both kidneys and the heart. When they finished they turned around and handed their weapons to the police.

They came and took what was left of Sheik away in a gurney, and when they pushed his body across the yard, everybody, all the cons, applauded. And the guards just grinned.

HOCKER HAD BEEN ON TO THE dope scene for a while. He knew we were handling the stuff even though he couldn't catch us red-handed. The gambling he always let pass, but he was a puritan about dope. He finally locked up everybody he thought was dealing in B-section on "Pending Investigation."

I was put in with a dude named C.D. Drake. He was pathetic. Used to be hard as a rock, but by the time I met him he was a split clam. He'd been a black motorcycle rider running with a white gang out of Oakland, pulling robberies. One night they took off from a liquor store they'd robbed and a motorcycle cop came after them. When he caught up with C.D., he pulled out a shotgun and blew the cop away.

They gave him ten-to-life, which means life, and slapped the Habitual Criminal Act on him. C.D. got deeply depressed.

Then he got fucked over by a homo he was in love with. By the time I got to him he was hooked on pyrobenzamine, boiling the pills down and shooting them up. He'd come out of his haze and talk about the streets for a while—to the point of breaking down. I felt sorry for the dude, but I was too disgusted by his wretchedness to help him out.

But it was through C.D. that I met Youngblood, crookedest cop in Quentin. He was a bull up on Death Row who came to work on B section. He knew we were in there for suspicion of dealing, and we could tell the first time he walked by that he was interested in talking to us. We gave him the high sign, and he came over for a chat. He was big—a black dude with a high ass—and he tried to look slick even in his uniform.

It turned out C.D. and Youngblood were both from Frisco and knew all the same bars and whores. Youngblood showed us pictures of his wife and girlfriends and was getting real friendly, so C.D. gave him some chick's phone number. Youngblood came back the next day saying he got a piece of ass from her, and slipped us a couple of joints.

He started coming around every day—wanted to know if we wanted any dope, what kind, and how he'd get paid. I lied to him about all my money and connections, and his eyes lit up. He supplied us regularly with a little dope, just enough for our own use. Later, once I got out of B-section, I started running the dude till the heels of his shoes looked like deer hoofs.

A popular drug at that time was Wyamine tubes—inhalers filled with enough amphetamine to get three people high for twenty-four hours. They sold for sixty cents on the street and five dollars in the pen. We gave Youngblood two dollars for them, which was pure profit because he stole them off the drugstore shelves. Youngblood would take these tubes and tape them all down his legs when he came to work, then point and sweat while I untaped him.

After a while Youngblood was driving a Cadillac and showing us pictures of his new house, He had operations going with people I'd never dreamed of. He was booking horses and running all kinds of shit. Finally they busted a guy in the honor block and he told them who'd brought it in. The next day, Hocker had about twenty employees searched "at random" as they came to work. He wanted to search and catch Youngblood (he didn't like black guards much either), but somehow Youngblood was tipped and that morning retired from the messenger business. Hocker couldn't pin a thing on him. He was mighty warm about it, so he sent the goon squad after Youngblood, hoping if he got beat up bad enough he'd quit. But Youngblood kicked six goon asses one morning when they jumped him, got in his Caddy, and drove off to work for the Alameda County Juvenile Authority.

LIKE ALL MY PREVIOUS BEEFS, I never got a one-fifteen out of this "Pending Investigation," just a bad report which in some ways is worse because it goes into the permanent jacket.

As soon as I got out after they dropped the investigation, I went around to the housing lieutenant's clerk (a con) and paid him fifteen packs to get me into the honor block. It's not much different from the mainline, except for your freedom of movement. You can shower, watch TV, go out on the yard, or lock up any time you want. It was nice for a while, but I knew I wouldn't last long there. It was filled with model cons and cons rich enough on the outside to buy their way on, and they had got a committee composed of inmates who think of it as a "community." If you don't go for that, or even seem like you're not going for it, the committee can vote you out. I stood out like a sore thumb; it was only a matter of time before they'd throw me out. My record couldn't use it; I decided to get out voluntarily.

I went to Hocker and applied for a job change that would necessitate living elsewhere. I told him I couldn't work on the ground crew any more because it was too close to the gate and therefore too tempting; I might try to get away against my better judgment (which was obviously bullshit, what with that machine gun). I told him I wanted to work in the psych ward. Hocker was so surprised and relieved that I hadn't asked to work with George, which I knew he wouldn't allow anyway, that he granted my request.

Three days later I got a ducat to report to Dr. Schultz's office for an interview. The psych ward is set off from the rest of the hospital by a grilled gate which is manned by a cop who's seldom there. Compared to the rest of the prison the place is well equipped with a stove, refrigerator, TV set, and steam bath, and the best food outside of Death Row.

Schultz's office was just around the corner from the ward. The walls were decorated with pictures of crazy people afflicted with things like catatonia, depression, and paranoia, along with photos of maniac murderers. The dudes' faces were so screwed up they looked like masks. I'd been in there with nothing to do but get uncomfortable trying to avoid looking at these photos when Schultz's secretary came in—This tall, gorgeous blonde walks over to me and says, "The Doctor will see you now." When I didn't grab her I passed my first test. Most dudes can't resist touching her. I had demonstrated self control.

Dr. Schultz was sitting behind his desk, looking like a German general with a bald, pointy head and a pair of those funny round rimmed glasses on. First thing he said was, "Vell, tell me, Chames, vy do you vont to vork here?"

"I want to help other people," I responded with all the sincerity I could manage.

"Good, good, good," he said, rubbing his hands together. "You vill do very vell here—you're a big boy." By the look he threw me over the top of his accent I got the idea he meant I could go up there and scare the nuts.

"These people are sick, Chames, because they've had bad family lives. Now, ve have to be understanding. But don't show them too much sympathy, my boy. They've got a long vay to go and they are going to have to make it on their own. Chust make sure dey don't hurt themselves. That's yer chob, Chames. I'm sure you'll be able to do dat, von't you, Chames?"

I nodded gravely. I couldn't say anything more. If I'd opened my mouth I'd have laughed in his face.

He outlined my duties. The psych ward was run completely by con staff. They took care of the patients, passed out the medications, and made out the reports that the doctors used in diagnosis. Schultz gave me a psychology textbook and told me to study it so that I could write out the reports in the proper technical language. That was it—I had the job. He showed me to the door and told me to report to work the next day.

When I got back out on the tier I asked some of the dudes about Dr. Schultz. He seemed weird, but I couldn't put my finger on how weird. Iron Man heard me asking some other dudes about Schultz and came running over. "Wait James, don't volunteer for anything till you hear about that dude." I told him I was going to be working for him, not be experimented on by him. He seemed a little relieved but insisted that I listen to the story of the good doctor.

Dr. Schultz and his assistant, Dr. Hagstrom, so the story goes, were the pioneers of the use of shock therapy in the California prisons. When it was first being used at the end of the '40s no one was sure of the proper voltages and tolerances, so some prison doctors did experiments, using the cons as laboratory mice. They recruited dudes from the Adjustment Center, which was a whole lot worse than it is today—it wasn't even heated— then promised them a "ticket to the mainline" if they "volunteered." They took a long time to find out the relationships between voltages and tolerances. They didn't want to give too little and not have the proper effect, and they didn't want to stop before results could be determined as "scientifically" conclusive. They were looking for the highest tolerable dose.

At least thirty dudes gave their lives to science in those pioneering years. They were all reported as having died of heart attacks, which was probably true enough. A lot of other dudes who got a jolt a little too heavy were turned into vegetables. Some walked around all right, but with their brains fried to ashes.

When the word got to the outside that these madmen were doing their little Nazi trip right there in Marin County, the local do-righters put pressure on the Penal Authority to have this "research" halted. The experiments weren't stopped, though. The officials simply moved them to Vacaville and renamed the place. They called it "prison hospital" which legitimized the butchery as far as they were concerned.

"Now, if that ain't enough to make you want to stay away from Schultz, I don't know what is," Iron Man spat at me.

I was confused. Before hearing all this shit about Schultz I had been looking forward to going in there and eating all that good food. I started to imagine all kinds of horrible things, like finding dead bodies hid away and being attacked by dudes gone berserk. I couldn't get out of the job now, though, it was too late for that. I didn't sleep very well that night.

ELEVEN

IRON MAN HAD PREPARED ME TO find an unreal scene, but nothing like the first thing I saw upon walking into the ward. Emerging from the steam bath in a big cloud of steam walked the Creature from the Black Lagoon. I yelled, "Oh, what the fuck are you?" as this dude—I could finally say for sure it was a man—stomped by muttering, "Yeh, yeh. It's me. It's me!" He was the ugliest thing I had ever seen.

This poor guy, whose name was Bobo, had poured a can of liquid metal all over his body and torched it up to protest the indeterminate sentence—made himself into a human bonfire. They saved his life by throwing sacks over him, but maybe they shouldn't have. Half his mouth and half of one eye were melted shut, he had shiny spots of dead flesh all over his body, and his nose sat over on his right cheek. Together with that, Bobo, who'd been a little off even before the torching, was turned completely paranoid looking like this. He ended up thinking everyone who stared at him was out to get him.

In contrast, the ward itself was bare as an empty wall, which there were plenty of. It was clean, flat, and boring, but Fat Ed, the guy who ran the place, made sure the dudes in there were as comfortable as conditions warranted. Not that Fat Ed didn't have a few kinks himself a former UCLA psych major, he got a child-molesting beef for fingering a three-year-old. He stood about five-ten and weighed three hundred pounds. Everything about Fat Ed was round, including his personality. The cons up there wanted to get rid of him because he took his job as seriously as Schultz did. Since he'd been to school to take this shit, he wrote reports on people that kept them in there for the rest of their lives. To Ed, anyone who got put in there was violent, or if they weren't actually violent they must be catatonic. Ed created a lot of nuts.

My ideas about psychology were a lot different than Ed's. All the patients in the ward were basically just having a healthy reaction to the insane environment of the pen, by either nutting out or pretending to. The guys who really nutted out were just like anyone else who runs a trip on himself and on the world, only inside it's more extreme. Ed and the shrinks treated them as if they were a different species: punishing them for being sick while at the same time going off on elaborate explanations of why these dudes couldn't cope. They were more cruel, if not always as brutal, as the mainline officials. With those cons whom the shrinks considered "extreme" patients, I found that if I was just straight with them and didn't play to their weaknesses, we got along fine. All I wanted to do was make it easy on them and easy on me. The other three ward attendants—Big Hamp, Bobby Beamon, and Horace the Cowboy—felt the same way. The only thing they had in common with Ed was that they were all fat.

The conscious goal of many of the patients was to get sent to Vacaville, where life was much easier. Just before they were going in to see the shrink they'd start acting sicker; it was obvious they were practicing. I'd tell them directly that I thought it was fine that they wanted to get transferred. I'd help them develop a good act, tell them what symptoms went together for a particularly serious disorder. To make sure, I'd write their report up so it looked as if they'd been that way the whole time they were on the ward. I was helping guys get to Vacaville right and left. The doctors took this as a sign of their success: their theory was that all cons were crazy.

For example, there was a guy named Red who got a stabbing beef inside and then nutted out in order to avoid going to outside court. When he got sent up to the ward, I told him his best chance lay in nutting out to the point where he didn't say anything at all; just stay up for two days straight staring at the wall, then all of a sudden fall out and sleep for a day. I wrote up reports on how the patient seems to be drawn into catatonia, but that every now and then he's extremely extroverted, which to the shrinks meant that he was schizoid. When I turned these reports in to Dr. Hagstrom, he just ate them up, sitting there puffing his pipe looking like a locomotive, saying, "Goood, goood, goood, goood."

One old man named Greer didn't need any help from me. When he was in the army he'd got in an accident and hurt his head. The VA hospital said nothing was wrong with him, but when he got to prison for a robbery there was "something" wrong with him. Every now and then he'd say he had these dangerous headaches that drove him up the wall and into the psych ward. The whole thing was a hustle to get pills, which he saved and sold on the mainline. Then he got a better idea and played his headaches into a transfer to Vacaville. He got his own room with lots of luxuries, plus outside work furlough. This contributed to Greer's miraculous recovery: for six months he was a model prisoner with no headaches. Everybody's happy: the authorities think they've rehabilitated someone, and Greer's been released to the streets.

Many of the patients were neither sick or nuts, but were in there for something related to homosexuality. The prison authorities condone and even promote homosexuality, but they'll separate a couple if they get too tight. Often they'll send a homo to Vacaville, particularly the ones that look like women and take hormone shots. Many times this homo's partner will cut his wrists or fake a hanging or just flip out on the yard in order to get sent there too. Usually, however, the farthest he gets is the psych ward.

I'd been working about a month before I saw any of the members of the Wolf Pack come into the ward—a dude named PeeWee who was Larry Green's partner. PeeWee's father was in Quentin too, and they looked exactly alike. The old man had been there for years, and the kid was trying to act like his father all the time. Now he'd made it: a life sentence for murder at the age of eighteen. And suddenly he changed his mind. The prospects of living in the pen for the rest of his young days depressed him to the point where he flipped out violently on the yard. Hocker had him put in the Death Row cell on the psych ward, where no one could get in except the guard from the main gate.

I talked to him every night through his window; he wasn't the same little dude I'd known on the yard. He'd tell me every night how he had nothing to live for, that he was going to kill himself. I never took it too seriously until one day he said, "Carr, I'm gonna kill myself tonight." He said it so weird, like he was already dead, but I could still hear his voice. I told him he had the right to do that, but that I felt he did have something to live for and that suicide would be a mistake. We talked for over an hour, and in the end the eeriness faded from his voice and it seemed like he was convinced. Next night, though, he was back at it: "Sorry, Carr, it's not gonna work."

When I left the ward that night I told everybody coming in on the graveyard shift to watch PeeWee because he was going to try to do himself in. The next afternoon when I came back on, one of the cons told me PeeWee had hanged himself. They couldn't talk him out of it, and they couldn't find the guard to open his cell. All they could do was watch the dude die.

IN EARLY 1965, BEN FALK GOT put in Segregation, probably as a result of Letters written by his debtors to the authorities. They put a picture of him on the bulletin board in the yard with a sign saying all debts to this man were cancelled. Falk's bust started a round of investigations and raids, which somehow led to a raid on the library—old Al's stronghold.

Alberto had been the main clerk there for a long time—years—and Mr. Spector, the librarian, loved him and trusted him as much as the cons did.

Back in '63, Spector had to leave town and left Al in charge of the place. Alberto put in a work order to the carpentry shop and had them come in and rebuild the bookshelves so they would slide; then Al and some guys in the clique built other shelves into the wall in back of them creating a huge secret storage space. It was our arsenal and our bank: Alberto stashed our cigarettes, knives, pipes, cash money, and weapons. This is where George and I and all the other dudes in the Pack stashed all our bread from hustles—the domino tables, poker games, lending, pressure, wine—and our equipment. This was particularly convenient for weapons, because we could always go from the main yard to the library, thereby avoiding the search coming in or out of the block. When we made money, we'd just give it to Al and it never got confiscated or ripped out of the cells. Altogether, we had over a thousand cartons of cigarettes, five thousand dollars cash, and two to three hundred weapons.

A few days after Ben Falk got busted, the library was closed down. Usually when we went to breakfast we'd meet Al out in front on his way to work, but this morning he wasn't there. Instead we saw a two-by-four on two sawhorses across the doorway and the goon squad all over the place. The goon squad, euphemistically known to the authorities as the "Security Squad," makes it their job to cruise the institution every day in their green overalls with little zippers and dunce caps, checking to see if any bars have been cut or holes dug and looking for contraband. They spent a week in the library taking the place apart; it was like a puzzle for them trying to figure out where to look next. Every day they'd come up with a gross of stuff they couldn't understand, and they sent it down to Inventory where the con clerks would tell us what they found. One day they'd come up with fifty cartons in back of Natural History; the next, they'd find a couple thousand dollars behind another wall. When they found the weapons they really freaked. They took a picture of all the knives and clubs and, together with pictures of two guys who had been ripped off recently they put them up on the bulletin board with a sign reading:

IN ORDER TO PREVENT THIS TYPE OF SLAUGHTER
INMATES MUST BECOME MORE COOPERATIVE
WITH THE ADMINISTRATION.
REMEMBER! YOUR LIVES ARE IN DANGER!

SIMULTANEOUSLY, THEY LOCKED UP THE ENTIRE library crew. We figured old Al had had it. But Spector came to work the next week and swore to God that Alberto couldn't have had anything to do with it. He said he needed Alberto back at work with him to reorganize the library. Al got out of the Hole after a week, while everyone else from the library got sent to Folsom.

The Saturday before Alberto got out of the Hole, I was working out in the gym when a brother brought me a message that George wanted to see me. George told me that that morning he had taken a ten-dollar bill to trade for cigarettes in order to buy canteen for Al, and had given it to a little homo named Freeman. Freeman's job was to run the bill to Chico of the Mexican Mafia, who was going to take it into the East Block. An hour passed, and no cigarettes had arrived. The homo went inside to see Chico. But Chico told Freeman to consider himself burned. When Freeman relayed this message to George, George advised him to tell Chico whom the money belonged to.

Chico told Freeman he didn't know what had happened to the money, that he'd given it to Darrell Cole, the white barber inside the block. The Mafia had set Cole up as the fall guy to use whenever someone got mad at being burned, so George went to him and said it was stupid to get killed over an affair that wasn't his responsibility, but that someone was going to get killed. It didn't matter about the money any more—it was the law. Cole said he didn't want to rat on anybody; I replied that he had five minutes to tell us who had the money, or I'd kill him—at that narrow strait he blurted that Chico had really given the bread to Indio, up in the Block.

Indio and his brother Pablo were obviously the ones behind the rip-off. George's plan was to kill Indio himself at lockup before dinner, and I'd down Pablo, who lived over in South Block, when he came to eat. I'd be at work in the ward then and could easily make it over to where he'd be going. I went and got someone to point for George, and then went to work and waited for the bell to ring. (Any time someone gets stabbed, this bell rings in the hospital and a light shows them where to take the gurneys. When this would happen I'd know George had gotten to Indio and I'd go after his brother.)

At five-twenty the bell went off, and I took a knife over to Pablo's cell and waited for him to come out for dinner. But he never came. A couple minutes after the chow bell, I began to think maybe he wasn't going to eat, so I started going up to get him. I looked around and pulled on the cell door, but it was on deadlock. There was nothing to do but leave. It turned out that as soon as Indio was stabbed, they'd taken Pablo into protective custody.

That wasn't the only thing that went wrong: George got caught by the cops. George was still too casual about killing people, so he was always going to have problems. The knife he tried to use was made out of a cast-iron paper cutter. It was brittle as hell. Besides that, he had on a new pair of "old folks" comforts; the shoes had slippery leather soles. As George stabbed Indio, he slipped on the concrete floor, breaking the knife as he plunged it in. He took the end of the blade and finished Indio off, but it took him so long that the cops arrived as he and the point man were running away. They caught them both and put them in AC.

After lunch the next day I saw Richard Gonzales, otherwise known to the cons as "Pelon." He said he thought the burn was stupid, so he wasn't going to do anything. Pelon had great influence on the Mafia, and he often used his weight to keep things from getting out of hand between our groups. I trusted him completely. He'd heard that Cole, the barber, was being harassed by the other whites for helping the blacks. He was all drove up and walking around with a knife. Gunning for me to save face. I hadn't even thought about that.

I was standing there talking to Pelon with my back to the canteen. Pelon whispered, "Don't look now, but when I tell you to, turn around," and went on talking to pass the time. A few minutes later he casually said, "Now," and I turned around and saw Cole had maneuvered around behind me. I didn't look directly at the dude; I could see he was trying to look unconcerned, as if he didn't see me.

I started staring at him as if to say, "let's get it over with." Cole never looked at me, but he started shaking all over. Then he began to run across the yard full speed, and three guards took off after him. He had decided to draw attention to himself to get off the mainline instead of tangling with me. He got more attention than he bargained for when the guards caught up with him and knocked him down with a flying tackle, the knife he was carrying popped out on the ground They took him to the Hole and gave him a five-to-life.

JEROME BOND—PEOPLE CALLED HIM THE Black Warrior—had spent most of his adult life in prison. Tall and lanky with a short torso and big long arms, his legs were small oaks. He could have been light-heavyweight champion of the world if he'd ever gotten out. As it was, all he had done for the last dozen years was beat every hotshot soldier or Marine fighter they'd brought in. At these so-called "athletic competition days," he'd get in the ring with a big cigar in his mouth and mock them: "Come on, Champ, have a go." No one ever touched him.

Bond had been in jail so long that all his highest aspirations were centered on winning three hundred cartons of butts and getting all the homos he wanted. He started talking to all of us in the Pack about going to work killing people to scare the pen into submission. All the hustles would be ours or nobody's. The young dudes respected Bond, the theory got put into practice.

I hooked up with him as soon as I got out of the Hole. He'd heard how crazy I was, that I'd do anything as far as fighting went, and we had trust in each other on that basis. He didn't trust many people—wouldn't let them within ten feet of him.

We'd be standing in line for chow and people would ask him to train them to fight. Bond wasn't interested, though. He'd become anti-ring since he hadn't been able to get out in time to win the crown; the only fighting he wanted to talk about was gang wars. When these dudes would come over to talk training, Bond would start screaming, "Get away from me, dog! Get your hands out of your pockets! What you got in your hands?" He'd back away, acting paranoid. "Back off or I'll knock you down."

He did want to train the Wolf Pack; get us into shape and get us in motion. "Okay, Champ," he says to me one day, "we gotta pick these dogs off"—referring to the Mafia and the Nazis. "Every day we gotta down a dog. And the more we down, the more respect we'll get. Pretty soon we'll have so many homos we'll be able to walk backwards and catch 'em. Whatdya think of that, Champ?"

I just thought, *Damn! This dude doesn't think about the streets at all.* The streets didn't exist for him; every time I mentioned some vague plans for outside he'd say, "Ain't got time for that, Champ," and change the subject.

Around this time there was a riot at Soledad, and the authorities employed their usual solution and transferred a bunch of young blacks and young white pseudo-Nazis up to Quentin, thereby merely transplanting the riot situation to more fertile soil. They knew this is what they were doing, since they put them all out on the mainline immediately, waiting for the tougher cons to "teach them a lesson."

The white guys called themselves Nazis, but they were nothing like the Quentin Nazis. In fact, the latter disowned them as punks who knew nothing about National Socialism but were rather just white supremacists. The pseudo-Nazis established themselves as pests by running around ripping old black men off for their canteens. We'd heard about them, but we hadn't done anything to stop them; we had quit taking care of blacks outside the group. Jerome Bond started agitating to change our tactic in this case and move on them. I'd really been dying to do it all along, since those dudes first got to the prison, mainly because I just like chaos.

Curtis South was a black dude, but outside our clique and a loner, who constantly messed with the homos. Every homosexual who came in, Curtis was after him. He wore a flip-flop jacket that no one knew for sure was the truth. (flip-flops, also called "knick-knacks," are dudes that begin by making the homos but wind up playing the female roles themselves.) When Curtis started messing with a white homo, the pseudo-Nazis told that homo to stay away from him or get killed.

I saw Curtis out on the yard, mad as hell at what the pseudo-Nazis had done to him. He was complaining and yelling at them. Alberto, George, and I stood behind Curtis as the pseudos told him it was tough shit what had happened; that's what he got for "messing with our punk." They did think they were tough. They'd been put in a trap by the authorities—still thinking in terms of Soledad but transplanted into a situation where there was much less tough talk and much more killing.

In the middle of their bullshit rap I jumped in and told them they were punks talking dumb shit. "Listen, you chickenshit fascist punks, you're messin' with me now, and if you're not real careful you're gonna sure wind up dead. If you think I'm bullshitting, ask Mike Nelson, he might just tell you the news." Nelson was a white I'd known since L.A. Juvenile Hall, who had later got into prison and into the Nazis. We were still friends.

They did ask Nelson and he laughed in their faces. They took his word as gospel (he told me the more he despised them, the more they worshipped him) and afterward crept around like "I don't like that nigger but I ain't gonna mess with him."

A week later, though, they piped Curtis, and a day later the dude died. I urged an all-out attack; by the time Jerome Bond had finished seconding me with his pep talk, the Wolf Pack was howling and ready for blood.

The pseudo-Nazis were smart enough to come in for lockup in a pack; our strategy was to sandwich them—twenty-five of us in front and fifty behind. Since they were so new at Quentin, they recognized only a few of us; they didn't know what we were doing until they'd bought the pig. The blacks in front got into the block, past the rotunda, and up on every tier and stairwell by the time the pseudos arrived. When they crossed the rotunda the rest of us came through the door.

They saw us behind them and started running into the tiers, only to find brothers with knives waiting for them. The dudes in front panicked and tried to run back but were pushed forward by the pseudos we were already beginning to carve. They couldn't shit and they couldn't run. All they could do was scream for help, and there wasn't much of that forthcoming. When the whistles started blowing, seventy-five knives flew off the tiers to the bottom as the cops came on and we ditched.

Alberto and I ran down the fourth tier to the end. One cell was empty; I tossed my blade in there. Alberto wrapped his in a chunk of paper and threw it off. We strolled back to our tier and stood in front of my cell, talking casually. Police kept running through, chasing dudes who had ditched too late and carrying pseudos off to the hospital. Pretty soon they called for general lockup.

I fixed some cocoa, put on my earphones, and kicked back in bed, reading Edgar Allan Poe. One of the pseudos was dead right there with a knife rammed through his heart. He was only eighteen years old.

At midnight a light flashed in and the cops told me to roll my shit up: I was under investigation for murder. They took me off to D-section, where the second tier had been turned into another Segregation unit.

The next morning a voice from the next cell woke me up: "Hey, next door, what you in for?" I said I was told that I was in on investigation for murder. He told me his name was Bond, and I asked him what he was in for.

"I don't know!" he replied, "I didn't do a damn thing. I'm just a poor Indian doin' my own time, goin' to school and associatin' with nobody, and then last night they drag my ass in here. I can't understand it. I asked the guard what I was in for. He said I had to ask Sergeant Hankins; but he won t even come near my cell. What do you think about that?"

Well, I didn't know what to think about it at the time, but I had some suspicions. This Sergeant Hankins was an old guard who'd been there for years—a good old dog, always trying to give people breaks when he could. For some reason Hankins loved Jerome Bond, had known him when he was in Quentin before and always got along with him. As soon as the pseudo-Nazis got hit, Hocker sent a memorandum out to have Jerome Bond locked up pending transfer to Folsom, because he knew about Jerome's agitation and figured him responsible for engineering the whole thing, whether he actually did the killing or not. When Hankins got this memo, he was supposed to lock Jerome up, but he locked up this Indian Bond instead so that the name "Bond" would still appear on the Segregation board outside the section. He told Jerome what was happening and left him up on the fifth tier, where he was a tender and could move at will. Jerome stayed there, still talking his shit but never going out on the yard. Whenever Hocker came around, which was seldom, he'd just hide. I never found out what happened to that poor fuckin' Indian.

THAT MORNING THE MARIN COUNTY DA called me out for a talk. The guards walked me out like I was a Death Row patient: one in front, one in back, and one on the catwalk above with a pump shotgun. I guess Hocker had had enough of me this time and there wasn't anyone gonna save me.

The DA said he couldn't put his finger on it, but from the information he had he knew that Alberto and I were standing near the dude who got killed, and he figured one of us killed him.

I said I wouldn't know this guy who got killed if I saw him and that I couldn't account for anybody else because I had walked directly from the yard to my cell. There was nothing more the DA could do; I went back to the cell in D-section.

I'd been the first person locked up in the section, along with the Indian Bond. By the time the DA finished with me I was joined by all the guys in our group, plus they put all of what was left of the pseudo-Nazis in there too. I didn't have long to enjoy it, though, because I was called to Classification right after lunch.

Hocker was there. When I walked in he growled: "How come every time something happens you wind up getting locked up?"

"Captain," I answered, "I wanted to ask you the same question."

Hocker fumed. "We got no time to get smart. We just wanna get to the facts."

"So do I, boss, so I can get out of here."

Hocker asked me if I was under anyone's influence. I said I wasn't. "What about Jackson?"

"Just a friend of mine," I replied.

"What about Bond?" he asked, almost spitting on the name as he said it.

"No, he ain't got any influence over me, just a friend—but I see you got him locked up, too."

"Thass right!" the Captain beamed. "And I don't even want to talk about that bastard." Lucky for Jerome, I thought. Hocker went on to say he was sick and tired of all this ruckus, and he was going to solve it by having me transferred.

Thinking he was referring to Folsom, I said I didn't want to leave because I liked it at Quentin. He said he was doing it for my own good, to get me away from the older blacks' influence. I had to go. He was going to see to it that George and I never saw each other in prison ever again.

In the meantime, he sent me back to the mainline, hoping, I suppose, that I'd get myself killed. They let everyone in the Wolf Pack out of Segregation except the dudes who were really on their way to Folsom. When the transfer list came out, all the guys in the group over twenty-five were sent to Folsom, but neither George nor I was on the sheets.

I WAS LEFT WITHOUT A JOB, roaming around the institution, so they decided to put me in close custody with a guy named Robert Wilson from Oakland. The next day when I came back to the cell from the shower, there was a box of candy bars on my bed. I figured they were Wilson's, that he'd thrown them through the bars on his way by. I put them up on his shelf. That night I asked him for one of those candy bars, and he said what candy bars? They weren't his either. I thought we'd got something for nothing and pulled them down. They looked just like they came out of the canteen. But when I broke one open to eat half of it, out came all this caustic soda and ground glass so fine I wouldn't have even tasted it. Wilson and I just laughed. We knew the pseudos had done it; Nazis were famous for poisoning and other impersonal means of murdering their enemies.

The next morning we went after the first Nazi we could find. I stuck a pock-faced punk named Harwood in the spine well enough to paralyze him, and let it be known that someone had seen him try to poison me.

A WEEK LATER SOMEONE ON THE yard told me I was on the list to go to CMC-East (the California Men's Colony at San Luis Obispo). I couldn't believe it—the cons call it "Paradise." It was the summer camp of the fuckin' prison system. But sure enough, when I got to the bulletin board, there was my name, right there at the top of the Cs, along with Davis behind and Bottoms in front, along with all the other younger dudes from the Wolf Pack. All of us bound for the sunshine prison!

TWELVE

"DISNEYLAND" IS WHAT ALL THE CONS call CMC-East. For homos it's dreams come true; for everyone else it's just unreal. More than half the cons were homosexuals living in this fantasy world they called "paradise." As the bus drove up to the place I saw cons out on the grass playing golf, tending flowers, and just lazing in the sun. It looked like a college campus taking the day off.

The buildings were all modern and clean. There were gun towers all around, but unlike Quentin the place gave off the feeling of being new. And the cops amplified that aroma. Unlike any of the other bulls I'd seen, and very different from the goons in other institutions, these guys were mostly clean-cut college dudes who greeted us politely as we got off the bus.

Out on the yard I was surprised to find that everywhere I looked were homosexuals of every description, size, and color. It was their institution. They were carrying purses, knitting, and primping themselves in little pocket mirrors and carrying on. Since the prison officials condoned this behavior and since the homos were the dominant group among the inmate population, the treatment they got from the straights was much better than anywhere on the streets.

When they saw me, the homos started twittering among themselves. One of them called out, "Look, girls, there's the new strong man!"

I just stood there not knowing what to make of it while this procession of beautiful-looking boys hurried across the yard and filed by me as if I was a judge in some fantastic beauty contest. These punks weren't the truck-driver types I was used to seeing in Quentin; they were real queens and dressed the part: tight short-shorts, teased hair, make-up, perfume, the works. Each one of them whispered a little sweet something in my ear as she (they didn't like to be called "he") swung by. I got right into the swing of things, introducing myself and handing out compliments.

CMC-East is a tight joint, though, even if they rate it only as a "medium-security" institution. The buildings are all lined with two way mirrors which the police use to keep surveillance over potential troublemakers. Even more effective is the quad system they use in which cons are assigned to one of four sections that they are not allowed to leave except to go to work. Dudes had to show their ID cards to a remote-controlled camera every time they entered the quad. It was a very efficient way of keeping people isolated from each other. They controlled you without coming in direct contact. You could only socialize with the five hundred or so cons on your quad, and the few cops you talked to kept up a front of polite efficiency.

I still maintained the philosophy that as long as I was

incarcerated I was going to let the police know I was there—
none of this hiding in-the-corner shit for me. I walked around
the place like I owned it. The homos loved me; they liked
looking for a strong man to take care of them. The police
noticed it, too, but they didn't find my style quite so appealing.

By the time I went for classification I had already established
a reputation as a bad-ass. Not that I had broken any rules or
anything like that; it was just that I didn't display guilt and
repentance the way they like in CMC.

I rode on in to my hearing confident that I would succeed in
throwing for no-control. De Angelo, the program administrator, and his lieutenant, Grapentine, met me at the door. De
Angelo looked like somebody I could handle: he was a short,
fat dago who just radiated insecurity, one of those obviously
strict Catholics who are threatened by everybody. Grapentine
was another matter. The opposite of his captain in every way,
Grape was a tall German, six-five and well built, in complete
control of this and every other situation. Whereas De Angelo
was nervous and talked with a squeaky voice, the lieutenant
was calm, collected, and sure of himself.

De Angelo told me to take a seat. He remained standing
while the other cops and counselors sat down; he relished the
rare opportuniy to tower above the crowd. "James," he began,
"this is a nice place, it's a place you can go home from; lots of
men have. You got the chance to rehabilitate yourself, to prove
to us that you belong on the streets." He paused again to see
how I was reacting. I looked down and noticed he was wearing
elevator shoes which brought him up to about five-seven. I
didn't move a muscle. All the time I could feel Grapentine
staring at me with hawk eyes, sizing me up.

De Angelo rambled on: "Everyone participates in our programs; there's no sitting around here. You'll learn a trade, go

to school . . ." I started to protest. He ignored me. "Now, where do you want to work?"

I said nothing.

"You don't have to decide today, James. We'll give you some time to look around so you make the right choice. Let us know by the end of the week what we can do for you. That's all, James. You can go."

I left without saying anything, my eyes on the ground, pissed off as hell. But I didn't want to blow it the first week I was there. The threat of being transferred to Folsom hung over my head. They didn't have to say it. I knew it could have just as easily been Folsom as CMC. I told myself over and over that it was best to stay cool.

After a week of getting my temper under control it was easier to go back to the Classification Board. I volunteered for the kitchen crew and enrolled in some classes, working toward a general education degree.

When I wasn't at work or school, I stayed in my cell. I concentrated on improving my reading. When I was running with George, I used to rely on him for considered opinions because he was so much better read than any of the rest of us. We sort of let him do our thinking for us. It was easier that way, more efficient, since we were usually under the gun.

Now I was on my own, with lots of time on my hands. I began to rework things for myself. It wasn't easy, either, since I had to use a dictionary about once each paragraph. But at least I was doing it. I suddenly realized how bad it was to be dependent mentally on anyone else, even George.

I was really an ignorant motherfucker. I knew a whole lot about doing what I wanted and about the streets, but I'd never gone to school, and since I'd spent most of my life in the pen I was even more limited. At twenty-one, here I was having to teach myself to concentrate and remember.

I decided to start at the beginning with philosophy. I got Russell's *History of Western Philosophy* out of the library and read it from cover to cover. Then I read through the entire philosophy section in the prison library. This gave me a rudimentary intellectual background so that I could read and appropriate the things that were more directly relevant to me.

From my experience I'd seen pretty clearly that the main force in people's life was conflict. The revolutionaries' (especially Marx's) explanation of class conflict as the motivating force of historical development made immediate sense to me. His theory of work and alienation was just as clear. I'd grown up hating work and had done everything possible to avoid it. I read everything in the library (and in other cons' possession) even remotely connected with revolution. My vocabulary increased to the point where I didn't need to use a dictionary, and my self-confidence increased until I felt confident of my own ideas and judgments.

The most important thing I learned was that people had always been rebelling against authority. On the street alone or even in a group, you don't talk about what you're doing, you just do it because it's the only thing to do unless you're gonna let the man run you over. Seeing that other people had done the same thing in different ways was a flash. It had never occurred to me before that we were anything but freaks. I began to feel like I was in good company acting like a motherfucker.

I was the big strong black dude who did a lot of cell time. That's what the guards and cons thought, and that's the way I wanted it. I left them to guess what I was thinking.

A year went by quicker than most. I went to the Board for the first time in July, 1966. One dude on the Board—"Mad

Dog" Madden they called him—I'd been hearing about all year. He'd been a lieutenant in the L.A. robbery and narco squads for fifteen years—put a lot of my friends in jail for a lot of years. He'd busted so many dudes that most of the cons who came before him on the Board were guys he'd originally arrested; he shot them down right and left. He was particularly hard on narcotics offenders. Madden'd bait people—calling them punks, telling them they'd have to do five more years when they'd already done six—in hopes that they'd react so he could shoot them down worse. I'd had plenty of warnings about his tricks.

As soon as I sat down he said, "Howya doin', Jimmy?" Calling me "Jimmy"—I knew right away there's gonna be shit in the game.

"I'm doing fine, Mister . . ." and I looked down at his nameplate like I didn't know who he was, ". . . Mister Madden."

He just smiled. "How'd you get into this institution, Jimmy?"

"I don't know," I replied, "I was just transferred here."

"Well," he snapped, "I don't think you *should* be *here*."

"Where do you think I should be?"

"You know just where I think you should be." Long pause. "What did you come up here to talk to us about today?"

I came to talk about leaving this institution, "I said politely. "To go out and get a job."

Madden started laughing, then turned red and yelled, "Don't pull that shit off your shoes, boy! *You* didn't come up here to talk about no fuckin' streets! Because you're not *going* to the streets. You got a *long* way to go. Boy, you still got a bad attitude. If you wanna talk about streets, you'll go to school, you'll take group counseling, you'll get a trade, you won't get any more one-fifteens. And I'll never hear any more about *violence* coming from you or about you. Then too, Carr, you'll have done some *time*! Maybe then you'll be ready for the streets. Maybe not. But until then, no streets. Come up here to talk about the streets! You must be outta yer fuckin' mind!"

He turned his swivel chair around and looked out the window. I sat there, waiting to continue. A minute later he spun around and frowned, feigning surprise. "You still here?"

"Yeh, man," I said. "We gotta talk."

"We ain't got nothin' to talk about, Carr. Nothin'. Now get out."

I KNEW NOW THAT IF I fucked up even once, I was never getting out. Madden had done me that favor.

I started treating all the officer dogs with courtesy. The head guard of my building always greeted me as I walked past him, but I'd programmed myself not to talk to police, so I never answered him. He was the classic cop—a tough, benevolent Irishman whose definition of peace was the absence of visible conflict. O'Connor didn't want to give or take any shit. After the parole hearing I walked into the building and greeted him before he had a chance to say hello. Surprised and enthusiastic, he replied, "Well, howya doin', James!"

Another officer, named Mach, had been wanting to get rid of me the whole time I'd been there. He was in my cell day in and day out, looking for contraband. One day while he was nosing around I looked up from my books and said, "You know, Mr. Mach, there's no sense in this shit. Society is a motherfucker. Here I've been rebelling all my life; now finally I want to do right, and you won't let me." Mach stopped fiddling around and looked at me. I continued, "I know I'm an asshole. That's the reason I'm trying to straighten up. All I want is a break. Now, can't a man have a break?"

Mach came straight up and stiffened out, "Yes, a man's entitled to a break." With that he walked off and never stepped into my cell again.

The prison library didn't have a lot of the books I was interested in reading, but I did manage to get hold of several volumes of the works of Lenin and Mao. I read them religiously. I didn't really get inspired, though, until I read Frantz Fanon. Here was this dude saying that the people of color who were murdering each other had displaced their hatred of their masters onto themselves. Fanon pinned down the enemy. His theory coincided with my own experiences since he maintained that violence was the only means by which Third World peoples could gain true self-determination.

It was clear to me that the struggles initiated by the ghetto riots were just as much a part of the anti-colonial warfare as the fighting in Africa. After reading Fanon, the Watts rebellion took on a different significance for me. When it happened I'd seen it as a whole lot of dudes fucking off; as far as I was concerned, the robbing and burning was the same kind of shit I had pulled as a kid, only on a bigger scale. Fanon made me see that the destruction was a beautiful expression of a community that could rise up only on the ashes of the old world.

I began to have deep fantasies about organizing a band of guerrillas—an urban counterpart to what Guevara was up to in Bolivia—structured on the principle of democratic centralism. In my visions, the comrades and I would redirect the violence of the lumpen proletariat—dudes who came from the same background as me—by providing them with a positive example: acts of sabotage directed against the white ruling class.

I didn't talk to anyone about these new ideas. To everyone else I was simply doing a lot of cell time studying mathematics. I couldn't keep more than one book on political theory in my cell at a time for fear the cops would find out what I was really up to and send me off to Folsom. On the outside I appeared like a changed man but inside I still had the same attitude, only now I had a lot of good reasons to hold my temper. The day I walked out of CMC-East was the day I would begin organizing the Red Army.

The second time I went to the Board, though, I was met with the same line. An ex-army colonel with a pie face started bawling at me before I could say shit. "You're not foolin' nobody, Carr— I know you and I know you like violence." I'd never seen this Loriano before. I knew what he said was the truth, that I was wasting my time tryin'. They weren't gonna buy my new program. I was blind inside. Loriano finished his speech by throwing me out, and I was ready to break some ass.

When I backed out I ran into this old con from St. Louis, who'd had asthma all his life, worked in the coal mines, been fucked over every imaginable way, and ended up a vicious and lecherous convict. But he had a sense of control. He'd come by the cell (he lived down the tier) in his old derby hat looking like Heckle and Jeckel and wheeze out, "Youngster, y'know these mo'fuckers got the world ruined, but Brewster's gonna always get his." Shit—he didn't have a thing but his hat and his inhaler, but he was a wise old man and I liked to listen to his stories.

Now he came to cool me down, telling me how they were gonna try to break me and "blow yo' mo'fuckin' cool" to send me away permanent. "They're gonna run a game on you, and they expect you to be fool enough to play. Watch out boy!"

The next day they moved. When I got back from my math class the cell was torn apart, all my shit strewn around the room. I knew the tier guard had to have been in on it and I went running for Abner with a vague idea of squashing his skinny black neck.

I ran up to the jerk, fuming, "What is the meaning of this? Why'd you go and do that shit?"

Cowering and asserting himself at the same time, Abner chirped, "We got a tip that you was wheelin' and dealin', so we shook your cell down. Simple as that."

"You find anything?" I growled.

"No, we didn't find anything . . . I don't wanna talk about it . . . don't bother me any more."

"That's all right with me, 'cause I don't wanna talk to your ass of a face any more. Yer a pup. You ain't got a lick of heart, and besides that all you are is a coward."

A crowd of cons had come around: they don't talk to cops like that in Paradise. I knew they couldn't transfer me for it, though. Sacramento doesn't want to hear about a con cussing out a cop. So I wet the wimp down like he's got nine tails, until he pushed panic and ran for Sergeant Myers, CMC-East's version of the Mississippi sheriff.

I didn't give a fuck about all hundred and ten pounds of this notorious little racist. He stammered out something about how I was a foul-mouthed bastard and had a violation.

I didn't care: "When you get through writin' that mother-fucker, write up twelve more, write until your chicken leg gets sore, you sorry son of a bitch." I had to let off the steam to stay sane.

They sent me to court in front of Lieutenant Grapentine for the violation. When I walked into his office, just to show my disrespect, I slid into the chair and sprawled out, looking crazy. Grape looked up and said, "You're pretty drove up, aren't you, boy?" He was sharp; he used an entirely different approach from the rest of the authorities. "I've read your record, Carr," he went on. "I know the kind of problems you've had in the past. You've been here a little while without any difficulties. Now this happens. What caused it?"

"Man, I just went to the Board and got shot down, and I was upset. Then I come back to my cell and all my stuff is thrown all over the place. I don't fuck with nobody here, I ain't had no fights mindin' my own business. Then these guys fuck with me."

He thought for a minute and asked me what my plans were. "I have no plans," I replied. "All I want to do is my own time and be left alone."

Grapentine did a strange thing—he just gave me a reprimand for the beef. None of the cops could believe it. Myers called me in the next day, madder than hell, mumbling something about how I was getting away with murder. I didn't need to cuss him; he'd been beaten and there was no sense driving him too far. "Look, Sergeant," I said, "I told the lieutenant that you caught me at a bad time. I ain't done nothing since I been here, so you know there must been something wrong with me to act that way. I'm tryin' to get that out of myself."

"Well, y'know you got a lotta work to do. *Sit down hyah!* I worked down in Georgia, worked everywhere. I nevah heard no one talk to an official like that an' git away with it."

I told him he ought to go up to San Quentin. "They do it every day up there. But, like I say, Mr. Myers, I'm a human being, too, you know, and I think I have the right to be treated with some respect. That's all I want. Now, if you don't mess with me, you'll never hear from me again."

And the Mississippi sheriff, who fucked up all kinds of people, never troubled me again.

IT WAS MY WEIGHTLIFTING, THOUGH, THAT really improved my image with the prison officials. I'd been working out with weights since juvenile camp, and training quite seriously since Tracy. There had been some gigantic dudes in Tracy who exercised methodically—nothing like the kids in reform school. I fell in with these dudes who were called the "hogs." They let me in the club which was limited to guys who could bench press more than three hundred pounds, even though I was still too weak to make the minimum requirement. But after a few months of their spartan routine and five hours pushing every day, I started to outgrow them all. In Quentin I continued the rigorous schedule with Iron Man Evans, who could do five hundred pounds of iron in the bench press. After a year of trying to keep up with him, my chest had expanded to forty-seven inches and my waist had narrowed down to twenty-seven. Weightlifting became for me like mathematics—a way of losing myself, of doing time quickly, and making some kind of progress.

By the time I got to CMC-East, I could bench press four hundred pounds. It seemed like I had reached a plateau; I couldn't get above four hundred in the bench and four fifty in the squat lift. CMC-East had excellent weights because the coach, Eppeley, was big on weight training. He had a white dude named Buck Browning, a middle-heavyweight, and a black guy named Ernie Matson, a light-heavyweight, on his team, and received a lot of recognition when these boys did well in the national prison championships.

I got into competition with Browning. A lot of the blacks wanted a black to be the strongest in each division so they urged me constantly to pass Buck by. We were even on the bench press, but his legs gave him the edge on the two other power lifts—the dead lift and the squat.

When Ernie moved to my quad we got together. He told me he was going to teach me how to lift real heavy weight—that was his game. When you see all that weight on the bar you just can't believe that you're going to be able to make it. Ernie gave me the confidence I needed to do it. He had perfect form and timing; besides which, he was a scientist and read everything possible on the subject. He discovered that the Hungarians radically increased their performance by eating huge amounts of protein. He had me downing huge amounts of protein powder and lifting twenty tons a day in the competition lifts. From then on I started making just a whole lot of progress.

Before the national prison meets, trials are held for dudes to qualify. The AAU officials come from the street with their measuring equipment and the whole con population gathers to watch the strongmen perform. I was extremely nervous since I'd never competed before. When Ernie put six hundred pounds on my back for warm-up and told me to walk around with it, I nearly freaked out. The dude was serious. The only thing he wanted to do was get out and beat the Russians, and he saw these competitive situations as his ticket to the streets.

After walking around with six hundred, Ernie put five thirty on his back and squatted down. The judges couldn't believe it. They knew he wasn't going to be able to lift that much weight because he weighed only a hundred and seventy-five pounds. But he shocked them by standing up like the iron had melted.

On my first lift with four hundred fifty pounds, I was so scared that I went down to the ground and couldn't come back up. I had to squat, burning with embarrassment, until the officials could take the weight off my shoulders. I felt like crying.

Ernie took me around the corner and talked to me. He didn't look at me as he spoke. He knew how scared I was. He told me to take four seventy-five on my next lift.

That didn't make any sense to me but I was too nervous to argue. Ernie told me my mistake was not watching the weights as I came up. Olympic barbells have springs on the end of the bar so that the heavy weights won't cause the steel to bend. When you dip down, the weight takes the spring down. If you don't start up when the weight does, you fight the spring and end by missing the lift.

I was so frightened on my second squat that I was in a trance. I didn't even remember lifting the weight. I went down and came back up without any difficulty. But I didn't lift anywhere near enough weight to beat Buck Browning.

I did get a second in the division, though, so the coach put me on the team. All the next year Ernie and I trained even harder, determined to win the whole show this time around. His fantasies about winning, getting out, and beating the fucking Russians kept both of us going harder and harder.

By the time of the middle-heavyweight trials, I weighed just over two hundred and twenty pounds. Thirty pounds heavier than the year before. I had to compete in the heavyweight class. The coach paraded me around in front of the officials like I was his prize steer. He hadn't done a thing. Ernie Matson was the one who had coached me.

Just before the meet, Ernie and I each drank a bottle of wheat-germ oil. I felt like I had taken a thousand bennies; walked out tingling with energy. I started out by bench pressing five-twenty, squatted six hundred forty, and did six-fifty in the dead lift, breaking all the national AAU records for my class. Prison meets don't count officially, though. After that I won in my division in the national prison meet every year I competed.

ERNIE AND I WERE WALKING ACROSS the yard to the gym past a bunch of low-riders who had been sent to CMC as a result of the Watts rebellion. I knew a few of them—a lot of them were brothers or friends of dudes I had run with—and most of them knew me by reputation. I recognized Larry Phillips, the younger brother of Jo, Iron Man's cellmate in Quentin. I said hello to him as we went by and he called me over.

"Hey, Carr, dudes are sayin' you think you're better than the rest of the brothers and that you've become an inmate!"

Ernie put his hand on my arm and told me to be cool. A lot of other younger dudes were waiting to see what I had to say for myself: "Listen, most of you are here for the first time. None of you have seen the insides of San Quentin; you ain't none of you convicts yet, you still got graduation coming up and just a lot of you ain't gonna make it. I've been here almost eight years and I aim to get out in the near future. I got things to do outside. If I fuck up one more time I'm gonna die in prison. Dig, I got no intentions of doing that."

Phillips was satisfied with my little explanation. Some of the others started raw-jawin' about how I was a sell-out bullshitter and talked like a white man. I turned my back on 'em and walked away.

After that a lot of dudes heard about the incident and would come by my cell and give me shit to make themselves feel tough. I ignored them. If they persisted I told them to swing first and I would defend myself. Nobody took me up on that offer.

I was just about flat broke when Fat Harry walked into my life: Harry Stavis, a nineteen-year-old black who looked like a puppy, round as he was tall. He'd been poor when he came in; then his grandfather died and left him a few oil wells in Louisiana. His mother had ten thousand dollars put on his books. Now, Harry didn't even know how to count—in fact, he'd had to be shown how to sign his name to get his money.

After Fat Harry'd got rich, dudes went after him like he was the greatest thing in the world. He'd buy loads of electric guitars, yet he didn't have a one. He was so rich he got in debt: he'd overdraw every month and borrow at ridiculous rates. Guys were cheating and pressuring him right and left, till Harry finally realized he needed some protection.

I was in my cell studying when Harry came to me and asked, "Is there any way you can help me and keep all these dudes from beating me up? I owe all these people and I can't draw enough to pay 'em."

"How much do you owe, Harry?" I asked.

"About thirty cartons." Among his other virtues, Harry was a habitual liar. His debts were closer to five hundred cartons than thirty, more than he could ever draw.

But it was still a situation I couldn't pass up. "Okay, Harry," I said, "I'm gonna get you out of debt. But after I get you out you can't go back in."

Harry used to trade at Pete McNair's store. Lots of people ran these stores in the pen: they'd buy from the Canteen and sell for a profit to cons who had cash but no draw, as well as to anyone who wanted something at night. The price was usually marked up 40 percent. Pete McNair was a slick swindler who'd been busted running bunko games on old ladies. He knew Harry's weakness for homos, so he'd hire some to bring Harry to his store and have him buy them presents at greatly inflated prices. Every month, in addition to the cash he'd spent there, Harry would go fifteen or twenty dollars further in debt to Pete.

I went to Pete, whom I barely knew at the time. I told him that Harry owed everybody money and couldn't pay it off so I was going to buy Harry out of debt.

"Buy him out of debt!" Pete shrieked. "You must be crazy."

"Not the way I'm gonna do it," I said, smiling. "And I can use your help. Before it's over we'll both be happy." When he'd heard my plan, Pete eagerly agreed to become partners.

We took Harry around to all the people he owed and who were out to get him. Typically, we'd find that Harry owed some dude twenty or thirty cartons on an original loan of a couple of packs. I'd go to the dude and say he shouldn't be messing with Harry that way.

"But he owes me!" the dude'd say.

"No he don't," I answered, "he don't owe you a mother-fuckin' thing, 'cause you fucked him over." If the dude put up a good protest I'd say, "Okay, you'll get five cartons," and he'd agree. But since I was the one who owed him now, he never got paid. I did this with everyone Harry owed; I wound up owing them all, and never paid a one.

We'd gotten Harry out of debt without costing a cent. He's got all this money on his books and no one to go for it but us. I went to him and said, "Harry, I went way in the hole to get you out, spent all my cigarettes . . . "

"Yes, and I really appreciate it, Big Jim."

"Yeh, Harry, you're all right with me. All you gotta do now is do what I tell you and there won't be any problems."

Fat Harry drew the maximum thirty dollars a month—that all went to me. Plus he drew the maximum sixty-five dollars a month for hobby-craft orders, credits which can be spent only on this—half of this went to me, and half to Pete McNair. We bought the stuff off Harry's hobby draw and sold the supplies in Pete's store for forty dollars cash. Painters and sculptors would make out lists of what they wanted; then we'd have Harry order it.

Pete knew two chicks in San Jose. He had one coming to see him and one coming to see Harry. Harry was out there in the visiting room, smoking cigars—Harry was so dumb he damn near couldn't talk. This chick was telling Harry how much she loves him, writing him all these sweet letters nearly every day.

After about a month I told Harry, "Look here, that girl really loves you. It'd be nice if we went and bought her a present."

"What should we get her, Big Jim?"

"Well, we should get her something nice . . . I'll tell you what—I'll have my sister get it."

"Can ya do that for me, Big Jim?"

"Yeh, Harry, I'll bring the applications over for you to sign tomorrow."

They have checks so cons can send money out of their books to people on the streets. I made one out to my Aunt Harriet for five hundred dollars, and after Harry signed it I sent it to her. Next week Pete's friend came and thanked Harry for the wonderful color television set.

Now we started doing this every month: between one and five hundred dollars for rings, dresses, car payments. In addition, we had Harry order things from the Sears and Wards catalogs—electric shavers, watches, radios—and sold them on the street at discount prices.

Morgan, the administrative head of hobby-crafts, knew what was going on, but he didn't do anything because he was the biggest crook of all and was afraid that we would expose him. He took the best paintings done by the cons, bought them dirt cheap, and sold them in his own gallery down in San Luis. Besides that, rumor had it that he was stealing money out of the Inmate Welfare Fund. Whether or not that was true, Morgan had a good thing going in his little hobby kingdom, and didn't want any officials nosing around.

Finally Harry's books were down to two hundred dollars; his mother refused to send him any more. He was going down fast, and it was time to cut him loose. Pete and I decided to take him off for his last draw.

We ordered a load of painting supplies for BJ, one of the con artists who Morgan was getting rich off. When his order came in, BJ met us at hobby-craft. Harry got his box from the clerk, but while he was signing for it the box somehow disappeared.

By this time the cops were waiting for something to happen; they'd seen Harry's books dwindle, checked Harry's property list and seen all this stuff catalogued, then searched his cell and found nearly nothing.

BJ paid us for the order and split; we gave Harry an empty box to carry back to his cell. Killian, the head of the goon squad, was waiting for him there. He looked into his box and asked Harry what had happened to his order. Harry told him he'd given it to Pete and me.

Killian came after us with Morgan and a couple of other goons, figuring he had us cold. But we had an ace in the hole. Our friend Louie was Morgan's clerk over at hobby-craft. Every time Harry'd bought something that we wanted ourselves, Louie would record that we, not Harry, had bought it, and give us the property slips. All these slips were signed by Morgan, too, who put his signature on everything Louie shoved in his face.

Killian looked through the window of my cell, saw all my tools and supplies, and started smiling: I hadn't made a regular draw in so long, he just *knew* he had me. He opened the cell and told me to get out. Morgan was out there and asked to see the property slips for all the tools I had.

"Sure can, Boss," I replied, "but you oughta have copies of all of 'em already, since I got 'em from you."

Morgan could see his signature on the slips, and not wanting to point out his own negligence, just muttered, "Well, he's covered for all this."

"What?!" cried Killian.

"Yes, here it is," said Morgan, giving me the dead fisheye. As the dust settled in their hands Morgan said, "Carr, you're not through yet. Report to Sergeant Swayne immediately."

I met Pete over near Swayne's office. The only contraband Morgan had found in his cell was a brush washer.

Inside, Swayne told us that ten thousand dollars in merchandise and cash were missing and they knew we'd gotten most of it. "Where," he asked us "is all that stuff?"

"Look, man," I drawled, "I don't know what you're talkin' about."

"Well, you've been seen runnin' around with Stavis, and he says he's been giving you his draws."

"I haven't got a thing of Harry's," I said. "As a matter of fact, I've been givin' *him* money to take care of all his debts, and now he owes me.

Swayne couldn't prove anything and he knew it, so he hardened up. "Since your name has come up in this case," he said, "I'm going to take away your hobby-craft privileges"—which meant they took all my tools.

"If you wanna do it, you got the power, I just don't want no trouble."

"If we catch you," he warned, "you're gonna have plenty of trouble."

"Well, you ain't ever gonna catch me . . . 'cause I ain't ever gonna do nothin'." And I walked out. Pete got and gave the same treatment.

I didn't think too much about it after that. Aunt Harriet sent me money every month, more than enough to get whatever I wanted, so I was in good shape. Or so I thought until I heard a rumor that Pete and I were going to be sent to Folsom on the next bus. When I told Pete he said, "There's only one man who can help us if it's not too late—that's Killian's secretary, Wally Covington. He's the only man who can touch the transfer lists besides the lieutenant."

Covington was a white-headed old homo, kicking the shit out of seventy and acting like he was twenty, swishing around saying, "my dear." He looked like Dagwood's neighbor, Herb

Woodley. Thinks his shit don't stink cause he's got so much juice—which in a way was true since he was so tight with Killian that the old boy even brought him special perfume.

When we went to see Wally, he started feeding us the shit: "I been hearing your names comin' through the office a lot. The lieutenant is concerned about you boys . . ."

"No speeches please, Wally," I told him. "We don't want to get on that bus."

"Well, my dear," he said, waving his rhinestone-studded cigarette holder, "I can keep anyone off that bus who'll give me a few cigarettes each month."

So we started paying Wally off, giving him cigarettes whenever he needed them. Which was often—he'd come "borrow" this and that, never intending to pay any of it back. We got tight with him this way, though, and got to be able to manipulate the transfer lists so that a few of our enemies unexplainably found themselves transferred underneath the walls of Folsom.

IN FIGURING OUT MY LITTLE-GOOD-BOY ROUTINE I used Mad Dog Madden's criteria as my chart. I'd done everything that he said was necessary to be eligible for parole except one—attend group counseling. I saved that for last so the cops would think that I'd changed gradually rather than overnight. They wouldn't go for any sudden transformation.

When I decided the time was ripe to join, I calculated that it would be best to get into Lieutenant Grapentine's group. I didn't go for Grape or Grape's line; it was his influence on the parole board that made joining his group fit the plan. Whatever he recommended they did—it was that simple.

I had my painter friend BJ, who was already in the group, start dropping hints to some of the other cons that I was interested in coming. When Grapentine heard about it, he had BJ invite me to the next session. I'd only had a chance to observe Grape in action from a distance. Now I was going to sit right next to this fox and watch him work.

It worked out fine because Grapentine wanted me in there: my presence added a new dimension to the group, which was previously made up of inmates and young fish. Grape wanted me in there to show the youngsters that crime doesn't pay before they got set into a criminal lifestyle.

The prison officials took the group program seriously. In fact, the whole place shut down every Friday afternoon for the sessions. Any free man employee can lead a group; a lot of them who did were fools who just got up there and talked about themselves. In most counseling groups, the cons know exactly what's happening. They have to be in there—even though it isn't mandatory, the Board lets you know you'd better go—and the instructors are stupid and transparently moral. Most of the groups get out of control: the cons just talk about fucking homos and pulling robberies, thereby subverting the intentions of the counselor, who wants to talk about going straight.

Grapentine, however, didn't tolerate that shit: you participate or you get out. He laid it on heavy with lots of books and modern psychological techniques. One of his games was a thing called the "Hot Seat." Every week somebody had to sit on the Hot Seat. The other prisoners would pretend to be prison shrinks and hold court on the poor dude. Grapentine furnished them with the guy's jacket so they could ask questions based on his record. They'd get a child molester up there sweating, asking him about his motives, his childhood and home life. It was sickening.

Grape had another thing called the "preparatory course for the Board," which was supposed to get you ready for your appearance. This was utter bullshit: when you go to the Board they already know what they're going to do. In this "course," the cons play the part of the Board members, trying to break the dude who's preparing, getting him to show he's not ready for the streets. Of course, anything he says will be used against him; Grape writes reports for the Board based on these "preparations."

Often Grape'd use a general group discussion both to instill morality and to judge how certain cons were coming along. This is where I participated, because I could tell Grape what he wanted to hear without helping him fuck over some other con. For example, one time Grape asked the group, "What makes someone commit an armed robbery? And if he's incarcerated and released, what's to keep him from doing it again?"

Before I could answer, a young black got up and said, "A dude robs 'cause he's hungry an' he can't get no job." That wasn't the correct answer.

I stood up and said, "No, brother, that ain't it. I came from a neighborhood where ripping off's a way of life. Dudes do it to get fancy clothes and cars so they can look slick. By not realizing that you can get what you want if you'll only work for it, I wound up getting busted over and over again until I realized that robbery is not right."

"And why," Grape asked, "is robbery not right?"

I had that one down, too: "Because you infringe on another person's property. After all, he's worked for it, it belongs to him. Therefore, you have no right to rip him off."

Grape smiled and nodded his head like I'm his prize pupil.

Grapentine had a thousand tricks, of which the following is a typical example: One Friday, after an hour of intense moralizing and manipulating, Grape said let's take a ten-minute break. BJ and I were sitting together bullshitting about this and that while the rest of the cons were gossiping about various people, cons and cops alike. Their conversation got looser and looser; everyone had forgotten that Grape was in the room. When Grape casually mentioned Larry Phillips's name, one of the fishes started talking about how Larry was running with the low-riders who were always talking about how we needed a little riot. When BJ and I heard this we looked up, surprised. I guess that snapped the spell: the cons realized they'd been giving dope to Grapentine, and they shut up.

CMC ALSO HAD GENUINE PSYCHOTHERAPY, RUN by two psychiatrists, Dr. Babcock and Dr. Bolden. Only a few cons went to therapy, but everyone was required to see these shrinks once a year for a Board report.

Babcock was a fool. Every year during my visit, he'd spend most of the time with the tests I'd taken at Chino in his hands, telling me I could never do what I wanted. The furthest I could go in math, he'd tell me, was basic algebra—I should set my sights on a career in welding. I'd just smile and say, "Right, Doc." I was doing calculus at the time.

The motherfucker didn't like me. Every year, no matter how sweet and docile I acted, he'd tell the Board that I was hostile and might explode at any minute. I guess he was scared of big niggers.

In '69 I wanted to get off psych referral; that way I'd never have to get another report, which'd mean they considered me psychologically ready to get out. When I went to Babcock's office, I started asking him questions before he could ask me any: what was his work like, where did he go to school, shit like that. Walking around the office admiring all his framed diplomas, I said, "Gee. Doc, it must've been a lot of work getting through school. How did you do it?"

He told me how he'd come from a poor family and had to study real hard to get into college and he'd had to work his way through school, sometimes two jobs at once but he'd struggled and made it without ever committing a crime.

"Yes, sir," I said reverently, bowing and scraping, "it just goes to show how far you can get if you just have patience and willpower."

I worked on him, gracious. He fell back in his chair and started talking dreamily about his college days, recounting stories of swim meets and all-night study sessions. When he came halfway out of this trance, I got to telling him how bad I wanted to get out, because I'd finally realized my debt to society and I'd never be able to pay it back till I got out. I needed to demonstrate my ability to live with humans and not be an animal.

Babcock wrote a report that got me off psych referral. While it doesn't have immediate effects, this is always a big step to the streets.

RIGHT AFTER GETTING SHOT DOWN BY the Board in July '69, I went to Classification for post-Board reevaluation, appearing before Grape, De Angelo, and one of Babcock's assistants. They told me that although the Board had failed to let me out, they'd most probably give me a date the following year. Since I hadn't had a real job in some time, they felt it was time I did some "good hard work."

I knew immediately what they meant. Here I was taking college courses—I'd even begun to find out about getting into the University of California—and they were going to get me "ready for the streets" by sending me to some fucking conservation camp to cut down trees!

I hated the thought of going, but I had to act more or less agreeable. "Look," I said, "I don't mind going to camp, cause it's good to be out in nature. But I don't wanna be anywhere that's going to take me further away from home. . . I haven't had a visitor in five and a half years. What I'd like is to be transferred to South Conservation Camp, since it's only forty miles from L.A. That way my grandmother can come see me." This was bullshit but sounded good, so they told me they'd send me to South CC.

I was mad 'cause I didn't want to leave. I had a soft setup, and I was in the middle of some college-credit courses. But at least South was the best camp.

Two weeks later the list came out, and my name was on it for Sierra Conservation Camp, six hundred miles north of L.A.

THIRTEEN

I WENT RUNNING INTO GRAPENTINE'S OFFICE, mad as could be yelling look what they've done to me. "That's Sacramento," he told me, "and there's nothing we can do about it." Which was a sack of shit: CMC had finally gotten rid of me, and since they couldn't send me to Quentin or Folsom, someone—probably Killian—had got his last licks in by shipping me off to hell and gone.

I was put on the Penal Authority bus—"the local"—which stops at every prison on the way north transferring dudes, mostly those bound for a year or two in camp on their way home.

Our first stop was Soledad, which made me happy since I'd get a chance to talk to George. We arrived at dinnertime and were to leave the next morning. I went to the chow hall and saw a bunch of old friends, but no George. Our friend Curly, who lived with Jackson in Y-wing, told me that George was in the Hole in the middle of a twenty-nine day sentence; the cops'd found a simulated .38 and a primitive chemistry set in his cell. I gave Curly some information about lawyers to tell George; Curly in turn told me about the situation at Soledad.

George had put together a little army there, teaching them political education and doing karate for two hours a day. Their tactics had changed from the defensive racist nationalism of our Quentin days to a concerted effort of dealing death blows against the prison structure. This movement had pulled together Mexicans, whites, and blacks, and had organizers in every wing agitating against racism. Even though these were the bare beginnings of anti-racist prison organization, the Soledad administration had already realized that the situation was getting out of control, and had moved to snuff it out.

WE LEFT FOR VACAVILLE THE NEXT morning. I spent four days there, mostly seeing old friends who'd been out and in again and were now in the Reception Center. Vacaville was the same old mellow facade with the backdrop of terror.

On the fourth day they sent in a busload of dudes from the Susanville Conservation Camp who'd started a food strike there and were being transferred to Sierra.

One of them was a little guy named Miles, a nineteen-year-old black with the first Afro I'd ever seen; he looked good but kind of crazy. He was a black belt in karate, and we worked out together that afternoon.

That night we rode up on the bus together to Sierra. Miles was saying that he'd started the strike to get to Quentin to be with all his friends. I told him how awful it was, but if he wanted to get there, I'd show him how, and I'd be able get back to CMC-East at the same time.

The first thing I noticed when I got off the bus at Sierra was the cold. We were way off in the mountains, deep in a pine forest, thirty miles from the nearest town, Jamestown. And it wasn't exactly a metropolis. We were up in redneck country, and all the police were racist cowboys. People said there wasn't nothin' black in Jamestown, not even a black cat.

There were twenty-four hundred prisoners there living in sixteen man dorms, and a picture of Ronald Reagan in a cowboy suit in every room. Actually, the dorms were nothing but log cabin bunkhouses warmed by a single heater. It was a cold motherfucker, and it was still a long way till winter. That picture of cowboy Reagan left me without any doubts: I hated the place.

The first night I was there, the Lieutenant called me in to tell me he wasn't going to take any shit from me.

Now, the last time I'd got into the kind of trouble he was talking about was back in 1965, so I said, "Man, I haven't had a beef in a good motherfuckin' four years. Now tell me what's on your mind."

"We're not gonna have any *shit!*"

"Listen," I explained, "I don't want you and you don't want me. The only solution is for you to transfer me outta here. There's no sense in us both bein' unhappy up here."

"You were sent here, Carr, and if you leave it's gotta be through Classification just like everyone else. My job is simply to make sure you stay here and don't try to run off and don't start no shit."

I figured this was a good opportunity to get off on the wrong track so they'd want to get rid of me. These authorities don't know how to deal with resistance 'cause most everyone there is so docile. They're not into tough habits. Furthermore, they're all from Jamestown and haven't been around uppity blacks.

"Listen here, boss." I went on, "I don't wanna be here. But as long as I am here I'm gonna do just as I please. And when you get tired of me you're gonna hafta ship me out, cause you ain't even got a Hole here."

That night when the cons came in from work, dog tired with red clay all over them from cutting fire trails all day, I asked them how in hell they could take it up here. They told me no one could apply for a transfer; you didn't leave unless you did something.

"Then why," I asked, "don't you do something?"

They all said no, no, they wanted to go home in a year, so they couldn't afford any beefs.

I said, "Well, how'd you like to get outta here without gettin' a beef?" About ten young blacks said they would. "All ya gotta do is what I tell ya," I continued, "and I'll show you a way outta here you can't refuse."

Later that night I started preaching some insane madness, fomenting against the police at the top of my lungs so they'd be sure to hear me. The guard came running into the dorm, waving and crying in a stage whisper, "We don't have any rallies here."

I smiled. "You do tonight."

The guard ran off and came back with the sergeant, who told me to keep it down. I told him we were doing as we pleased and didn't care to have him interfere. Miles called him a sack of motherfuckers; the sergeant told Miles he had a one-fifteen. Miles said to write him up a few more if he felt like it. The sergeant stood there waiting for me to say something so he could give me one, but I just stood there grinning, not saying a word, till finally he left. Then I started back agitating—riled the cons up until three a.m., when I let them get some sleep.

The next day, Saturday, they didn't have to work. I took my group out to the yard and lined them up. Then Miles put us through a routine of karate exercises. When the lieutenant walked out on his porch and saw us, his mouth dropped open and he ran back inside. Emerging with a pack of guards, he charged out on the yard yelling, "What do you think you're *doing*?!"

"Well, Lieutenant," I replied calmly, "right now we're warming up, and in a minute we'll start karate. Wanna watch?"

"We don't do that up here, Carr."

"Where I come from, Lieutenant, we do it every day, and we're not gonna stop training just 'cause we got sent here. So you better get used to it, Lieutenant, since you don't transfer nobody." We started back to work as the lieutenant retreated.

By the time of my Classification hearing the next week, I'd built up such a terrible reputation in the camp that I figured they'd ship me out. Before the hearing I told everyone in our group to pack up all their shit and follow me over to the administration building 'cause we were going to get out of there.

We marched in two abreast. I sat my troops down in the lobby, telling them to stay on top of their boxes and not give them up. The guard, with eyes bulging at the sight of us, ran into the Classification room, after which we heard a loud buzzing in there for several minutes. Then the door opened and they peered out.

"There's ten of us here," I shouted, "and we all wanna leave!"

They called me into the Classification room and tried to be nice, grinning and carrying on about how nice it's going to be here at camp.

"Look here," I interrupted, "you people are racists. The population here is half black and you don't have one black worker here. The only one you ever had got beat up and run off by the Jamestown police for dancing with a white girl in town. It's dangerous. I'm not here to mess around and get a case on me. One of these ridge runners is gonna say something to me and I'm gonna knock the top of his head off. That's the *last* motherfuckin' thing I want."

"We're gonna keep you here," the smiling man insisted.

"I was railroaded, double-crossed, kidnapped, and brought here. They told me I was goin' to South CC, and that's the only way they got me out of CMC-East. I'm goin' to South or I'm goin' back to CMC—take your choice."

One of them whispered, "Give him a job! Give him any job he wants!" But I knew what *that* meant: if I took a job and tried to quit later, that would be a beef; but now, with no job, there's no rule to break.

"You can't give me *no* job, from pickin' up cigarette butts to cuttin' down redwoods. All that shit's dead. I'm just gonna sit down as long as I'm here. Now, if you got any facilities for people sittin' down, you can give me an assignment for sittin' down. I ain't doin' nothin' else. Now that I've told you what's happening, let's not waste our time arguing about it."

The smiling man was no longer smiling: "We're gonna send you to Folsom!"

"I could not care less. Just get me away from here." Then I walked out. Miles ran in, cussed them out, and kicked over the table.

They locked all ten of us up in a dorm. Three days later a bus pulled up and took us to Folsom. Apparently they couldn't make room for us on their mainline there, for after a month in the Hole they shipped us all off to Quentin.

But Quentin didn't want us either. The cops had just managed to transfer all the troublemakers to Folsom; I was the last person they wanted to see. We weren't there more than a week when they put us on the bus to CMC-East. This "bus therapy" is famous in the California pens: anyone who's hard to handle without committing violent acts gets to see a lot of the state.

After an absence of only two months, I was back at CMC-East.

When he saw me on the yard, De Angelo almost went through the roof. Grapentine came up and said, "You're gonna have to walk mighty light around here, Carr. First thing you do, they'll ship you out."

I went to the academic counselor's office, collected my mail from the University, and got readmitted just before finals to the courses I'd been taking. I passed math with ease and got a good grade in anthropology by writing a term paper out of the encyclopedia.

When I went to Classification I knew there'd be some shit: Wally Covington had already told me about the rumors that I'd be sent back to Quentin. As soon as I walked in, De Angelo said: "As far as I'm concerned, you manipulated your way out of camp, and I don't appreciate it one bit. You're gettin' pretty slick at this kinda shit, and it's gotta stop. I ought to be sending you back to Quentin . . . but I'm gonna give you the benefit of the doubt. What we're gonna do is put you to work. Ever since you been here you done nothin' but what you want. You got an education out of us and now you owe us. You're goin' on Arbini's crew"—Arbini was called "The Slavedriver"—"and you're goin' outside the fence on minimum custody."

"I don't want minimum," I said. "I want to stay medium and inside the fence where it's safe." I wanted minimum custody so bad I could taste it: that means you're goin' *home*. I just pretended to object so he'd feel good about giving it to me.

"You got minimum, Carr."

"I don't want no trouble, Mr. De Angelo. But I don't want no minimum and I don't wanna work for Arbini 'cause he's gonna try to work me to death. Can't I work in the gym?"

"No, Carr, you've always wiggled your way into jobs like that. Now you're goin' where we want you. We're puttin' you out in front of the institution where we can all see you. And when I come to work in the morning and look across that field, I wanna see you *shine.*"

"Yes, Mr. De Angelo."

"And one more thing: if you try to manipulate your way out of this, the only thing that's gonna beat you to Folsom is the headlights on the bus."

They were really happy because they just *knew* I'd try to get out of it. But I wasn't going to play into their hands: I was going to the Board in July, and it was already January. I couldn't afford a single one-fifteen, so I was mighty cool. No hustling whatsoever, plenty of quiet cell time. And I worked my ass off.

Arbini's crew deserved its reputation. We had to take big blocks of lime, grind them up, and load the hundred-pound sacks on trucks. We had to move boulders, cut grass, and pull weeds out around Highway 1. It was colder than a witch's tit out there in the morning, but I had to do the work.

Arbini had heard about me and singled me out: "Ah, Mr. Carr, so you're the guy who likes college, huh?"

"Yes sir," I answered, "I want to go when I get out."

"Ah, but you don't like work, do you?"

"Who says that?" I asked politely.

"That's what they say inside."

"Well, sir," I promised, "any work you got for me to do, I'll do it."

Arbini's a mess. He's got a piece of paper he got in boot camp in World War II saying he's got the equivalent of a high school diploma for going through basic training, and he's jealous of anyone who's read more than the military code of justice. He's a short fat dark dago with hair coming all out of his shirt—must shave three or four times a day—and got an inferiority complex like a motherfucker. Always messing with people, especially me.

He'd read in the prison bulletin that I'd been a weight-lifter, so whenever anyone came to an extra big boulder Arbini'd yell, "No, no! Let Carr get it!" Pretty soon I'd just go after them without his even asking me, taking out all my aggression ripping these big rocks out of the ground, then run up to Arbini asking for more. Whenever the prison officials came by to go to the snack bar I'd work even harder. We'd be out cutting elephant grass and I'd be working with two sickles, one in each hand. My friends'd see me from out of the windows of the institution and cry "Shine! Shine!" laughing their heads off—

Arbini was proud as hell that he was the one who'd got me to work. He was always trying to kiss ass with his superiors, and he'd point at me, telling them, "Look at Carr—never thought you'd see that, did ya?"

Arbini loved fishing. When he got to talking about it one day, I took him on a trip about fly-casting and different kinds of flies. Now, I'd never been fishing in my life, but I knew something about flies from the guys who used to make them in hobby-craft. I'd get to razzing Arbini about how I'd catch every fish in the ocean before he'd catch one out of a trout farm; he'd get all worked up, laughing and saying, "You lyin'!" Pretty soon everybody'd be working their asses off while Arbini and I talked about hunting and fishing. I even got him to the point where we called each other "Arb" and "Jimmy," and he'd let me go in early on the smallest pretext.

I WENT TO THE BOARD IN July, appearing before a black named Walter Gordon and another liberal named Lymon. I'd gotten a lot of letters from the University about how bad they wanted me, as well as an offer of a job as teaching assistant to a math professor.

"Well, Mr. Carr," said Gordon, "you look good. Look like a different person. We're going to let you go, and we don't expect to hear from you again."

"Boss," I said with a big grin, "that sounds more like a warning than a compliment, but I'm awfully glad to hear it just the same."

Ten days later I was on the streets.

FOURTEEN

I've been struggling all my life to get beyond the choice of living on my knees or dying on my feet. It's time we lived on our feet.

As a kid my rebellion was pure: unthinking, arbitrary, devilish; sometimes for fun or because I was bored, more often because I saw adults standing over me at every turn—parents, teachers and preachers—and sought ways to get even, to avenge my submission, I was always caught and punished in such a way that my feelings were only intensified and reinforced.

Along with the stick, of course, they always showed me the carrot: clothes, cars, cigarettes, and whisky and women—telling me that to get these things I'd have to be a success. Telling me out of the other corner of their mouths that I'd been born to be a failure. Always taunting, jeering, and lecturing me. I was completely disoriented, caught between acceptance and rejection of an alien world at once fascinating and disgusting. It's a trap, *the* trap. I became a rebel—still caught, but proudly defiant.

This defiance, however, was constantly frustrated and unfulfilled. The "criminal mentality" (what I prefer to call the "philosophy of crime") is born to lose. The criminal acts out his role the way he's been taught it, taking a series of huge risks with very little reward, until he gets caught. His confusion in the face of bourgeois values is shown by the fact that, while he often can't stand work even if he can find it, he squanders his hard-earned money so fast and so senselessly that he has to go to work again and pull another job. As a consumer—and he consumes with a vengeance—he is flashy, over-conspicuous and demonstrative, behavior which leads to arrest in poor black neighborhoods. As a thief, however, he's thoroughly secretive, isolated and paranoid. It was me against the world, locked in a battle which wound up in San Quentin. I rejected dominant values such as work and respect for private property without understanding their source or function. The most positive word in my vocabulary was "bad." So when I was presented with the California Penal System, with its hierarchy of punishments (that is, more and more severe prisons), I could only spit in their face by aspiring to go all the way to the top. It was not until the gates of Quentin closed on me that I realized the trap, and only several years later that I began to figure out how to escape it. This is the period during which many cons—in fact, most—are broken.

Once they have him in prison, the authorities do everything within their power to promote the convict's individualistic, paranoid side, fostering competition and suspicion by holding out limited rewards, spreading false rumors, deliberately putting enemies together so they'll destroy each other, and so on.

The first widespread, active reaction of the prison population to this chaos of mutual hatred and uncertainty was to seek identification with cons of their own race and define themselves in opposition to the rest. This process began in the California prisons in the mid-'50s, then got a terrific boost from the development of African and Afro-American nationalism on the outside in the early '60s.

Nationalism—the development of large cliques by race—broke down the most basic isolation of the individual con, and started the development whereby he could at least *begin* to see his relationship with the outside world. Naturally, this led to a breakdown in the authorities' control; so, just as naturally, they fell back on their second line of defense: racism. Now all the petty intriguing and gross manipulations that went on before on an individual level were transferred to the interracial scene, made more frantic and vicious by the officials' fear of total loss of control. Obviously, every con who is not an inmate knows who has the keys and guns and why, but *practically* this is often forgotten. The object of those who exercise oppressive social control is to keep the immediate enemy (in this case, the whites and Mexicans) ever before your eyes so that your knowledge of the real enemy doesn't affect your actions.

When the cons began to break down racism at Quentin and Soledad, the system fell back to its third line of defense: the vicious cycle of militancy and repression. Here, even when the cons realized that they were all opposed to the system, they were prevented from locating themselves realistically within it: rather than recognize that they were on the margins of society and study strategically the development of society as a whole, they[1] saw themselves as a class apart from the proletariat, or as its vanguard, and adopted an ideology of class war by which the only battleground was the prison itself. They mistook the system's arm for its heart.

---

1 I say "they" because at this point I was at CMC-East, physically isolated from the development of the "prison movement."

THEY WERE, OF COURSE, CONSTANTLY REINFORCED in this false consciousness by the attitude of the Left, with its own romantic fetishization of crime, its moralist protest against the penal system,[2] its rhetoric of guerrilla warfare, and its solicitation and exploitation of convict martyrs (which brought about a humiliating image of the prisoner as victim, the way the civil rights movement reduced all blacks to victims—an image which every con writer in the last three years has gone for hook, line, and sinker).

Guerrilla ideology reduces all revolutionary questions to quantitative problems of military force. Nothing could be more disastrous, even on the outside. In prison the results of this ideology are as horrifying as they are insane: George Jackson's death and the Attica revolt are two obvious examples. Nothing could please the most reactionary prison official more than a fight to the finish.[3]

The few prison militants who get out alive usually get killed or rearrested within a few months. They have been trained, by the guards and by the Left, to expect a fight to the death at any moment, and they provoke such fights on the outside even in those cases in which the police don't. Of course, every one of these militants is trailed and harassed; the cops feel they've lost a case whenever a troublemaker gets out of the joint, so if

---

2 Marx said that basing a revolutionary movement on prison reform was like basing an abolitionist movement on better food for slaves. Of course, this criticism isn't literally applicable here, since the New Left was never a revolutionary movement. These fools always feigned surprise and shock that bourgeois punishment could be "cruel and unusual."

3 It must be kept in mind that the prison system is not yet an advanced capitalist institution, and that the prison bureaucracy, manned for the most part by flunkies and psychopaths, has until now successfully resisted all attempts—and there have been damn few—by the overall State bureaucracy to rationalize it. For the prison authorities, this is not just a question of opposing liberal politics—even Reagan's commission is against them—but of protecting their entrenched position, indeed their very jobs. No reformed prison system is going to include these gorillas, and they know it.

they don't shoot you down directly, they work on you until you play their game and shoot yourself down. Most militant cons fall into this trap, remaining just as isolated from society on the outside as they were in the pen, seeing a world made up chiefly of cops and cons (or "revolutionaries").

I WAS NO EXCEPTION. DESPITE MY five years of insulation at CMC-East, where at least I learned some of the cops' more subtle tricks, I came charging out in 1970 expecting to find a Red Army ready for revolutionary war. What I found was a handful of red criminals with the same world view I'd had as a poolhall hustler, reinforced with heavy doses of ideology and drugs. But my disappointment at their lack of power was softened by the tremendous amount of money they had to spend on me.

At the same time, to fulfill my parole, I had to be in school in Santa Cruz. So being a "revolutionary" consisted mainly of tripping back and forth between there and the East Bay—target shooting and attending classes and small-time protest meetings in Santa Cruz, snorting coke and puttin' on the style in Oakland.

The main difference between these people and a non-political criminal gang is that here the ideology of Leninism greatly solidifies the position of the leadership; this is, in fact, the main purpose of that ideology. Never a leader myself, I contented myself with guarding those at the top and reaping some of their material benefits for myself. Caught up in this environment, I sustained my illusions for nine months more. I had doubts, but I swallowed them down with heavier doses of white powder and red book.

By this time, George had become a Soledad Brother. I worked a little for the defense committee, more out of loyalty to my friend than from any great passion for legal work. The meetings were endless. The strategy of radicalizing the masses by "exposing" the prisons and courts was contemptible to me even then; but since I was a celebrity to them as George Jackson's friend, and my presence seemed to inspire them to maybe do something to save his life, I went to the meetings. (This is not to say that I didn't eat up all the attention I got there!)

I had started working as a teaching assistant at Santa Cruz and on April 6th, 1971, I took several of my students to see the Soledad trial in San Francisco. As the court session ended, somebody handed George a newspaper. The deputies grabbed it from George, and the old boy started swinging, as did half the people and all the cops in the courtroom. I was caught right in the middle, and downed a couple of dogs as I was coming up for air. The pigs grabbed whomever they could, took us upstairs to County Jail, and charged us with felony assault.

I couldn't believe it. After all my efforts to "reform" myself, here I was faced with the possibility of going back to prison for the rest of my life just for this little scuffle. The police had acted in their typical stupid, brutal way, and I was madder than hell. Almost immediately, though, I realized that as a militant I would always be at the mercy of such arbitrary acts. The militants and the Tactical Squad[4] live symbiotically since the leftists speak in the language that these goons can understand: the purely military resolution of power relations. ("Political power flows out of the barrel of a gun.") If I continued to run around with a bunch of fools who said that legal work and socialist soup-kitchens were subversive, and carried guns to prove it, then I'd be treated as an enemy by the police even though I was no threat to the system.

---

4 San Francisco's crowd-control specialists—huge bulls with four-foot clubs whose main job is combat against the Left.

This realization left me disgusted with my recent activity and my "comrades," but it didn't get me out of County Jail. My stay there dragged on for nearly nine months while the State tried to decide whether to hang me or let me go and give me a chance to hang myself even better. I was kept isolated from the other prisoners most of the time, with only the guards to talk to (except for limited visiting privileges for my friends and several ingenious message systems worked out by the cons at County); a lot of guards hung around my cell to talk politics or just bullshit to while away the time. Some of them were punks tucked up there because they weren't mean enough to be real pigs; others were criminology students working part-time, the "new breed" of "humane" cops; one was just a nice old Tom seeking his black identity so he could get himself laid. They don't get many cons from Quentin in S.F. County—half the inmates are vagrants—and since, furthermore, I was George's friend, I was once again a celebrity.

Most of the time I read and thought, more intensely than ever before in my life. Except for my math, the direction of these studies was always revolutionary theory or strategy. I spent a lot of time examining my past activity in terms of what it offered me immediately and ultimately, and found it sorely lacking on both counts. In addition to the obvious limitations of guerrilla strategy in and out of the pen, I saw that all the alternatives I'd set myself were reactionary in that they were merely direct respones to crimes committed by the State. The terms, the terrain, and the weapons of my past struggles had all been dictated by my enemy. This had increased my rage, but had also increased my willingness to enter combat in such a way that I couldn't win. This pattern, set in prison, had continued since my release from CMC.

Getting out of the madness of that past year was the best thing that could have happened to me; I'd like to take this opportunity to thank the San Francisco Tac Squad for providing me with the means to do so. Other than the constant psychological torment of being in a cage, however comfortable, my life during the nine months I spent in County wasn't that bad. I lived kind of like a medieval monk—though the subject matter of my studies was a little different—turning myself on and calming down at the same time.

In December 1971, my lawyer, after months of running around, made a deal with the DA whereby the felony assault charge was reduced to a misdemeanor and I was given credit for time served. Then the Adult Authority played out a sadistic little charade, keeping me guessing for two weeks whether or not they'd send me back to prison on a parole violation anyway. (Hundreds of ex-cons make deals on misdemeanors, only to get sent back. This can happen even if you go to trial and are acquitted, or even if all charges are dropped!) Finally they ordered me released as part of their annual Christmas show of goodwill toward men; but the guards didn't tell me, so I didn't get out until the 30th.

To a great extent, I have written about my past here in order to get over it, to appropriate what I've learned and cut loose the remaining dead weight. It hasn't been easy. When my life was at its most sordid, when prison had almost turned me into a caged beast, I never looked as closely at *anything* I did, and when I thought about it at all it had to be completely detached, as if it were about somebody else. Life was just too brutal and uncertain. You'd think tactically, planning how to survive, but you couldn't go deep into yourself or you'd nut out. You had all the time in the world in one way, but really you had no time at all.

Now it's different, of course, if only because I can do much more about my situation. By and large, I can think about everything I've done in a critical way, basing my judgments and tactics not on the reflexes of a trapped animal but on general ideas which themselves are constantly scrutinized and developed. Still, some aspects of my past that are irrevocably finished continue to haunt me in peculiar ways, and it's been very hard to relate to them. I sometimes start telling an amusing little story about myself and a couple of friends and then suddenly realize they're dead. Needless to say, I've had to detach and harden myself up a little even now to get the story out.

BEFORE GETTING BUSTED AGAIN, I GOT married—me!—and entered for the first time into a large, pretty closely knit family, where I was generally warmly accepted. However, I didn't have time to get very far into that before my arrest. It was only when I was in County Jail that this "alliance" had its full effect: where in my last seven years in the pen I'd never had one single visitor, now every week I had at least a couple of people there, and sometimes half a dozen, all concerned with my welfare. Their visits and letters—and work to get me out—just plain melted me. I learned to let down my guard with them to the point where I could trust and give. There had been something like that among some of us at Quentin, but it had been forged as a result of the constant warfare with the rest of the population and the goons. I had known then the love of comrades together under the gun, and I still treasure its memory, and the other survivors of the forge. But never before had I known love so unconditional as that of my wife and her family, and of some of their friends who became mine as well.

I WAS REINSTATED ON PAROLE WHEN I was released; now, too, because of my misdemeanor conviction, I was on probation. Two sets of cops following me around, two sets of rehabilitation standards to live up to. Clearly, even if I'd wanted to, it would have been foolish to go back to my same old tricks. Now I couldn't even *appear* to in any way. For the next year I not only have to *be* straight, but *look* square. Not that I'd even want to pick up where I left off, but I have to maintain appearances to such a degree that I can't even go to see my old comrades to tell them how wrong they are for fear that the police would get ideas.

It's not so bad, though, being straight. Everything's new to me out here: fresh air and freedom of movement are things I could barely remember. Add to that a baby, woman, family, food, and fire (in the fireplace this time). . . seeing the stars at night, swimming in the ocean, having a garden and a dog, calling an old friend up the night he gets out, being around lots of kids, going to someone's house for dinner, sleeping late once in a while . . . getting used to the little freedoms of the outside world.

Of course, the fact that it's not all that free keeps coming up. I can see the dead weight of the daily grind, even if I don't yet feel it completely because it's all so new. (I start work soon; that should help me feel it.) In part I've just talked myself into enjoying the novelties so as to combat my restlessness while on parole and probation. Even so, or maybe especially so, this attitude serves its purpose—it's a different time.

So I'm just kicked back, getting soft and old and a little lazy, reading a little, thinking a lot, taking a year off—I dare say I deserve it.

James Carr, with wife Betsy and daughter Gea

AFTERWORD

BY BETSY CARR

WHEN I FIRST MET JIMMY I was totally immersed in the prison movement. I was on the Central Committee of the Soledad Brothers Defense Committee, lived in the SBDC house in San Francisco, and ran their office like a Red Army bureau. One day in September, 1970, I went to San Jose to help George Jackson's attorney put together a legal brief; Jimmy was sitting in the office, reading Marx. He knew me, was waiting for me. He pulled my photograph from his pocket and said hello.

I was scared. George had told me that Jimmy was the baddest motherfucker in the world, that I'd fall in love with him and I'd be sorry. Now here he was, with his huge arms and his shaved head, not saying much and smiling almost shyly. I talked a lot to hide my nervousness, carrying on aimlessly about some guy I hated who'd said he was Jimmy's friend. Jimmy let me go on. I was so attracted to him that I did go on, despite my discomfort.

When the work was done we went over to my mother's house. Joan, who was also working on the SBDC, had met Jimmy a few weeks earlier when he'd first gotten out of jail, and they were pretty good friends by now. Jimmy sometimes stayed in San Jose on trips between Santa Cruz, where he was enrolled in school, and Oakland, where he was being introduced to the world of militant politics on the outside. Before going back to San Francisco, I gave him my number and told him to come see me at the office. He said that it would be very unlikely since his parole restricted him to San Jose and Santa Cruz.

The next morning I was very busy with a small staff meeting when Jimmy walked in. He leaned against the wall and didn't speak to anyone. The others there knew him only as the "Jackal," knew that he was a friend of George's and that they shouldn't inquire further.

I tried to keep busy but it was impossible. He eased himself off the wall, went out, and returned with a bottle of Jose Cuervo and said he wanted to talk to me in the back room. We didn't talk much. We made love till dinnertime. At one point Jimmy sent one of the staff members out for another bottle of Jose.

Next night I got a call from a Black Panther I knew. He told me I'd be picked up at nine, then hung up. Two dudes I'd never seen showed up, told me to come with them and took me by a tortuous two-hour route to Berkeley, dropping me off at a fancy apartment filled with tropical fish. An old lady appeared, gave me some tea, and disappeared. An hour later three obvious Panthers walked in, sat down and asked me a lot of meaningless questions. Then Jimmy and Huey Newton came in. Jimmy waited in another room while Newton chatted with me, checking me out and apparently concluding that I was all right. After half an hour Newton went to sleep, the other three got drunk, and Jimmy and I went to bed. We finally talked—all night.

We talked about George Jackson: how we both loved him, how I was stupid to think he'd ever get out alive. We talked about how there was nothing happening on the streets, no red army waiting for Jimmy to lead them to victory. Legal work had no place in his idea of revolution. His reaction to anyone helping George was gracious thanks—he was nice to all of them—but he knew their work had no use beyond keeping George a little happier and less isolated.

Jimmy told me what he was doing at UC Santa Cruz, a place I despised for its nauseating liberal image and its zombie student body. Jimmy hadn't started classes yet; he was tutoring in math, helping a couple of professors outline courses, and fucking all the girls. In 1970 every school had to have either lots of black students or a few and one big one. Jimmy was the big one. They all loved him.

He was living with Herman Blake and his family. Blake, Santa Cruz's showcase black professor, had gotten Jimmy into school. They all got along well, even though Jimmy could never stomach Blake's nationalism. (Even then, at the height of his militancy, Jimmy had no racist tendencies; I had so come to expect them that I was quite surprised.) Besides the Blakes, he ran with a houseful of black women students and a houseful of my friends—some white militants who worked for the SBDC in Santa Cruz. At this point he wasn't taking me down there because of all his girlfriends; he had a big keyring full of dorm and house keys which he was making good use of.

After that night we were friends. I was in love with Jimmy. He was still mythy to me—and I got off on myths. I was completely fascinated with the Panther elite—the glamour, the bizarreness. It was my Hollywood. I'd never discussed anything with any of them, just watched in total awe. I didn't think I should talk to them or try to know them. They were the vanguard; I was a helper. I figured they were grateful for my help, and I knew I loved having them lead me. I loved the way they looked, with their shiny leather coats and beautiful shoes (I wore a fatigue jacket and work boots), I was always very polite and obedient, never expecting them to show me any courtesy; but they always showed me respect, which made them just that much more awesome.

At first, I had this same reaction to Jimmy, except that I talked to him. I knew he was friendly with the elite and he looked smooth, and for a little while I acted accordingly. But there was a difference which became obvious almost immediately: Jimmy wouldn't let me slide. He wanted to know what I thought. He criticized me and wanted me to criticize him. I don't think it ever entered his mind that I would think of him as elite, though he knew others did. He had no front with me,

Jimmy came by the San Francisco office nearly every day, often on made-up business. His hanging out with me became more casual, even though he still kept up his anonymous, heavy, jackal-dog image with the others.

One night soon after we met, he came by the house where I was talking to a dude I'd been running with before I met him. We were just discussing business but Jimmy didn't like it. He kicked my friend out and hit me very hard. It surprised both of us. He explained, as only someone fresh out of the pen could, that I was his woman, that I was not to talk to people he didn't like (that is, other boyfriends). This was news to me, but I ate it up for a while.

The next night Jimmy called while I was in a meeting, and I told him I was busy. He walked into the meeting, announced that we had something very important to do, and took me out. We got loaded, drove to Santa Cruz and played on the beach, then went to San Jose and stayed in bed all day.

I never sat through an entire meeting again, even though by this time we were both on the Central Committee. For two people who couldn't wait for the insurrection to begin, endless circular strategy sessions were an unbearable waste of time. We stuck around because George wanted us to, but we couldn't sit still. Sometimes we'd get silly and giggle our way through a meeting; often Jimmy would get very mad and holler his way through it, grabbing me and stomping out when he couldn't take it any longer. (At the first meeting he attended, Jimmy hadn't realized that it was natural to get mad when he was so frustrated; he kept running into the kitchen. When I went back there I found he'd punched a hole in the wall.) At several meetings we got drunk and wound up going into the back room to fuck. We weren't very well liked.

JIMMY HAD A COUSIN, BOBBY TUCKER, who had been busted at fifteen and sentenced to ten years at Quentin. He did the sentence but just a little while before his release date Bobby hit a guard and had to go to outside court. When his time was up at Quentin they put him in Marin County Jail. Jimmy got him bailed out and brought him over.

Bobby had grown up in Q; he had no idea how to be on the streets. He'd had lots of homos in the joint but had never slept with a woman, never even talked with one since he was a little kid. Jimmy wanted all the women to sleep with him, but Bobby wouldn't come near me because I was Jimmy's woman.

Bobby was the opposite of Jimmy—the other side of what the joint does to people. He'd had shock treatment an amazing number of times: he was very quiet and smiled a lot. He had scars all over his arms from "suicide attempts" faked in the vain hope of being transferred to the Medical Facility at Vacaville.

The first night Bobby was out he was blown out by everything—windows, toilets with doors, double beds, refrigerators (he opened the icebox at least a dozen times, saying, "I'm not hungry now," as he took food out and put it back again).

By the beginning of October Jimmy had moved most of his shit into my old room at Joan's house, and I started to spend a lot of time there. At first I always made excuses to come to town on business, but little by little I took more time off to visit. On my nineteenth birthday we got very drunk in the course of a walk with a bottle of Jose. We ran into some neighbors who had some cocaine; it took us forty-five minutes to walk the three blocks home.

The next morning neither of us could move, so we talked all day. Jimmy asked me to marry him and have a baby. We really loved each other, so we dropped the marriage idea, but a baby was perfect. We both loved kids, and his ideas about having children were based on passion and trust.

Of course, there were problems that we discussed. It was quite possible, we knew, that Jimmy or I would get busted or killed. We would have to slow down to avoid this. We discussed the possibility of a time when we wouldn't want to live together, but both of us knew we'd still love each other and wouldn't let that stop us raising kids. Jimmy and I were already opposed to the Stalinist ideas of childrearing prevalent on the left. We wanted to change this, to come up with a more loving alternative to the bourgeois family and its cold socialist counterpart. Jimmy even wanted to adopt some kids from the County so we could start immediately, but the Department of Corrections wouldn't allow it. As for the black/white thing, we never talked about it. Neither of us wanted a kid hung up on race. Jimmy was worried that I would be overburdened (although he planned and did lots of work), but I wasn't worried about it.

In early November I moved back to San Jose. Our activity in the movement was slowing down, but it was still taking up too much of our time with meetings and shitwork; between bureaucracy and commuting, we didn't have enough time to have fun. So we laid back a little more, tried even harder to get me pregnant, went for rides in our new jeep, and spent a lot of time hanging out together. We fought a lot, but that was just part of our understanding. We were really so much in love, it surprised the hell out of us.

ONE DAY WHEN JIMMY WAS COMING down from Oakland, he picked up a hitchhiker—a kid from Alabama who'd come to milk cows in Stockton, made it to Stockton, but couldn't find the cows. Jimmy brought him to San Jose and fed him huge amounts of food, then took him to the bus station and sent him off to Stockton.

A week later we got a telegram: STILL NO COWS. So Jimmy sent Clarence fifty dollars. A few days later, he showed up.

Clarence was country like I didn't know existed. He was young, very dark, and very naive. I thought he was funny. So did Jimmy, but at the same time he felt paternalistic toward him. Clarence sort of moved in and gradually made himself at home.

One night when we all went out to dinner, Clarence said he didn't feel good and stayed home. When we got back Clarence was gone, and so were Jimmy's clothes.

I was mad and thought Jimmy'd be furious. But he really got off on it, laughed for hours imagining this country boy milking cows in much-too-big San Remo boots and a two-hundred-dollar leather coat. He thought it hysterical that his hick had turned bodacious and ripped off just him, the Champ. I finally had to laugh too.

IN LATE NOVEMBER JIMMY NOTICED THAT the quarter was almost over. Things were hot because of the Angela Davis grand jury, and school was the only thing that made his parole officer love him. So we retired to Santa Cruz.

After looking everywhere for a cheap apartment, we finally found a terrible one between the campus and downtown. The most together person in the building was a destitute, pregnant heroin addict who'd borrow things like a spoonful of sugar or seven cents. The woman in the next apartment had a cop boy friend who came over on his lunch hour while her husband was at work; they'd grunt for forty-five minutes, then he'd leave. On the other side was an old lady who was at least eighty-five. She loved me and often came calling.

Our apartment was tiny; the living room was about the size of a king-size bed. It was literally filled with our ammo reloader. Every night after dinner we sat around making bullets. ("So nice you have a hobby," the old lady said.) We were loose. Lots of dope and guns.

On Christmas Day, as we were leaving town for San Jose, two cops stopped us. They said there'd been a robbery at a pawnshop and that guns had been taken. We fit the description, I had a nine millimeter automatic in my purse and my new twenty-two rifle, a Christmas present from Jimmy, in the back of the car. Somehow Jimmy talked his way out of a search, but I was scared because I thought one of the neighbors must have reported us to the police. To play it safe, we moved back to San Jose for a week, then found a new place in Santa Cruz.

When the winter quarter started, Jimmy decided to do school right. He really loved math and wanted to get it all down; often he stayed up all night doing numbers. We cut way down on our trips north and settled down for a few weeks.

Jimmy got a job as TA in a sociology class on prisons, and thus got slightly involved in black school politics. The UCSC Black Student Union was like similar big-city university groups except that instead of urban reform projects they had Soledad prison, which was fairly close to Santa Cruz and offered them a chance to consider themselves "superoppressed" just like the cons. Jimmy treated them like he treated the white militants: he was glad they were helping his friends in the pen. He didn't like their nationalism or their bickering with the whites, but he was usually polite.

At the time there were very few blacks at Santa Cruz. All of them I met were middle-class nationalists (except for a converted Jewess who told me I should be proud of my race). Three of the women were after Jimmy and would do anything he said. Of course, they hated me. So Jimmy would flaunt me around, hold me under his arm when they were around and mutter, "Every dog's got his day, and a good dog's got two."

One night Red Nelson, the warden at Quentin, came to speak at College Night, a formal dinner at the University attended by a large number of students and faculty. Jimmy had prepared a list of very specific questions—like, Why did you throw tear gas into a certain cell on a certain date?—and had the girls mimeograph and distribute them. Nelson came and gave a speech about how everything was going to be all right. Then he asked for questions. Blam! The students started reading off the list. The poor dog was almost in tears. Then he heard the unmistakable laugh of the old jackal and ran off the stage.

Things were good. No parole hassles. All this time Jimmy told his parole officer he was living with a black woman, and gave the address of one of his friends. On mornings that the P.O. was coming up from Salinas, Jimmy would go to this chick's house and scatter his clothes around. And I was pregnant—we were both in hog heaven about that. But neither of us liked Santa Cruz, so we moved back to San Jose.

Jimmy wanted a kid more than anything. He became very protective of me. He wanted to get married, too. Finally I gave in, but I was so embarrassed that I made him promise not to tell anyone.

Jimmy sent our San Jose address to his parole officer, who dropped in one day soon afterward. He was one of the new breed of CDC employee: thirty-five-year-old social-worker type, quasi-liberal, pleasant-looking and pleasant-talking. He covered his gut reaction (which showed in his face) against a nice girl in a big house marrying one of his cons by asking us parental questions: How would we support the kid? Did I have a doctor? Would the kid be raised in any religion? (Jimmy and I both said, "Huh?") I'll never forget the scene of the two of us sitting under a huge poster of Lenin, telling this cat that we wanted to settle down and raise a family.

Right after the move to San Jose we had a surprise visitor. As soon as I answered the door I knew it was Jimmy's sister Gwen. She was a typical fox, with a bleached natural, a really short dress, fleshy body, beautiful almond eyes, and high cheekbones. She looked a lot like Jimmy.

She came in crying hysterically. When Jimmy saw her he didn't have much sympathy for her (a few months before she'd taken off with some of his money after he'd brought her to Santa Cruz and given her a place to live). She told me that her husband had beaten her up and that she was leaving him for good.

Gwen was married to Louis Tackwood, whom Jimmy had met once and didn't like. He didn't like anyone who didn't think, and that was Tackwood all over. I was torn between oversympathizing with her and following what turned out to be Jimmy's good judgment.

The next morning she changed her mind about leaving her husband. We took her to the airport. A few months later Tackwood confessed that he was an agent of the CII (Criminal Investigation and Interrogation—California's FBI), and that he had sent Gwen up to see us to plant a bug in the house. When he read this in the paper Jimmy wasn't as resentful as one would imagine. I was.

We were very clandestine all this time, mostly just tripping, but always plotting. We spent hours writing out plans: we'd figured the house was bugged even before Gwen actually did it, so we always wrote notes. One night we made a very intricate plan to kidnap Bing Crosby off the golf course; as I was burning it in the bathroom, the toilet seat caught fire.

Jimmy was quite late coming home one night. I thought he was with a girl I didn't like until I heard him, about three. (He always threw a pebble against the window and shone his flashlight up; if I was in a good mood I'd look down.) Moments later he walked into the room with a huge bag of clothes. He and a friend had been tripping around, looking for something to get into. They saw a little hip boutique full of handmade clothes, and they most definitely got into it.

We went through the clothes. Almost everything was too big for me but I kept the few things that fit. Nothing had labels, so we had no worries. Jimmy gave away or sold all the clothes I couldn't use.

On April 6, 1971, Jimmy took a class of Santa Cruz students up to San Francisco to watch a preliminary hearing in the Soledad Brothers trial. He arrived late, just before the judge came in, and had to sit at the back of the courtroom. (I'd gone up earlier and was in front.) Jimmy hadn't seen George in six years. I couldn't wait.

George walked in looking better than ever, grinning, happy. Then he saw Jimmy . . . I almost cried, I was so happy.

The hearing was fast and uneventful. As the Brothers started to walk out, a pig stopped George, who had some underground papers that one of the lawyers had given him. The guard tried to grab them but George wouldn't give them up. The guard hit George. George said, "Please don't hit me." The guard hit him again. George said, "Don't hit me." The guard hit him a third time. Finally, George hit back and it was all over. Millions of police came out of nowhere. Somebody jumped over the partition to help George, who by this time was on the floor. Then I saw Jimmy's arms flying around up there. I had two thoughts: cocaine and parole. After a few seconds, Jimmy had at least one of those thoughts and jumped back over the partition.

I met him at the back door. We calmly waited for the guards to unlock it. When they did, it was only to let the Tac Squad in. Undersheriff Scanlon was hysterically yelling, "get the man in the black leather coat!" The whole scene was riotous: people trying to run out of the courtroom, newsmen fighting to get in. We stayed cool. I pointed to the staircase. Jimmy gave me a little kiss and split. He never made it to the stairs. A minute later I found him handcuffed, surrounded by police. He and two other dudes in black leather coats were booked for felonious assault on a police officer.

Three young lawyers from Berkeley were on the scene immediately. I went around quietly collecting bail money. Under California law anyone who is busted while on parole can't be bailed out without his PO's permission. I called Jimmy's PO, who already knew all about it an hour after the bust. He told me that Sacramento had to approve the request. By the time we reached them they had already decided to hold Jimmy for violation of parole.

Next morning I went to City Jail to visit Jimmy. It was his birthday, the first one he would have spent on the streets in sixteen years, and he was back in jail. The visiting room was decorated in the ordinary sterile style, beige with big glass partitions between the cons and their visitors, little phones to scream over. It was very loud. You were allowed to visit thirty minutes each day.

I watched through the big window for Jimmy to come. I was pissed off until I saw him; then I started to cry. He asked me what was wrong, why was I so upset. He dug what had happened, was relieved that George hadn't gotten busted, and glad that someone else had fought. He didn't like jail but felt certain he'd be out soon since none of the police got hurt. (He wasn't used to fights where no one was killed or badly injured.) I guess I knew better. Jimmy was in City Jail for two weeks. I went to see him every day. It was an hour's ride each way, an hour's wait, and a visit that was usually less than thirty minutes. I wrote him two or three letters a day, all full of chatty news.

Someone found us a lawyer, Henry Ramsey, who was young, black, and into moderate Berkeley politics. I didn't like him because he had that cultural-nationalist attitude common among black professionals, but he seemed competent. He asked a lot of questions, wanting to know every detail and thinking of obscure legal technicalities to help Jimmy.

The arraignment was great. The police all contradicted each other. The black liberal judge seemed fair. For a while I thought the charges might be dropped. But the three defendants were bound over for trial and Jimmy was transferred to County Jail.

All of this, the courts and both jails, was happening in the same building, the Hall of Justice. Some of the guards at County Jail were the same ones who'd beaten up George and busted Jimmy.

The first time I visited County, one of Scanlon's best friends was on duty at the desk. My driver's license was in the name of Elizabeth Hammer. Jimmy had said that his wife's name was Betsy. I was under twenty-one and had no proof of marriage. The cop wouldn't even look at me until I threatened to sue. Some of the women standing in line backed me up, saying that they would tell their husbands who wouldn't take the matter lightly. He let me in.

Jimmy looked great. He liked County Jail much more than City because of its more experienced group of cons—less turnover and more rebellion. He was enjoying the night life on the block, and was already beginning to make a few friends.

He gave me a list of books to get for him—Marx, Mao, math, and a few sociology texts to keep up his professor image—but when I brought them next time the guards wouldn't allow it. I had to get a fucking court order and a letter from the university. It took two weeks, and Jimmy was mad.

I learned quickly that it was going to be hard for both of us. For one thing, it was hard to have fights that only lasted a quarter of an hour. We'd fought a lot before—neither of us ever believed in swallowing our opinions—but we'd always had time to make up. Now there was just fifteen minutes and lots of added tension.

But we also learned that we really loved each other. Jimmy had been a little reluctant to believe that I loved him, mostly because no other woman had been given the chance. He had done seven years in the pen with no visits, and only a few letters. Now he had lots of visits, not only from me but from his friends, his students, and my family (and from some people who considered him a goddamn hero). He got plenty of mail every day. He told me that this was harder than the isolation he'd known before because now he knew he was missed and needed.

I've never been a believer in monogamy, but watching women in the visiting room mess with their men's heads, playing with them until they got shipped off to prison, was really depressing. After several of Jimmy's friends got fucked over he started to think about me doing the same thing to him. I found that being in jail makes even the most under-standing man jealous and possessive—jealous because the "competition" seems so uneven (they see only the women who come to visit, while their women see all the men on the streets), possessive because there is so little to hang on to. Jimmy had had these tendencies even before County Jail, after having spent so much time in the joint and seeing so many men abandoned.

One day he came out mad. He'd had a letter from me saying that a friend of his from CMC-East had dropped by and I'd cooked the guy dinner. He decided I'd said that to get a reac-tion. I laughed. I didn't even particularly like this dude, and I had no intention of doing a trip with anyone. I told Jimmy that I was in love with him, I hadn't needed anyone on the side when he was out, and I still didn't. He believed me but made me promise to tell him when I was ready to do a trip with this dude. I got mad, told him if he didn't trust me I would split. We hollered at each other and I ran out crying. I found a friend of mine downstairs who was also crying. We went upstairs again, asked to visit each other's husbands, and traded places. Jimmy was very surprised to see me again, apologized, and we straightened it all out. Still, about once a month Jimmy would write me a letter saying he would understand if I wanted to leave him for someone else—I always got mad, but I could see what started him off thinking like that.

Jimmy was trying very hard to do clean time. He never gave the guards any reason to mess with him—but they did anyway.

They all got off on him one way or another. The rednecks and most of the old guards called him the "Professor." Some of them stood outside his cell, heckling him as they fondled their keys. The vast majority were borderline liberals who joked about having a hero in their midst. Most of these were decent; a few were overly friendly. Then there were a few—young blacks and Chicanos, and some young whites working their way through law or criminology school—who really dug Jimmy and honestly thought they could learn from him. They hung around his cell asking questions, borrowing his books, and coming back for more.

Some time in June, Ramsey quit the case. I can't remember his reason, but I assume it was money. I started looking for another lawyer. Most of the people I called were too busy. After about a week I went to see Patrick Hallinan, one of a famous San Francisco family of leftist attorneys.

The first thing he said to me was that he'd have to charge us. He explained very proudly how he'd just finished success-fully defending one of the Soledad Seven, a less popular but still heavily martyrized group of cons busted for killing a guard a few months after George was busted. Of course, he hadn't made any money on that case, he said, and a man has to make a living. I told him we expected to pay.

Hallinan asked a lot of questions, all about Jimmy's rela-tions with various leftist groups and his degree of friendship with the current superstars. I sensed that he wanted another feather in his crusader cap, but I thought we could keep him under control. The last thing I wanted was for Jimmy to be made into a martyr. I'd heard that Hallinan was one of the best criminal lawyers around, so I told him just enough to whet his interest. He said he'd take the case (without asking one legal question, and ignoring the background information

I'd volunteered) and quoted me an outrageous fee (which I never intended to pay).

When he went to see Jimmy, Hallinan changed his tack, talking only about the business of the case; but the questions he asked were too obvious to indicate much interest. (Who was there? Were there any witnesses? Who arrested Jimmy? What happened at the preliminary hearing? He could have gotten all this from the transcript.) Jimmy disliked him and wanted me to check up on him. The people whose legal opinions I trusted agreed with me about the man, but they all felt he was a good lawyer, so I gave him a little bread. Nevertheless, I kept looking—with no success. It was interesting that after all the time I had worked with prison lawyers it was so hard to find one. Some were busy and several weren't experienced enough, but more than a few just made themselves hard to find.

Hallinan went to see Jimmy a few more times, but he never did any visible legal work. Jimmy felt that he meant nothing to his new attorney, who seemed interested in making him into a martyr, into another proof of the injustice of the bourgeois judicial system. Jimmy didn't find this exercise very radical, certainly not worth sacrificing his life for.

Jimmy's only previous exposure to the martyr syndrome had been with George Jackson, and then it had seemed to happen by accident. He had never worked for a cause in his life and never considered that the purpose of his work for the Soledad Brothers was making George into a martyr. So he was quite surprised at the depersonalized and calculating way in which Hallinan and others were sizing up his own case. I had been into martyrdom—religiously—at one point, but only to the extent that it was my goal as a militant. I was, in a way, even more surprised than Jimmy to see the process from the beginning: how it could happen with the martyr having no say in the matter and the martyrizer being the Left rather than the State.

We began to see martyrdom as an essential part of the movement—the mark of its failure. We saw that the leadership of the Left fell into two groups: those who sacrificed themselves and those who preached to the followers how this sacrifice demonstrated the evils of the system, then organized them to make a few changes. At this point most of our criticism was confined to the "organizers" but we saw how the martyrs—usually strong, independent people who wound up needing organized support fell into the rut of fighting the State on its own terms in order to prove its evils.

For a few visits we talked about George's brother, Jonathan. It had been a year since the Marin County Courthouse scene.

Through George, Jonathan and I had become very close. I saw him become desperate; George meant the world to him, and he had no hope of his release. When he was killed, I felt sad, of course, and furious, but I'd felt that his death would have some lasting effect on the people. I'd interpreted his desperation as revolutionary sacrifice, and fanatically believed it my duty, as his comrade, to show people that whatever he did was for them, and that he was the most effective kind of revolutionary warrior because he fought the hardest.

As I looked back on it a year later, I realized that Jon had disappeared; that even his action was virtually forgotten by all. Nothing had changed. I wanted to remember Jon for what he was when alive, not for how, or even why, he died; by thinking of him as martyr, I'd almost forgotten. I told Jimmy about him, his love for George, his hatred of all authority. One day in Salinas we were walking toward the courthouse where George was to have a pretrial hearing when Jon saw a County car. He hit the hood of it hard enough to leave a big dent, grinned, and said, "If I don't

destroy a little property every day, I get these headaches. . . . "
Jimmy laughed, saying that sounded like George. I laughed too,
relieved that I could think of Jonathan as a person again.

As for Hallinan, at first we saw the problem as being more
related to his privileged position in the movement than a logical result of the movement itself. Movement lawyers were
already famous for keeping one foot on the side of the bench,
always around for the applause, but jumping behind their pro-
fessionalism at the first sign of heat. But with so much time to
think and talk, we began to extend our criticism. The leaders
of the Left objectified us as much as the State did. They saw
society divided into masters against masses, and made themselves the masters of the masses (and for the masses). There
was going to be a bit of a delay while they waited for the masses
to step into place; meanwhile, they had only the movement to
manipulate. Each of the little vanguards did the same thing,
each thinking it was the true leadership. We still didn't reject
the idea of a vanguard, but we criticized more and more the
fools who claimed to fill the bill.

Meanwhile, my brother Dan and his friend Isaac started
coming to visit Jimmy. I was quite surprised, because we hadn't
been very close the last few years; Dan had long been making
what I'd considered an ultra-leftist ("infantile," in Lenin's
word) critique of the Left, and the Left had been my life. I
took his criticism personally and didn't listen to a word he
said; soon he'd stopped wasting his time. I was pleased now
that they were coming; I realized that what they'd said was
what I was beginning to think. Jimmy loved Danny, was amazed
at how quick he was. It was a while before I talked to him since
I was still rather defensive, but I always asked Jimmy to repeat
their conversations.

I WAS LYING IN BED, FEELING lonely and eight months pregnant. I got a phone call saying George Jackson was dead. I couldn't cry or move. I felt only the finality of it. I had avoided thinking of George as a martyr, only as a close friend and comrade. Yet now I could only think of his death as inevitable.

A few hours later Jimmy called, crazy with love and anger. A guard had told him his best friend was dead. He wanted to know everything and he wanted someone down there fast. I told him the few facts I had pulled together and told him I'd get someone to see him. We talked for only about a minute, but I felt the terror of his shock, which was multiplied by his feeling of isolation, of being locked up when he wanted to explode.

Our first few visits after George was killed were very hard. Jimmy cried, yelled, and exclaimed his love for George. He was very confused. He wrote me six or seven letters in one day, none very comprehensible. The press was coming around all the time. He hated them, but he wanted very much to convey his feeling that George had been forced against the wall by the Left's use of him. He felt pretty desperate for a while, and very much alone.

When the shock started to ease and things became clearer, the smell of the Left's garbage became more offensive. Of course, the reaction to George's death was varied, but the most common was to carry on, without stopping to think critically. To keep bearing witness and demonstrating moral outrage. They gave George a big hero funeral and everyone talked about how, this time, they really wouldn't let the State slide.

This was too much for us. I didn't want any part of it. Jimmy, for a while, thought he could straighten a few people out. I agreed that if ever there was a point to stop watching and proving, it was now, but I didn't think I could say anything to make it any more clear.

I was pretty cynical. I didn't want to talk to anyone about anything. I tried very hard to stay away from the movementeers (though they kept dropping by to share their misery), even stopped reading the papers. I wanted to be in a void for a while. I didn't yet want to offend the people on the Left, and since I didn't have anything nice to say I said nothing.

Jimmy thought differently. He tried, when people came to see him, to give them his thoughts on what was happening. He blamed our ideology for George's death, and blamed the leadership more. He even sent a few messages to the elite on how the movement had to change itself or perish. Those who didn't resent what he was saying simply didn't understand it. After a few weeks he gave up.

THE SHIT KEPT COMING. ED MONTGOMERY, a red-baiting reporter for the *Examiner*, printed a story tying Jimmy in with George's "escape attempt." According to Ed, Jimmy had written to George from Santa Cruz and George had written back on the same paper detailing an escape plan, sending the letter through an attorney. Supposedly, Jimmy had left the letter in his pants pocket; when I'd taken them to the cleaners, the cleaners had found it and called the CII, and the CII had xeroxed it and returned the original to the pocket to avoid suspicion.

I knew this was impossible since I always checked all Jimmy's pockets for dope and money (usually with some success). Even the police had grown to ignore Montgomery, whose fondness for exposing militant scandals had led him to create a number of them. They went to see Jimmy once at County, gruffly interrogated him for a few minutes, and apparently dropped the whole thing.

Hallinan called to say he was dropping the case. I asked him why but he didn't answer. I think he'd given up on making

Jimmy a saintly hero. I sent a friend to talk with him; he agreed to stay on if he could have more money. I got together close to a thousand dollars and sent it to him. A few days later he quit again.

We were both really frustrated: Jimmy'd been in for five months with no legal help; now George was dead, our old ideology was shattering, the legal shit was heavier than ever—and this fool quits.

The search for a lawyer began again. I wasn't in any kind of physical shape to go from office to office, so the woman who'd talked to Hallinan, a young lawyer who had worked on George's case, went to see a number of lawyers all over the Bay Area. Most said no out front or made up stupid excuses.

The first who didn't was Dick Hodge, whom I'd seen in action in the Los Siete case (a trial of seven Chicano militants accused of murdering a policeman). He was willing to meet Jimmy; then he'd decide if he wanted to defend him. He went to see him on a Sunday right before visiting time. After their meeting I met him downstairs; he smiled and said he'd just been upstairs with Jimmy, talking about Nietzsche.

Jimmy and I trusted Hodge immediately because he didn't bullshit or come on with the old crusading radical-lawyer line. He checked into the background of the case and agreed to take it.

Two and a half weeks after George was killed we were having a very good visit, full of new thoughts. A nice guard was on duty and he let me stay for over an hour. We talked about how we were going to lay back when Jimmy got out. We laughed a lot. I kept having weird pains, but I didn't tell Jimmy. Finally the guard told me to split. Jimmy called me back and told me to name the baby George. I just grinned; I knew all along she was a girl.

Late that night I went to the hospital. Gea was born early in the morning. A few hours later I called County and got a friendly guard who gave Jimmy the message.

Though I couldn't visit Jimmy for a week or two, he was getting plenty of visits from my family, his new lawyer, and the press.

By the time I got back it seemed like years. Jimmy was very glad to see me and especially excited about Gea. We'd really missed each other. A sympathetic guard allowed us a long visit, but it still wasn't enough time for me to answer all of Jimmy's questions. He wanted to know every detail of the birth, everything Gea did all day (he was disappointed when I said she didn't do anything), and what her toes and elbows looked like. He had pictures of her but he hadn't seen her; kids aren't allowed in County Jail.

When Gea was a few weeks old, Jimmy had a pretrial hearing and I took her to court. I held her way up. Jimmy couldn't take his eyes off her. The judge was mad, and made no reply when Jimmy said he wanted to see his kid for the first time. After that I started sneaking her up the lawyers' elevator, which opens onto the visiting room, when Jimmy was in there with someone else.

The next few months were fairly calm. I was busy with Gea. Jimmy played it cool and hung out with his two close friends, Tom and Hector. Tom was a white dude charged with murder who had never thought about politics but was quickly becoming a radical. Hector had been a movement hero as a defendant in the Los Siete trial. Now he was in for robbery; he had an incompetent lawyer and almost no visitors. The three of them were on the same cell block. They spent a lot of time talking, reading the books I gave to Jimmy, and just fucking off—pulling pranks or getting high on the drugs they had smuggled in. Once they were sitting around stoned when they heard this fool they called the "Moaner"—a con who complained loudly about everything, day and night. They made a fire bomb out of matches and paper and lowered it into his cell. After that he complained a lot less.

One young con had such a good singing voice that Jimmy asked me to write down lyrics of Motown love songs for him. (A few months earlier I'd been writing down the catechism of Nechayev.) For a little surprise I sent him Martha and the Vandellas' "Dancin' in the Street." Jimmy said later that when he heard that kid sing the song, he knew that his political philosophy had really changed, that he wanted to overcome the duality between Martha and Nechayev and make the revolution a dance in the street.

In late October we gave serious consideration to an escape plan we'd been working on for a few months. We'd been dreaming them up, partly as a diversion, the whole time Jimmy was in County. This plan involved Jimmy's getting into County Hospital. A few times in the past months he'd faked injuries in order to check out the prisoners' ward there. (Once, in fact, he really did get hurt in a fall from his bunk; I thought it was just another check and didn't sympathize.)

We worked out the final details during visiting hours by holding up notes and gesticulating. If anyone had seen us it would have been all over, but we didn't worry about it; we were too far into it to notice such details. Jimmy was going to fall off the top bunk and get sent to the hospital for X-rays. I was to meet him in the X-ray unit dressed as a nurse, with three guns in my purse. Without anyone seeing me, I would slip two to him and keep one for myself. When he announced his intentions I would play innocent and be taken as a hostage, but be ready to become his crime partner if necessary. To go along with my double role I'd have two sets of ID for myself—one with nurse's registry cards and the other with a fake Canadian passport—and one for Jimmy. We would send for Gea when we were safe.

In November, Hodge pulled off a deal that made us hesitant to use the plan. Jimmy's charge was lowered to a misdemeanor, and he'd be sentenced to six months, with credit for time served (already almost eight months). This was somewhat of a relief because something was finally going to happen, but it was very scary. Jimmy would then be completely in the hands of the Adult Authority Board, which had the power to revoke his parole and send him back to prison for life.

My reaction was to go ahead with the hospital plan, but Jimmy reasoned that the Adult Authority didn't want any of George's friends in the joint at the moment. He thought none of the other charges (conjured up by Montgomery) could stick, and they knew they could always get him later. For now they were probably afraid of a "leftist uprising" if Jimmy was sent back.

His hearing was set for December 23. The last few weeks of preparation were hectic, exhausting, and endless. It was hard to reach the frame of mind we needed: we couldn't give up hope but we couldn't be too optimistic because the disappointment would then be too great. Jimmy was looking forward to moving either home or to Quentin. Anything was better than limbo.

On the 23rd I got up enough nerve to call the Adult Authority in San Francisco. The secretary told me Jimmy's case had been held over another week. Since no one ever bothers to tell prisoners things like that, I sent him a telegram, which he never received.

The next day we got the following letter from Jimmy, who at the time had no idea when he'd ever get out of jail:

Monday 20 December, 1971

Dear Family,

Though you all know that I personally don't relate to Christmas, I find that I do relate to it through you. I'd like to thank each one of you for this feeling, for it's been quite a few years since I last experienced it. Love surely must be the greatest force that we shall ever know. Your love has given me something that no political philosopher ever could, and I know, for I've read them all! You have given me something to live for. It's a very deep something to know that you're loved and that someone loves. I spent seven dead years in prison and in all that time I was alone except for a few friends inside the walls, so you can imagine what Christmas or any other day must've meant to me! In prison I learned how not to have feelings or, rather, how to suppress them. This was necessary in order to adjust to complete isolation from the outside world: I never received one visit. When I got out I was 65 percent human and 35 percent defense mechanism and other various maladies. You people have enabled me to feel again and not be ashamed of it. I shall always love you!

My friend, George, used to say, "I'll love you so hard that you may get burned." I don't see life quite as passionately as that, but one thing that I'm positive of is that my love will endure. It can never end, just grow. I'm hoping to be there by Christmas, but if I don't make it that won't make any difference, for I couldn't love you anymore than I do right now. Exchange kisses for me. If my dog is back from the mountains, give the old boy a steak for me.

Merry Christmas and Happy New Year.

Love and plenty of kisses, Jimmy

I KEPT BUSY WITH LITTLE TASKS for a week, wrote letters to Jimmy and his friends. The morning of the 30th I called again. When the secretary told me Jimmy'd been reinstated on parole I almost dropped Gea. I really didn't believe it.

Then Jimmy's new parole officer called and I believed it. A few minutes later Jimmy rang up to say that Dan was giving him a ride to San Jose.

IT TOOK FOREVER FOR THEM TO get home. I was inexplicably nervous. Poor Gea got two baths and I changed her every few minutes. I didn't know what else to do. Finally I heard Jimmy running upstairs.

After a lot of kissing and hugging and looking at each other, Jimmy picked up Gea and kissed her even more than he had me. She was almost four months old, and they were meeting for the first time. Watching them made me cry.

That first night was very slow and quiet. We spent the evening talking with Dan and Sally and the rest of our close little family. We went to bed early, made love, talked about how the last eight months had been good for us by bringing us close together. But we didn't talk so much as we exclaimed love for each other.

Jimmy kept getting up to look at Gea, bringing her to bed with us, watching her nurse (he was really disappointed that my milk tasted so funny).

The next day we went to see the new PO, an overly friendly dude who felt so guilty about being a watchdog that he reversed roles with us and made us look at *his* life. He kept us in his office for hours, telling stories. We were floating and hardly noticed he was there. We spent the rest of the day in the same euphoric mood. It was New Year's Eve. We had dinner and champagne with friends and went to bed early.

We talked more seriously that night about the changes we'd made in the past eight months; while Jimmy was in County we'd discussed everything, but that glass between us had been a hindrance.

Our political changes were like day for night and, of course, that changed our everyday life: now we *had* an everyday life. We were both relieved of the militant compulsion for "revolutionary busywork," of thinking that nothing would change unless we were either passing out leaflets or blowing up PG&E plants. This was a great feeling in itself; we had time to think and to learn and just to trip. It was important for us then to make no plans.

We talked about Gea, a few good friends, and a few former friends. We didn't mention George.

The next day, New Year's, Jimmy watched football and drank. That night he got quite drunk. I sensed that he was down and followed him upstairs. George was on his mind. I loved George as much as anyone on the streets ever could. But Jimmy was his brother; they had grown up together. When George was killed, Jimmy had to force himself to stay together.

That night I held him while he cried. He could barely speak. He tried to say something once, but nothing came out except the pain. (I thought I understood, but when Jimmy was killed I realized I hadn't.) He cried for a few hours before falling asleep. Neither of us ever mentioned it.

The next few weeks we did a lot of playing, something which had been taboo in the movement except as a way of letting off steam from the pressures of militancy. Finally Jimmy could be himself, be spontaneous. (There were a few old habits he never broke. The worst was waking up at three minutes before 6:30, which he'd always done to avoid being awakened by the guards. What I hated was that he woke me up.)

We did everything as if we were brand new, which was easy with Gea around. She was really new. We went to the ocean and to the mountains and to a nearby reservoir. Every night we went to bed early, made love, talked, and made love some more. We talked about anything. When we couldn't think of anything, we'd read Nietzsche out loud, and Jimmy would laugh his I-told-you-so chuckle. One of our favorite passages was: "Shedding one's skin: the snake that cannot shed its skin perishes. So do spirits who are prevented from changing their opinions; they cease to be spirit."

A few weeks after Jimmy came home, he and Dan and Isaac started taping for the book. This was much harder than any of them thought it would be, as I came to know only too well.

After they talked for a few hours Jimmy would let his pressures out on me. I was used to this from militant days, but I didn't like it, so I'd bitch. It was hard—I realize how hard as I write this—for Jimmy to talk about the ups and downs, the good and bad times, without being overwhelmed. What bothered me was that he wouldn't say what was bugging him unless it hit a tender emotion like George. He would just blow up at me. We were fighting again. It wasn't constant, but it was frequent. When we were feeling good we didn't want to talk about it, so it just dragged on.

Finally we talked about it. Jimmy explained that he had to use me to vent his frustrations because he could trust me. Things got better because I made him talk about the shit that hurt, but the fighting kept up as long as the taping did.

When it was finally done and Jimmy could move back into his new life, we went to L.A. to see his family. After the treacherous weeks of reciting the past it was important for him to see his relatives and their reaction to his present. It was great: he said he'd never felt so close to them.

We stayed with Jimmy's Aunt Harriet in Central Los Angeles. She is a wonderful lady who has worked too hard for too long. She opened her house to us, loved and cared for Gea, treated me like she'd known me all my life. Jimmy was closest to her of any of the family. We all had gin and milk and talked about all the problems Jimmy had had with his mom while growing up.

We saw all his aunts and uncles and some cousins. We tripped around L.A. like tourists. He showed me Juvenile Hall, the rebuilt Mellowbar Elementary School, Hollenbeck Park, and his foster homes. We laughed, ate, visited old friends and showed off Gea.

The Sunday we were there we went to church with Jimmy's eighty-year-old grandmother. She is beautiful, looks like Jimmy, only little with gray hair and the best smile in the world. She is very religious and very together, which for her is somehow not a contradiction. She also took me in, totally. She told us stories about when she was young and talked devotedly about all the family (except Tackwood) and their hassles.

Before we left Los Angeles I convinced Jimmy to call his mom. He hadn't talked to her in eight or nine years. He told her about me and Gea and asked if we could see her. She said no, she didn't want to see him until he was dead. Neither of us could believe that she really felt that way. (I found out recently that Louis Tackwood had told her we didn't like her. She was sick with cancer, which we didn't know. Tackwood said that if Jimmy loved her he'd have visited her in the hospital; he was in County Jail at the time.)

In L.A. we got right down to analyzing more deeply the causes of our fighting. Other than the book pressures, Jimmy's temper, and my laziness, it was mostly caused by feelings of being tied down by obligations. For too long we'd had our decisions made by some other forces—the movement or the joint. As for our marriage, it wasn't particularly vowful, but since vows are part of a deep-rooted cultural pattern, their negation had be emphatically stated.

We came back up north feeling very refreshed. We both did a lot of reading during this period (mostly Korsch, Lukacs, the Situationists and the revolutionary classics) and listened to our favorite music (Mingus, Miles, and Ike and Tina Turner).

When the weather got better we started working in the garden. Jimmy had fantasies of being a farmer, and was good at it. We got up early—the now-familiar 6:30—put Gea on a blanket, and worked. We also did a lot of laughing, dirt throwing, and very off-key singing. Jimmy tried to convince me I was a farmer. We started looking for land despite my joking protests: our garden was beautiful, but forty acres is another story.

The "land question" brought up another problem: we didn't have any money. Jimmy wanted to pull a big robbery. When he told me this I got very mad. We both knew how the police would love another chance to send him up for life. I talked him out of it, but it took a lot of convincing.

Jimmy had been paroled to go to school, but now he had no intention of returning to UCSC. The Department of Corrections insists that parolees have visible means of support, so he started looking for work.

But he didn't look very hard. He was spending most of his time with Gea. She was about six months old and very responsive. He took her on his back for walks and bike rides, and often they'd take off for the day in the jeep. She'd giggle and say, "dadada." They talked a funny little language and sang (Gea sings off-key, too). Jimmy had always been playful and pranky, and now he had someone who felt the same way. I tried to keep up with them, but I played all night so I had to rest during the day.

After a few weeks of asking around and doing odd jobs, Jimmy got into the construction workers' union. He had to wait a week for his first assignment, so we finished off some gardening and loafed around. Saturday we went to San Francisco to visit my brother. Sunday we colored Easter eggs. Jimmy's favorite food was dyed hard-boiled eggs (he didn't like the white ones). Sunday night he ate two dozen.

The workday routine came easy for us. We'd always gone to bed early, talked and played until three or four, and gotten up early. I made him a huge breakfast, packed a big lunch with all his favorite food and money for beer, and sent him off. I really didn't know what to do with myself, so I played with Gea until he came home. (He called twice the first day to say it was hard.) He came home like a kid from kindergarten. He was building a cheap motel and made me promise never to sleep in one: he was convinced they were doing it all wrong.

On Jimmy's third day of work it rained and he got to come home early, bringing two co-workers with him. We listened to music and talked for a few hours. The dudes were from the Valley, and traveled around the state doing construction work wherever they could get on. They lived in campers during the week and went home to their families on weekends. They made pretty good money and spent it all feeding their families and their boredom. Jimmy spoke to them in a very elementary way of their position in class society. They were boggled and interested to hear they had a role in history.

When they left we were exhausted and took a nap on our new bed (Jimmy's birthday present). When we got up Jimmy played with Gea. She'd just started crawling that day, with her feet flat on the ground and her ass up in the air. Jimmy was very excited, and the two of them crawled around for hours. I fed them together on the floor, put Gea in bed, and Jimmy and I started talking.

We always talked at night, but this night was different. I rarely talked about my past, except about specific incidents. Jimmy wanted me to tell him how I had become what I was. He could finally appreciate the good aspects of writing this book and thought I should do the same. He asked questions, but didn't say much. We laughed; I cried a little. We talked about my father who died when I was eleven, about my miserable years in junior high school, my strange forms of rebellion. The conversation was interrupted a few times by lovemaking. Jimmy fell asleep for about an hour, but I couldn't. I wanted to cuddle and talk. I remember my exhaustion and a strange fear of sleep. Jimmy woke up. I needed comforting and got it. We talked for a couple more hours.

This time we talked about work, about us, about Jimmy's birthday the day after next. It was then April 5th. The year before, on April 6th, he'd been busted. He'd been in some kind of confinement on every birthday since he was eleven. We'd both developed heavy doses of birthday paranoia. I wanted to lock him in the house for two days. Jimmy said he'd go to work, come right home, and not do anything even remotely against the law until after his birthday. If it worked we'd celebrate on the 8th maybe even get some coke. About three in the morning we fell asleep.

Gea was hungry at 5:30. Jimmy brought her to bed and I nursed her till six. He was sleepy and I was grouchy, but somehow we got up. I made him a little breakfast and a big lunch to take to work, then sat on the kitchen floor to nurse Gea some more. We quietly read the paper while Jimmy hummed to us. At a quarter to seven he patted my head and said, "Got to warm up the jeep. Back in a minute, babies."

Seconds later I heard shots.

I started upstairs to get my gun, but I stopped. I sensed that it was too late.

Jimmy was dead.

The terror that followed, the intensity of my pain and dis-belief, I am unable to explain. I can only remember images. Within minutes there were police everywhere. The phone kept ringing; people kept coming. I remember faces filled with shock and sadness. The sidewalks were filled with people from the press. I couldn't imagine Jimmy dead: I could see him in the jeep, felt I had to touch him. The police wouldn't let me out the door. I felt less than half alive.

Finally, when the spectators and press and police started thinning out, when the morgue truck was gone, I split. I needed to find some space to be anonymous, to find out if I was dreaming. I walked around for a while, then saw a news-paper with the headline AMBUSH SLAYING, with pictures of two strangers and one of Jimmy from his prison file. It was real.

The next few days, all intermingled in my recollections, were long and unbelievable. We didn't do any funeral trip. Those of us who loved Jimmy stayed very close together; the comfort was vital. I dealt with those things one can't avoid: the motherfuckers at the mortuary, the slimy police who loved to hear me say I hadn't seen anything, a few phone calls of the caliber of sympathy I didn't really need (leftist heroics).

But the general reaction was overwhelming. I learned a lot about friendship. I received hundreds of letters, many from the joint and County Jail, even a few from County guards. Our friends, even those Jimmy'd known only briefly, and our fami-lies really gave me the strength I needed. But knowing how much Jimmy was loved made it all even harder to understand.

Bourgeois justice was served with the arrest and conviction of two men, Lloyd Mims and Richard Rodriguez. The DA explained in his opening statement that these dudes were hired killers, only the triggermen in a well-planned murder.

But, he added, he wouldn't try to prove who had hired them. They were convicted anyway and got life sentences.

There is no easy explanation for why Jimmy was killed, and I have no desire to speculate. I do know that Jimmy hadn't done anything public or clandestine in a year, since his arrest in San Francisco, except for trying to wake a few people up after George was killed. But someone felt threatened enough by his silence, and by some assumed change, to go to the risk of having him murdered. (Of course, Jimmy had changed, and he felt alive for once because he had. I guess feeling alive is dangerous.)

It's been two years now and I'm just beginning to sleep a whole night without waking to visions of Jimmy in his jeep that morning, or seeing him on that cold table at the mortuary with a sheet where his heart once was, or the empty faces of Mims and Rodriguez at their trial. The nightmare is fading. The pain is forever.

But the memories are much more important than the pain. To dwell on Jimmy's death would contradict all we learned together and shared till the end. Jimmy taught me to shed my skin. Together we learned how to love.

Jimmy is in me all the time. I can even hear his laugh when I need to. Every moment we had together was based on growth. And I can't stop now.

RECENT AND FORTHCOMING BOOKS FROM THREE ROOMS PRESS

FICTION

Meagan Brothers
Weird Girl and What's His Name

Ron Dakron
Hello Devilfish!

Michael T. Fournier
Hidden Wheel
Swing State

Janet Hamill
Tales from the Eternal Café
(Introduction by Patti Smith)

Eamon Loingsigh
Light of the Diddicoy
Exile on Bridge Street

Aram Saroyan
Still Night in L.A.

Richard Vetere
The Writers Afterlife
Champagne and Cocaine

MEMOIR & BIOGRAPHY

Nassrine Azimi and
Michel Wasserman
Last Boat to Yokohama:
The Life and Legacy of
Beate Sirota Gordon

James Carr
BAD: The Autobiography of
James Carr

Richard Katrovas
Raising Girls in Bohemia:
Meditations of an American Father;
A Memoir in Essays

Judith Malina
Full Moon Stages: Personal
Notes from 50 Years of The Living
Theatre

Stephen Spotte
My Watery Self:
Memoirs of a Marine Scientist

HUMOR

Peter Carlaftes
A Year on Facebook

PHOTOGRAPHY-MEMOIR

Mike Watt
On & Off Bass

SHORT STORY ANTHOLOGY

Dark City Lights: New York Stories
edited by Lawrence Block

Have a NYC I, II & III:
New York Short Stories;
edited by Peter Carlaftes
& Kat Georges

Shadows and Sound: Music Noir
edited by Jim Fusilli

Songs of My Selfie:
An Anthology of Millennial Stories
edited by Constance Renfrow

This Way to the End Times:
Classic and New Stories of
the Apocalypse
edited by Robert Silverberg

MIXED MEDIA

John S. Paul
Sign Language: A Painter's
Notebook (photography, poetry
and prose)

TRANSLATIONS

Thomas Bernhard
On Earth and in Hell
(poems of Thomas Bernhard
with English translations by
Peter Waugh)

Patrizia Gattaceca
Isula d'Anima / Soul Island
(poems by the author
in Corsican with English
translations)

César Vallejo | Gerard Malanga
Malanga Chasing Vallejo
(selected poems of César Vallejo
with English translations
and additional notes by
Gerard Malanga)

George Wallace
EOS: Abductor of Men
(selected poems of George
Wallace with Greek translations)

DADA

Maintenant: A Journal of
Contemporary Dada Writing & Art
(Annual, since 2008)

FILM & PLAYS

Israel Horovitz
My Old Lady: Complete Stage Play
and Screenplay with an Essay on
Adaptation

Peter Carlaftes
Triumph For Rent (3 Plays)
Teatrophy (3 More Plays)

POETRY COLLECTIONS

Hala Alyan
Atrium

Peter Carlaftes
DrunkYard Dog
I Fold with the Hand I Was Dealt

Thomas Fucaloro
It Starts from the Belly and Blooms
Inheriting Craziness is Like
a Soft Halo of Light

Kat Georges
Our Lady of the Hunger

Robert Gibbons
Close to the Tree

Israel Horovitz
Heaven and Other Poems

David Lawton
Sharp Blue Stream

Jane LeCroy
Signature Play

Philip Meersman
This is Belgian Chocolate

Jane Ormerod
Recreational Vehicles on Fire
Welcome to the Museum of Cattle

Lisa Panepinto
On This Borrowed Bike

George Wallace
Poppin' Johnny

Three Rooms Press | New York, NY | Current Catalog: www.threeroomspress.com
Three Rooms Press books are distributed by PGW/Perseus: www.pgw.com